FERTILITY CHANGE ON THE AMERICAN FRONTIER

STUDIES IN DEMOGRAPHY

General Editors
Eugene A. Hammel
Ronald D. Lee
Kenneth W. Wachter

1. Douglas Massey, Rafael Alarcon, Jorge Durand, Humberto Gonzalez, *Return to Aztlan: The Social Process of International Migration from Western Mexico*
2. Ronald R. Rindfuss, S. Philip Morgan, C. Gray Swicegood, *The Transition to Parenthood: Temporal, Social, and Demographic Dimensions*
3. Judith Blake, *Family Size and Achievement*
4. Lee L. Bean, Geraldine P. Mineau, Douglas L. Anderton, *Fertility Change on the American Frontier: Adaptation and Innovation*

Fertility Change on the American Frontier:
Adaptation and Innovation

ERRATUM

In Studies in Demography, page ii:

The listing of books in this series, after number 3, should read as follows:

4. Ron J. Lesthaeghe, ed., Reproduction and Social Organization in Sub-Saharan Africa
5. Lee L. Bean, Geraldine P. Mineau, Douglas L. Anderton, Fertility Change on the American Frontier: Adaptation and Innovation

FERTILITY CHANGE ON THE AMERICAN FRONTIER

Adaptation and Innovation

LEE L. BEAN,

GERALDINE P. MINEAU,

& DOUGLAS L. ANDERTON

UNIVERSITY OF CALIFORNIA PRESS
Berkeley · Los Angeles · Oxford

University of California Press
Berkeley and Los Angeles, California

University of California Press, Ltd.
Oxford, England

Library of Congress Cataloging-in-Publication Data

Bean, Lee L.
Fertility change on the American frontier : adaptation and innovation / Lee L. Bean. Geraldine P. Mineau, and Douglas L. Anderton.
p. cm. —(Studies in demography : 4)
Bibliography: p.
Includes index.
ISBN 0-520-06633-2 (alk. paper)
1. Fertility. Human—West (U.S.)—History—19th century. 2. West (U.S.)—Population—History—19th century. 3. Utah—Population—History—19th century. I. Mineau. Geraldine P. II. Anderton, Douglas L. III. Title. IV. Series: Studies in demography (Berkeley, Calif.) : 4.
HB931.B43 1990
304.6′32′0979509034—dc20 89-5045

Printed in the United States of America

1 2 3 4 5 6 7 8 9

The paper used in this publication meets the minimum requirements of American National Standard for Information Sciences—Permanence of Paper for Printed Library Materials, ANSI Z39.48-1984 ♾

Contents

Tables

FIGURES

Acknowledgments

Fertility Change on the American Frontier is the product of a research program that began at the University of Utah in 1974. In that year Dr. Mark Skolnick initiated the development of a computerized database that was built around a set of family records made available by the Genealogical Society of Utah, an organization of the Church of Jesus Christ of Latter-day Saints. These records were originally intended to be the core of a complex record system in which medical records would be linked to the population file.

The notion that these records provided an unusual opportunity to merge genetic and demographic analysis originated in two events. First, the idea that the records maintained by the Utah Genealogical Society might prove useful to historical demography was suggested to Lee L. Bean, the senior author, by Prof. Ansley Coale at the IUSSP conference in Liège, Belgium, in the late summer of 1974. Second, the plan to apply Coale's idea to Skolnick's research project emerged during a faculty seminar organized by Skolnick and Bean, who joined the faculty of the University of Utah at the same time. Active, original members of that seminar who contributed to the shaping of the research program were Dr. Carol Werner (Psychology), Dr. John McCullough (Anthropology), Dr. Dean May (History), and Dr. Lawrence Nabers (Economics). Funding for the seminar was provided by the Institutional Funds Committee of the University of Utah.

Development of a database as large and rich as that used in this study required the support of a number of investigators. Two must be credited with major roles—Mark Skolnick and Roger Williams. Grants for which these individuals were principal investigators[1] were critical to the development of the database, as were the grants provided by the National Institute of Child Health and Human Development / National Institutes of Health, which supported data analysis.

At the time the project was initiated no database management systems were available which would meet the data entry, storage, and retrieval requirements of the project. Consequently, under the direction of Skolnick, an original database management system was developed. Initial work was completed by Val Arbon, with subsequent extensions and improvements made by Tim Maness and Sue Dintleman. During the initial phases of the project, analysis would not have been possible without the programming assistance of Klancy de Nevers and Peter Cartwright.

It is difficult to identify all of the people who have provided suggestions, comments, and advice helpful in shaping the analysis in this volume. To all we are grateful, and we wish to particularly acknowledge Jean Pierre Bardet, Ansley Coale, Gene Hammel, John Knodel, Katherine Lynch, Dean May, Thomas Pullum, Arland Thornton, T. James Trussell, Etienne van de Walle, Kenneth Wachter, and J. Dennis Willigan. Tim Heaton reviewed a draft of the manuscript and provided helpful comments. Ellen Bartholomew copyedited several versions of the manuscript, and Yung-chang Hsueh was responsible for the preparation of many of the graphs. None of these individuals, of course, should be held responsible for any errors of judgment or interpretation. Whatever those errors might be rest with the authors of this volume.

The authors would like to express their appreciation to the University of California Press and in particular Dr. Nancy Atkinson, who was responsible for the editing of the manuscript. Dr. Atkinson not only clarified the writing greatly but also identified many points that perhaps only the authors would have understood.

The order of the authors' names on the title page of this volume reflects seniority and nothing more, for this is truly a jointly produced manuscript. Lee L. Bean initiated the demographic analysis, and over the past several years has been responsible for the overall supervision of the project. Geraldine P. Mineau was the first graduate assistant recruited to work on the study. She employed the database for her Ph.D. dissertation in sociology and subsequently joined the project on a full-time basis as an investigator. She, more than any other person, understands the internal structure of the computer file and knows how it might and might not be used for analysis. Douglas L. Anderton later joined the project as a graduate research assistant and has remained associated with the study in a critical and central fashion following the completion of his Ph.D. in sociology. Anderton also used the database for his dissertation, and it was within the context of his work that the first evidence of birth spacing as an early strategy of fertility limitation was found. Anderton is primarily responsible for whatever statistical sophistication our analysis possesses. Anderton received support from the University of Chicago and The Center for Advanced Studies in the Behavioral Sciences, Palo Alto, California. Noriko Tsuya and Rebecca Emigh provided research assistance to him while graduate students at the University of Chicago.

The joint production of a volume in which each writer's work is continuously critiqued by coauthors is perhaps as stressful as the first few weeks of an arranged marriage. As one finds in arranged marriages, however, tolerance, understanding, and mutual appreciation often follow the birth of each child. So it has been with *Fertility Change on the American Frontier*.

Introduction

This volume is a report on social change in America, yet its focus is specific. It deals with one of the myriad forms of social change which have marked American society: changing fertility behavior. In addition, it is not a study of American society as a general entity but a study of a specific population—one that was involved in the colonization of the western American frontier in the last half of the nineteenth century and that encountered during the early decades of the twentieth century increasing urbanization, commercialization, secularization, and modernization. A detailed view of individual fertility behavior during the period of tumultuous social change on the frontier is captured through the analysis of a set of data generated by using Utah genealogies and focusing upon women born during the nineteenth century, 1800–99.

One reason for limiting the study of fertility change in American society to a specific population is that patterns of fertility behavior have varied among the populations of the various regions and social categories. Fertility of American women in the original colonies was uniformly high, approaching levels observed among groups such as the Hutterites, who are used as models of high fertility among populations with minimal social, environmental, and personal constraints on childbearing (Coale 1969; Eaton and Mayer 1953). Consequently, Malthus selected the colonial population of New England to illustrate his principle concerning the level of growth which might be observed in the absence of resource limitations (1965). By the third quarter of the twentieth century, however, the fertility of native white American females fell to or below simple replacement (U.S. Bureau of the Census 1984, 1985). Some contemporary populations in Western Europe, particularly the residents of large metropolitan centers, have lower fertility rates, yet their fertility decline started at levels considerably below that of the colonists of New England (Coale and Zelnik 1963).

Neither Western European nor American fertility change can be fully described by reference to average, national rates. John Knodel, Etienne van de Walle, Ronald Freedman, and others have reported that the timing of the introduction of fertility limitation was often specific to subcultural areas in Western Europe (Knodel and van de Walle 1979; Freedman 1979), although a significant number of greatly different areas initiated the shift from moderately large to small families within a relatively narrow time period (Coale and Watkins 1986). Throughout the nineteenth and twentieth centuries, major differences are also found in levels and rates of fertility change among different regions of the United States (Smith and Zopf 1976, pp. 366–372). Moreover, the American pattern of decline from high to low fertility emerged at different times among different groups.

When the American population expanded from the New England colonies to fill its current territories, many frontier families, drawn from the settled, declining-fertility regions of America or from Western European nations with moderate levels of fertility, achieved family sizes—that is, their number of children—exceeding those produced by their parents or siblings who resided in the more developed regions. Typically, within a generation after the settlement of frontier regions, fertility limitation became more common, so that falling frontier fertility rates subsequently mirrored the earlier fertility decline of the populations in the northeastern states. Second-generation fertility in the frontier regions, however, often declined in advance of fertility in many Western European nations. Only France preceded or shared the early fertility decline observed in the United States at the national level (Coale and Zelnik 1963).

If one recognizes such variations, then stating that the decline of American fertility was early and of unprecedented magnitude obscures as much as it illuminates. The long-term secular trend in American fertility which began with the opening of the nineteenth century hides periods and regions within which fertility initially exceeded the levels in more settled regions and only subsequently began to decline. A complete picture of the magnitude and timing of fertility change in the

United States therefore requires study of different population groups defined geographically, economically, culturally, ethnically, or racially.

The number of studies of particular American populations during the eighteenth and nineteenth centuries has increased in recent years, but there have been fewer than one might wish. To a large extent the absence of such studies stems from the absence of what one would presume to be relatively unambiguous data: a simple count of births and their timing, linked to mothers. The systematic recording of such simple data, within a system designed to produce routine statistical summaries and analyses, is only recent, dating from the early part of the 1930s for all states in the union. Alternative data sources such as population censuses have a somewhat longer history than official registration systems and may be used as indirect, or in some cases direct, estimates of fertility. Nevertheless, it has only been within the past few decades that systematic efforts have been made to exploit alternative data sources and develop techniques to utilize historical census records more effectively. Fortunately, the recording of births for religious or political reasons has been important among some literate populations, who have thus produced various forms of potentially usable records reflecting the demographic history of families, communities, and religious groups. The study reported in this volume employs such alternative data sources.

This volume is based upon a study designed to describe explicitly, and to analyze extensively, the process of changing fertility in one population over a time period that predated the availability of official vital statistics. Our study deals with women born between 1800 and 1899 who participated in the migration from Europe, the New England States, and the Midwest to settle and develop Utah. Because most of these women and their descendants were associated with the Church of Jesus Christ of Latter-day Saints (Mormon, or LDS), their history is recorded in a set of genealogies that provide detailed individual records of childbearing as well as information on selected social characteristics typically employed to explain the patterns and processes of fertility change. The computerized file constructed from these genealogies is large, including approximately 185,000 families, or slightly more than 1.2 million individuals. Therefore, one distinguishing feature of our study is the access to a massive data file of individual records covering more than one hundred years of childbearing experiences.

These records enable us to replicate the procedures used by investigators of other historical populations and to extend the analysis in three significant ways. First, the use of an extensive, individual-level data file enables us to study the fertility behavior of theoretically specified subgroups rather than groups specified by the arbitrary political boundaries used in data collection systems. For example, because the file gives religious information for most of the people listed, it is possible to create a scale of religious commitment in order to study the relationship between this constructed variable and fertility behavior, within and between various types of communities.

Second, the type of data available in the file enables us to extend the analysis to the timing of life course events (Hareven 1978; Elder 1978), including birth intervals. In addition, the data make it possible to study the relationship between migration during various stages of the life cycle and fertility. Individual cases are not lost to observation because they leave a particular politically bounded unit.

Third, we specifically contrast two competing explanations of fertility change among Western societies: an adaptation argument based on the work of Gösta Carlsson and an innovation argument based on the work of John Knodel and others (Carlsson 1966; Knodel 1977; see also Retherford 1985).

The evaluation of the adaptation-innovation issue involves the test of a series of assumptions and propositions. First, we test the assumption that, prior to the initiation of the secular fertility decline, the concept of natural or uncontrolled fertility is applicable only at the aggregate level and that, within such populations, subgroups composed of couples who limit family size may be identified. Second, we test the hypothesis that the introduction of parity-dependent fertility limitation primarily involves a new, innovative mode of fertility behavior described by the term "truncation"—stopping childbearing late in the life cycle after a given, desired number of children have been born. Third, our data and previous analysis have suggested an alternative "spacing" hypothesis. The hypothesis is that with access to imperfect contraception technologies, subgroups of the population who aim to limit family size implement their goals by adopting longer birth intervals throughout the childbearing years. Additional tests of hypotheses arise logically from attempts to associate these behavioral changes with the patterns of social change stressed in recent fertility theories. For example, we are led to an examination of the timing and sequence of the introduction of family limitation among specific subclasses of the society defined by economic and cultural regions and by religious affiliation. Moreover, we place these family-formation patterns in the context of broader developmental processes at work on the frontier.

Our study focuses on an American frontier population, representative of groups that—as suggested by such writers as Yasukichi Yasuba, Colin Forster, and G. S. L. Tucker, and Richard Easterlin—have larger families than populations in older, more densely settled regions (Yasuba 1962; Forster and Tucker 1972; Easterlin 1971). The context within which this population lived is described in chapter 2, with an emphasis on the critical forces of social change stressed in recent fertility theories. The development, strengths, and limitation of the Mormon Historical Demography Project (MHDP) are discussed in chapter 3. Chapter 3 also outlines the innovative methods used in the organization and analysis of the data. These two chapters along with chapter 1 constitute Part I of the volume and are a prelude to the analysis of the data presented in chapters 4–8, in Part II.

Chapter 4 outlines the general levels and trends of fertility using a variety of measures and indices to provide a basis for comparison with other historical demographic research. Chapters 5 and 6 examine compositional factors associated with the process of changing fertility levels. Chapter 5 is specifically concerned with the migration experience, examining origin, ethnicity, and the timing of migration to the frontier as determinants of fertility differences. Exploiting migration histories provides an opportunity to reexamine differences in fertility among the native-born and foreign-born, and the potential conceptual significance of assimilation. Chapter 6 explores the independent and interactive effects of two dimensions of social structure: the changes in internal structure as "urban" centers develop within a population, and again as "secular" groups develop. Taken together, these two chapters then provide a view of the adaptive responses of fertility behavior to the formation and development of social structures on the frontier.

Chapters 7 and 8 focus on changing individual-level fertility behavior within the population. Going beyond the confines of previous fertility studies, chapter 7 explores the timing of life course events to determine both the specific forms of behavior responsible for fertility limitation and the possibility that these patterns were already extant in some social groups rather than unique innovations within the population. The analysis both defines groups on a behavioral basis and assesses the importance of the distribution of behaviors across groups. Chapter 8 explores the distribution of significant fertility patterns across the geographic frontier. Allowing the possibility that fertility control went beyond adaptation to changing social structure, this analysis looks for patterns of innovation and subsequent diffusion not explicable by concrete dimensions of social change (agricultural, urban, ethnic, religious group, etc.).

These five chapters in Part II then bring a central question of recent social theory into the arena of historic demographic analysis. The alternatives of changes in social structure and fundamental changes in "rational" human behavior not directly attributable to changing social structures are posed and assessed as competing explanations of fertility change on the frontier.

Chapter 9 summarizes the results of the study and outlines the contextual factors that must be considered in evaluating fertility change, in historical populations and in contemporary populations marked by varying levels of social and economic modernization. The results of the study are then used to evaluate previous fertility theories and efforts to draw policy conclusions from historical demographic research based primarily on studies of European populations.

PART I

Theory and Data: The Mormon Historical Demography Project

CHAPTER 1

Fertility Change on the American Frontier

Adaptation or Innovation?

A hallmark of industrial Western European society was the emergence of increasingly smaller families. Our understanding of this Western European fertility transition—the shift from high, uncontrolled marital fertility to low, controlled fertility—is based upon a set of "interesting partial hypotheses," according to Charles Tilly. Therefore, over a decade ago, he suggested, "By studying particular experiences closely, we hope to get a sense of the actual process by which fertility changed and to start ruling out a few of the available hypotheses" (1978, p. 4). The study presented in this volume is responsive to that suggestion. It extends the study of "particular experiences" from Western Europe to the American western frontier, where it deals with the particular experiences of a specific population. The study is concerned with the processes of fertility change. It evaluates a set of competing explanations of fertilty change in an effort to "rule out a few of the available hypotheses."

Our study differs in other ways from many historical demographic studies that describe the modern fertility transition. First, a majority of published studies deal with the "fertility transition" among national or regional populations from Western Europe, but we deal with a population as it moves into, settles, and develops a frontier region of the United States, namely, Utah.

Second, we are concerned with historical fertility change in America, not simply with a "fertility transition" as generally understood when the term is applied to the modern secular decline in Western Europe. A fertility transition usually implies a shift from high, uncontrolled marital fertility to low, controlled marital fertility. It is associated with a variety of social and economic changes described as modernization, industrialization, urbanization, and secularization. During initial stages of modernization, however, fertility may increase rather than decrease. The pattern of an initial rise is inconsistent with the general use of the term "fertility transition," but the phenomenon of an initial rise is proving to be more general than previously thought (Fridlizius 1979; Hirschman and Fernandez 1980; Hull and Hull 1977; Mosk 1979). It has been observed among indigenous populations of North America and a variety of populations in Asia, Africa, and Latin America. The population we study also demonstrates an early rise in fertility. Because of the ubiquity of the term in the literature, we shall use "fertility transition" to refer to the shift from high, uncontrolled to increasingly lower, controlled fertility. We recognize, however, that Western demographic transitions are not monotonic, and that there are "multiple paths of fertility decline in contemporary developing countries" (Hirschman 1985, p. 35).

Third, almost all historical demographic studies deal with a geographically bounded population; they are forced to do so by the types of data employed for historical demographic research—that is, parish and community registers, manuscript censuses, and other official records established by community authority. Our study population also has a geographic context, being composed of individuals who experienced demographic events in the territory, and subsequently in the state, of Utah. The sample is, however, open rather than closed to migrants and thereby contains a wealth of information often discarded from other historical studies. The initial population of the territory of Utah was composed primarily of migrants from the midwestern and northeastern states and Western Europe. Therefore, its demographic history extends beyond the geographic boundaries of Utah. We examine the migrant population, its regional and national origin, and its behavior following settlement and movement within a specific region.

This study is part of a research program entitled the Mormon Historical Demography Project (MHDP hereafter). The MHDP study population is dominated by members of the Church of Jesus Christ of Latter-day Saints (LDS church, or Mormons); but the population is diverse, and the initial cohorts were not Mormon at least until their later years of life. We study the fertility of women born between 1800 and 1899, and the LDS church was not established until 1830. Moreover, even though Utah has consisted largely of an LDS population, the LDS members have been marked by varying degrees of commitment to the church. Thus the term "Mormon" in the project's title is not a complete description of the population but rather a description of the data source.

Family-group sheets from the files of the Genealogical Society of Utah (GSU), an organization maintained by the LDS church, provide the basic data used in the MHDP. From these records a series of linked genealogies have been computerized, and it is the analysis of this machine-readable database which is reported here. The analysis of the database is viewed as important for two reasons.

First, the study provides an unusually extensive description of the processes of family formation and change during periods in which detailed demographic data were typically unavailable. This description augments the body of linked data sets that draw on a variety of nineteenth- and early twentieth-century records—records that usually come from the eastern United States—with a careful documentation of demographic processes that occurred in the western region of America during the same period. This study therefore broadens the literature of historical demography in the United States.

Second, the analysis presented is theoretically driven, attempting to distinguish between two general explanations of the process of fertility reduction which became common among Western industrialized countries of Europe and North America. Although the time of the initiation of the secular Western fertility decline varied among various communities and countries, the general process involved in the shift from moderately large to increasingly smaller families has been described typically as a form of innovation: the adoption and diffusion of a newly acceptable social norm, the small family. In contrast, some writers have suggested that some form of limitation of family size, in some degree, existed prior to the onset of the general fertility decline, and that the shift simply reflected an adaptation to a new set of costs and benefits. Therefore, the major theoretical goal of the present study is to determine the degree to which these two general explanations—innovation and diffusion versus adaptation—fit the changes in family formation and fertility behavior documented by the MHDP database.

In the following sections of this chapter we first discuss the notions of adaptation and innovation as applied to the study of fertility change.

We then discuss the importance of the American frontier for the evaluation of these concepts.

ADAPTATION OR INNOVATION: AN OVERVIEW

The juxtaposition of the concepts "adaptation" and "innovation" was suggested by Gösta Carlsson two decades ago (1966). Although Carlsson uses the term "adjustment" rather than "adaptation," we use the latter term throughout the study. Our reason is that "adjustment" implies a normative change (namely, to bring to a more satisfactory state), while "adaptation" simply implies a modification of behavior to fit changing conditions.

Carlsson stated that the secular decline in marital fertility began around 1880 in many Western European countries. He suggested that the phenomenon represents an unusual change of mass attitudes and behavior. The change was linked to the growth of industrialization, the decline of agriculture, the spread of education, and other factors associated with modernization and secularization. Carlsson noted:

> But within this widely accepted framework at least two types of theory are possible, one of which, the **innovation** approach, seems to dominate the current thinking on the subject. The other, the **adjustment** approach, may at first glance not appear very different, but . . . the two approaches should be distinguished and . . . the innovation thesis has been stressed too much. The main objective of this paper is to demonstrate this, and to show that the notion of adjustment fits the decline more easily. (1966, p. 149)

Carlsson also stated that the innovation orientation is based upon a series of assumptions: (1) birth control, especially contraception, is a recent invention, essentially new to Western European cultures; (2) the innovation occurs in a population where there has been little or no practice of birth control; and (3) once the innovation is introduced the information spreads (rapidly) as knowledge, positive attitudes, and use skills "trickle down" from the middle class to lower classes and from urban to rural areas. Operationally, these assumptions imply the following conditions: no evidence of fertility control prior to the adoption of the innovation (contraception or a small-family norm); no prior variation due to volitional control in levels and patterns of fertility within marriages independent of age of marriage among significant geographic, class, or other social groups; and sequential initiation of fertility decline, first in urban and then in rural areas, or first in middle-class groups and then in lower-class groups.

Carlsson outlined an alternative explanation:

> The adjustment theory differs from the innovation hypothesis in most of these respects. Birth control, especially contraception, need not be regarded as new or recent in human society. There may have been a "steady state" in which birth control was practised by part of the population, or it may have been practised with higher targets. The decline in fertility is then regarded as an adjustment to a new set of forces, defining a new equilibrium level of modern or "controlled" fertility. The role of motivation, and structural factors bearing on human desires and values, is stressed more than knowledge of contraception. This type of theory is not dependent on lags or a "trickle down" pattern of spread. (1966, p. 150)

Carlsson tested his hypothesis by examining Swedish fertility data. He relied upon relatively crude measures of period fertility, and the units of analysis were rather large: Stockholm and other urban areas contrasted with rural or agricultural districts. Analysis indicated that there were major differences in levels of fertility prior to the onset of the secular decline among the various regional units of analysis, that the decline commenced among all areas almost simultaneously, and that subsequent change by district was described by a series of parallel curves maintaining regional fertility differences. Carlsson argued that, prior to the initiation of modern birth control, differences in fertility levels existed among significant subgroups of the population exposed to different social and economic conditions. Because of the simultaneous initiation of the decline and the subsequent parallel patterns, no evidence of diffusion or a "trickle down" effect can be demonstrated; thus the notion of adjustment fits the pattern of fertility change more easily.[1]

Carlsson drew upon Kingsley Davis's argument that the reaction to population pressures stimulated by a decline in mortality is multiphasic, involving out-migration, delayed marriage, increased celibacy, and birth control within marriages (Davis 1963). He therefore evaluated the effects of other types of change which might influence his conclusion regarding birth control within marriages. For example, it is evident that variations in nuptiality may have played a major role in the regional variations in fertility levels in Sweden prior to the onset of the fertility decline. Regardless of variations or changes in nuptiality, however, Carlsson concluded that birth control within marriages may have been a contributing factor of some strength (1966).

INNOVATION AND ADAPTATION: A FURTHER EXPLORATION

Approximately a decade after the publication of Carlsson's article, John Knodel provided the results of new, more refined historical demographic analysis to reaffirm the importance of the notion of innovation in explaining fertility transitions. Yet Knodel posed innovation and adaptation not as conflicting processes but rather as complementary ones:

> It is unfortunate that Carlsson posed the question of innovation or adjustment since few observers doubt that the fertility transition, in at least a general way, is related to motivational forces stemming from changes in socio-economic and demographic (especially mortality) conditions prior to and during fertility decline. The real issue is whether or not fertility control within marriage typically represents a new form of behavior at the onset of the fertility decline which can then spread with the force of an innovation and in this way contribute to the speed and breadth of fertility decline once the diffusion process within the broader segments of the population begins. (Knodel 1977, p. 240).

Knodel did not deny that some form of birth control may have been practiced prior to the onset of the "transition," but he did question the existence of parity-dependent control. He conceived birth control to be of two forms, either parity-dependent or parity-independent. The former, parity-dependent control, is defined as family limitation "since it alone is directed at stopping childbearing at some given number of children. [It] . . . requires that couples anticipate fairly long-range benefits as a result of preventing further births" (Knodel 1977, p. 241). The innovation underlying the fertility transition is thus the adoption of parity-dependent family limitation—a decision to terminate childbearing after a certain number of children have been born.

The innovation-plus-adaptation argument requires the refutation of an assumption made by Carlsson, namely, that there is evidence of premodern birth control. Knodel noted the importance of this assumption: "[C]entral to Carlsson's rejection of the innovation perspective is the assertion that birth control was widely practiced prior to the beginning of the modern fertility transition" (1977, p. 240). This assertion is supported not only by Carlsson's analysis of fertility differences among various regions of Sweden but by the suggestion of other analysts of historical demographic data that birth control may have been practiced by married couples in selected provinces. J. D. Buissink cited evidence from the Netherlands (1971), and E. A. Wrigley's detailed analysis of

Colyton, England, suggested that early practice of birth control was followed by a period in which control was relinquished (1966). Carl Mosk's study of Japan also suggested that the practice of birth control existed among populations of some prefectures prior to the onset of more general fertility decline (1983). (See also Blake 1985.)

Knodel stated that evidence of the type employed by Carlsson and Buissink, however, does not suggest widespread parity-dependent control—family limitation. The data they employed emphasized levels of fertility rather than patterns of fertility, and it is the latter which is the key to the identification of family limitation, or parity-dependent control. The work of Louis Henry and the mathematical extensions of it by Ansley Coale and T. James Trussell have demonstrated that changes in age patterns of marital fertility evidence the adoption of parity-dependent family limitation. The foundation of that argument is the concept of natural fertility.

THE SIGNIFICANCE OF THE CONCEPT OF NATURAL FERTILITY

The concept of natural fertility was originally developed by Louis Henry (1961). By definition, natural fertility exists when married couples do not change their conception-related behavior as a function of the number of children ever born, that is, as a function of parity.

Henry's first analysis of natural fertility was based upon data for a limited number of populations. He observed that, while each population followed the predicted age pattern of fertility, the populations differed from one another in terms of levels of fertility, that is, completed family size. The differences arose from the fact that although various populations may follow practices that might delay each birth, as long as these practices are followed consistently, regardless of parity, then the shape of the curve approximates the ideal type, the convex curve. Practices that produced consistent differences in birth intervals, or spacing, might have included breastfeeding and postpartum abstinence (or taboos), among others. Birth intervals independent of such practices increase across the childbearing years of life as a consequence of increasing infecundity associated with the aging process, although as Jane Menken has demonstrated the decline in fecundability associated with aging occurs moderately late (1985). Levels of fecundability may vary among populations (Knodel and Wilson 1981; Menken, Trussell, and Watkins 1981), but there is no evidence that the age pattern of fecundability is significantly modified even though the overall level may vary.

In contrast to natural fertility, controlled fertility (family limitation in Knodel's terminology) exists when couples modify their behavior after a certain number of children have been born. In general, the notion of controlled fertility implies that couples, after a certain number of births, adopt methods that will prevent additional births; that is, they attempt to eliminate future conceptions in order to truncate the childbearing experience prior to the onset of age-related sterility. If such behavior is present among a population, then one would anticipate certain empirical regularities. Because couples attempt to stop childbearing after a selected number of births, success is indicated by the elimination of higher-order births. Women complete childbearing earlier than the previous generation, and as a result, the mean age of childbearing declines across successive cohorts of women.

Because parity is related to the age of the mother, the increasing elimination of higher-parity births would imply that the fertility decline that marks a controlled-fertility population would be greatest among older women. Thus, comparing age patterns of marital fertility over time, one would find that there is a proportionately greater relative reduction in age-specific marital fertility rates the older the mother. The change is, of course, relative rather than absolute because fertility normally declines with age as subfecundity or sterility increases with age. In the presence of natural fertility, the marital age-specific pattern is described by a convex curve. Increasing parity-dependent control is represented by a shift in the typical curve from convex to concave, as shown in figure 1. Evidence of natural fertility and the shift toward controlled fertility, that is, parity-dependent control, may also be provided by examining numerical indices of the ratio of age-specific fertility rates in each group of ages 25–29 and older to the marital fertility rate for women of ages 20–24, assumed to be the highest level. Coale and Trussell have added a mathematical procedure for measuring the degree to which an observed age-specific marital fertility schedule approximates an ideal natural fertility schedule or deviates from such a schedule (Coale 1971; Coale and Trussell 1974, 1978). The index "*m*" may be computed as a summary measure of the degree of difference between a model natural-fertility schedule and an observed-fertility schedule among all age groups, as well as a measure of the degree of variation at specific ages. An additional index, "*M*," represents the degree to which the level of fertility in the observed population approximates the level of fertility in the natural-fertility population.[2]

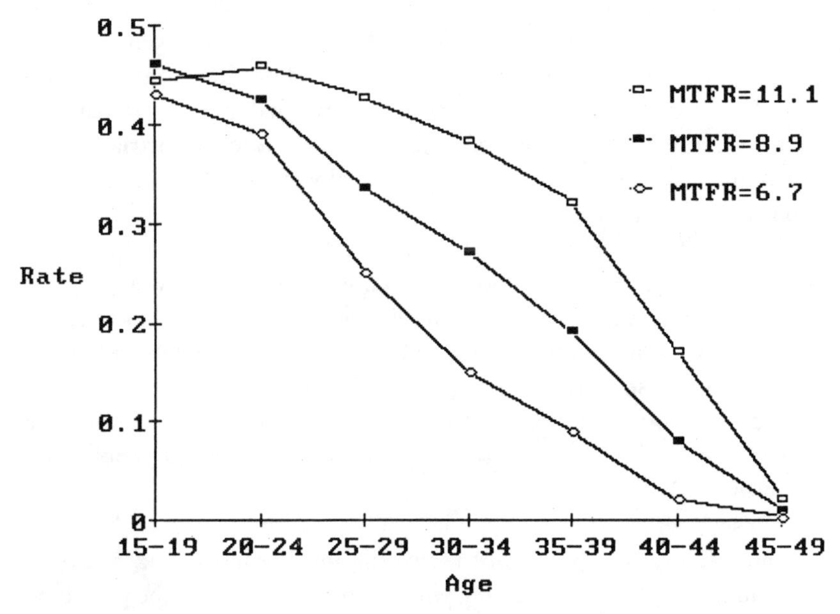

Figure 1. Patterns of Marital Age-Specific Fertility Rates (MFTR = Marital Total Fertility Rate)

In summary, the term "family limitation," as developed in this literature, refers to a type of fertility control which is specified by parity-dependent behavior. That is, once couples achieve a desired family size (or parity), they attempt to prevent further births. In contrast, natural fertility is the absence of parity-dependent control; that is, natural fertility exists where the number of children already born does not influence the likelihood of another birth. Parity-dependent family limitation has been identified through (1) a declining age of last birth; (2) a declining ratio of age-specific fertility rates at ages 25–29 and each older age category relative to the marital age-specific fertility rate of women aged 20–24; (3) increases in the length of the last closed birth-interval and perhaps the penultimate birth-interval as a consequence of "contraceptive-failure" after the achievement of the desired final family size; and (4) an increase of Coale and Trussell's "*m*" value. In spite of the multiplicity of techniques available to identify the adoption of parity-dependent control, we argue that further tests are required.

First, any population will evidence a range of final parities at age 49 for women whose marriages remain intact to that age. Variations in the age of onset of infecundity will produce some variability. Differences in the intensity of breastfeeding, even in the presence of a well-accepted norm related to length of breastfeeding, would produce some variability. Therefore analysis of birth spacing by final parity for natural-fertility populations should be able to demonstrate that variations in birth intervals can be accounted for by biological factors, that is variations in levels of infecundity.

Second, if the truncation process of achieving smaller family sizes is the predominate mode of behavior modification, within family-size groups early birth-intervals should remain relatively constant across successive birth cohorts; only ultimate and penultimate birth-intervals should increase. Of course among populations adopting parity-dependent limitation and having access to modern, highly effective contraception, one might also predict little or no change in the ultimate and penultimate birth-intervals.

These additional tests designed to clarify the forms of behavior adopted during the process of increasing fertility limitation, however, are equally applicable to dealing with the problem cited in the preceding section. That is, the innovation argument hinges upon the assumption that parity-dependent, family limitation is absent, or not widespread, among natural-fertility populations. The arguments developed above suggest that this assumption requires disaggregation of natural-fertility populations by completed family size and the comparison of birth intervals by parity within completed-family-size groups. Comparison of moderate- and large-family-size groups should find no significant variability in birth intervals among the first few birth intervals.

Extension of the analysis to include birth intervals within completed-family-size groups, however, is insufficient to indicate the absence of parity-dependent control among some subclasses of a natural-fertility population. The adaptation argument suggests that one must demonstrate that such differences, if identified, must be related to variations in social and economic conditions. One would begin with an examination of age-specific marital fertility schedules for various regional populations to demonstrate the existence of parity-dependent limitation as a response to variations in socioeconomic conditions. Knodel examined some evidence of this type for Sweden and was lead to reject Carlsson's conclusion that regional differences in fertility levels prior to the general Swedish fertility decline demonstrated that some groups were practicing deliberate birth control.

Thus we agree with Knodel that differences in levels of fertility observed by Carlsson in Sweden and by Buissink in the Netherlands are insufficient to confirm the presence of volitional, parity-dependent family limitation. Our argument presented above, however, applies in this case. The traditional analysis of the adoption of family limitation, which uses a variety of indicators, is incomplete, requiring more detailed analysis of birth spacing within final-family-size groups. The innovation-diffusion view of the process of increasing family limitation requires examination of variations among subclasses of the society not simply, however, to demonstrate the initial absence of parity-dependent limitation among subclasses of a society, but also to demonstrate that the acceptance of the small-family norms spreads throughout various subgroups in a predictable way.

THE DIFFUSION OF INNOVATION

Confirmation or denial of the acceptance of family limitation based upon the analysis of age-specific marital fertility patterns, however, cannot rest on the analysis of national, aggregate data, but requires analysis for subsections of the population which might vary with respect to access to or control over various socioeconomic resources. Even at the most general level of variation—rural-urban differences—data are often not available. As Knodel noted, "Unfortunately, rural-urban comparisons of age-specific marital fertility are rarely available for periods that clearly precede the secular fertility decline" (1977, p. 242). However, even where such data are available, analysis of rural-urban differences may be insufficient. Aggregation of data at this level may obscure significant variation within these areas. Ideally one needs access to data for distinct classes of society which vary with respect to access to or control over resources, investments, and consumer goods.

The innovation proposition implies more than simply the absence of family limitation prior to the onset of the secular decline in marital fertility. The innovation is the decision to stop after a given number of children have been born, as well as the acceptance of technology or techniques to implement that decision. According to the literature on innovation and diffusion, which is derived in large part from rural sociology and the study of new technologies, the innovation should diffuse, spread rapidly, from a limited set of early adopters throughout the balance of the population. Consequently, one should observe a sequence of time-related patterns. Initially the population should be undifferentiated by patterns of age-specific marital fertility. Next, one should observe a shift away from natural-fertility schedules among those population segments assumed to be early adopters of limitation—for example, the urban, secular, upper middle class. As other sectors of the society accept the innovation, the overall pace of fertility decline escalates, and eventually a new form of homogeneity is achieved with the uniform practice of family limitation, although differences in levels may still exist and some pockets of nonlimiting couples survive. Another way of describing the predicted changes is simply by the sequence (1) homogeneity, (2) divergence, and (3) convergence. These are states and processes common to literature on social change.

TECHNOLOGICAL EFFICIENCY AND FERTILITY LIMITATION

As a study of changing human values and motivations, however, the test of the adaptation-innovation argument remains incomplete. It is devoid of any consideration of explicitly formulated "learning" processes and technological efficiency. Discussion of such issues is important, and we suggest reasons for this through a simple illustration.

Assume the following two conditions. Under the first condition, we have available an imperfect technology to limit family size. Under the second condition we have a perfect or near-perfect technology—sterilization, the contraceptive pill, or the IUD backed up with legal abortion. Further, let us assume that in each case certain socioeconomic changes have occurred which lead some couples to decide that they wish to have fewer children than their parents had or fewer children than seems to be the norm for other classes in the society.

Couples living in a society marked by the first condition, access to an imperfect technology, may be motivated to test these imperfect methods prior to reaching the number of children desired. To delay testing the technology leaves the couple with two equally unacceptable alternatives after reaching the final desired family size: uncertainty or complete abstinence. Moreover, one would anticipate that the smaller the family-size target, the more assiduously couples would attempt to prove the effectiveness of their use of the imperfect technologies available.[3] Under the second condition, couples can delay use of the perfect technology until desired family size is achieved, if the technology is known and little practice is required to achieve maximum effectiveness.

Different forms of behavior may be prevalent under these two different conditions. Using an imperfect technology, couples have moderately long birth intervals at the aggregate level, and birth intervals increase with parity because (1) efforts to avoid conception may intensify when family goals are achieved, (2) practice with imperfect technologies may make couples more efficient, and (3) birth intervals are compounded by normal age-related infecundability. Having developed relatively effective control over conception, couples are more likely to be successful in terminating childbearing after the target has been achieved. There will be less subsequent error, and thus the mean age of childbearing declines. The perfect contraceptive population is also effective in controlling after achieving a certain target, and the mean age at last birth for this population also declines. Yet both populations are subject to some error in the last closed birth-interval, the period between the penultimate and the ultimate birth. Consequently, both populations may also be marked by relatively long final, closed birth-intervals. Examination of all birth intervals, however, should demonstrate that couples using imperfect contraception with limited-family-size targets have moderately long birth intervals, and the size of the birth intervals across all parities will vary by final parity. Those with smaller targets will be more highly motivated to test techniques earlier than those with higher targets.

The first condition, the population's having access to imperfect contraceptive technology, may be further distinguished. Assume a differentiated class structure, one in which socioeconomic and demographic conditions motivate some classes to want to terminate the number of births at a lower level than other classes because they have access to health facilities that ensure a greater probability of survival of infants or because the cost of caring for or educating children is greater. Such a class would be more likely to experiment with the available imperfect technologies earlier in the life cycle. Therefore, class-related variations in practice with the imperfect technology will also produce variations in spacing within the society among different class groups.

Note the implications of such practice-spacing behavior with respect to the indices of natural fertility. Increasing birth intervals associated with increasing effectiveness in use would be age related, producing declining age-specific marital fertility rates. Similar changes in the shape of the age-specific fertility curve would also be present owing to physiological changes. Therefore, the examination of age-specific marital fertility curves may be insufficient to identify the timing and the conditions under which parity-dependent family limitation exists or changes, the conditions under which change represents adaptation or innovation.

TESTING FOR INNOVATION

The notions of adaptation and innovation do not represent grand theories but rather reflect a set of modest propositions: ones that have the advantages of being falsifiable and that therefore provide the framework within which a series of specific hypotheses may be tested. The nature of the data set employed in the MHDP makes it ideally suited for the tests of the competing propositions suggested by the concepts of adaptation and innovation. The data set also provides the opportunity to examine a series of other independent hypotheses; for example, the hypothesis that immigrants tend to have higher fertility than natives. We shall exploit opportunities to examine subsidiary issues insofar as they do not detract from our central objectives. But our major focus is the adaptation-innovation argument, because it contains a series of critical assumptions regarding changes in human behavior. Some of these become evident through a summary of falsifiable propositions derived from the notion of fertility change as an innovation process. These propositions follow from the above discussion of the literature on innovation and adaptation, and fall into two sets.

First, the innovation argument suggests the hypothesis that prior to the onset of the change in fertility from high to low associated with the processes of modernization, populations are homogeneous with respect to parity-dependent family limitation. Variations in fertility levels may be present, but these would be limited to parity-independent constraints on fertility largely due to variations in selected proximate determinants of fertility, such as age at marriage. To distinguish between parity-dependent and parity-independent fertility, it will be necessary (1) to control for selected proximate determinants (Bongaarts 1978) of fertility, such as age at marriage, (2) to introduce tests for other proximate determinants of fertility, and (3) to focus primarily on patterns of fertility within marriages. To test the notion of homogeneity, one must demonstrate that there are no significant differences in marital fertility patterns among significant subcategories of the population, theoretically specified. Such subcategories are discussed in chapters 3, 5, and 6.

The universal absence of parity-dependent behavior in advance of the anticipated secular decline in fertility cannot, however, be tested simply on the basis of controlling for selected proximate determinants of fertility, examining patterns of marital fertility, analyzing age at last birth, and examining changes in final and penultimate birth intervals. We argue that specific attention must be given to the tempo of childbearing across all parities. The innovation argument predicts that during periods when parity-dependent control is absent, the length of the birth intervals during the initial stages of family formation should be independent of final parity. An inverse relationship between birth intervals and final parity would suggest that couples who desired smaller families began to test their ability to stop childbearing earlier rather than later because access to control methods is limited to imperfect contraceptive technologies. These analyses involve consideration of additional proximate determinants of fertility, including variations in fecundability.

Second, assuming the first proposition cannot be falsified, the innovation argument predicts the adoption of parity-dependent control emerges among selected groups and then diffuses throughout the balance of the population. Several specific tests are involved. Comparison of theoretically identified subcohorts over time should confirm the implied "lag" hypothesis: change occurs initially among a group of early adopters and occurs later among other groups. Change occurs at different times among different groups. Simultaneous change among theoretically meaningful subcohorts is less likely under the lag hypothesis. Note, however, that both simultaneous and lagged diffusion are compatible with an adaptation perspective if the diffusion parallels that of the changing social characteristics to which individuals are adapting.

A related test of the same principle involves an analysis of the geography of change. Theoretically, according to the innovation view, one would anticipate that the adoption of parity-dependent control would emerge among urban populations and then diffuse through the more rural sectors of the society. The innovation argument predicts that change does not occur simultaneously among all geographically defined populations.

The innovation argument therefore suggests a series of interrelated tests. These are presented in Part II, and where appropriate, each of the analytical chapters begins with a brief additional specification of the theoretical basis of the tests presented.

While our analysis of fertility change is proposed as a series of specific tests of a general set of propositions concerning fertility change, our study is specific to a particular population during a particular time. Yet it is a population observed over a series of years which represents an important phenomenon in American society, the settlement of the American frontier. We therefore turn in the second part of this chapter to a discussion of the setting, the meaning of the frontier and its significance for demographic change generally and fertility change specifically.

FRONTIER SETTLEMENT AND FERTILITY CHANGE

In the introduction to this chapter, we suggested that the fertility experience of the population studied in this volume was influenced by its frontier experience and the timing of that experience. The importance of the frontier for understanding social change in America has been explored extensively since the presentation of Frederick Jackson Turner's paper "The Significance of the Frontier in American History," but his frontier thesis is perhaps inapplicable to the study of levels and changes in American fertility. His thesis, briefly stated, is this:

> American development has exhibited not merely advance along a single line, but a return to primitive conditions on a continually advancing frontier line, and a new development for that area. American social development has been continually beginning over again on the frontier. This perennial rebirth, this fluidity of American life, this expansion westward with its new opportunities, its continuous touch with the simplicity of primitive society, furnish the forces dominating American character. The true point of view in the history of this nation is not the Atlantic coast, it is the Great West. (1921, pp. 2–3)

Turner's thesis strongly influenced, if it did not dominate and guide, much American historical research over more than forty years. Little work, however, emerged dealing with the effect of the frontier on demographic processes.[4] While historians have appeared to ignore the importance of the frontier to demographic processes in America, economists and demographers have not. The characteristics of the American frontier have indeed strongly influenced the work of demographers concerned with the analysis of American fertility.

Whatever the intrinsic meaning of the concept of the frontier, up to the late nineteenth century census officials of the United States government operationally treated the frontier as simply a region of low population density. Acceptance of this definition is current. Murray Melbin defined a frontier as "a pattern of sparse settlement in space . . . located between a more densely settled and a practically empty region" (1978, p. 6). The frontier environment, conceived simply as a region of low population density, is discussed in several important studies of regional fertility variations and change in American society. Yasuba's study of fertility ratios in the United States during the middle of the nineteenth century notes significant regional variations, with the highest ratios among the frontier or recent frontier states or territories (1962).[5] He concludes that the higher the population density, the lower the fertility.

> [In] a community where the supply of land is limited, the value of children as earning assets is low and hence the demand for children may not be so great as where there is plenty of open land nearby. The increased cost of setting up children as independent farmers and fear of the fragmentation of family farms may further encourage the restriction of family size in densely populated areas. (1962, p. 159)

Further analysis by Forster and Tucker (1972) found support for Yasuba's conclusion. Density as an environmental characteristic emerged subsequently in the study of Easterlin, who presented what is essentially an adaptation interpretation of regional and community fertility differences: "A plausible case can be made that the secular decline in American fertility was a voluntary response to changing environmental conditions" (1971, p. 400). Examining child-woman ratios for various regions from 1850 through 1960, Easterlin finds lower ratios among the earliest settled regions and higher ratios among the more recently settled regions, the frontiers. These differences appeared as early as 1800. The changing levels of the ratios, from high to low and again to high during the post–World War II recovery, occurred simultaneously across all regions. Thus, with minor fluctuations, the regional differences persisted, although tending in most recent times toward convergence. When a region is initially settled, the population begins with a fertility rate higher than that found among the populations of previously settled regions. But relatively quickly the rate begins to decline, paralleling the downward trend previously initiated in the settled regions. Thus these data suggest similar fertility change, beginning from different levels but declining at roughly the same pace. If all regions were "adapting" fertility to changing environmental or socioeconomic factors simultaneously, what then is the significance of the frontier for fertility change in the United States?

The American frontier experience was a continuous process affecting segments of the population from the period of initial colonization in Virginia and New England through the beginning of the twentieth century. Political considerations were important in the pattern of settlement, but the basic attraction of individuals and families to the frontier was resource availability—mining opportunities, open land for cattle and sheep, and cheap arable land for agriculture. Melbin has suggested that the commitment to western resource exploitation became a national policy underlying governmental encouragement to settle western regions: "In 1862, with the passage of the Homestead Act, it became a deliberate policy of the U.S. government to use the western territory to help relieve the conditions of tenant farmers and hard-pressed city laborers" (1978, p. 17). While historical studies have emphasized circular migration to the frontier and back, it is obvious that expansion into the frontier absorbed a substantial population growth that would otherwise have been confined to increasingly crowded urban centers and marginally productive eastern farmlands.

Movement to the frontier involved not simply "pull" factors but also "push" factors; the two components underlay many migration streams. The relative limits on economic opportunities in established areas were often the stimulus to move. Absence of economic opportunities, economic exploitation, and restrictions on individual liberties separately or collectively stimulated movements of families and individuals.

In addition to perceived access to unexploited or uncontrolled resources, other considerations played a role in the settlement of America's continuous frontier during the seventeenth, eighteenth, and nineteenth centuries. In some cases religious, ethnic, or political persecution stimulated groups of individuals to migrate to new frontiers. The initial settlers in the Utah territory represent a particular group of frontier settlers motivated by political conflicts and religious persecution, but the selection of the settlement area was strongly determined by economic considerations. Mormons who initially colonized Utah sought not simply an area in which they could avoid conflict with neighboring groups but also an area in which an independent economic empire could be established to sustain and develop this "chosen" people. Drawing upon biblical analogies with the "people of the covenant" (i.e., the Jews), the Mormons sought to establish their own Zion—a political and economic state that would protect the welfare and rights of a religious group.

Although movement to the frontier provided access to certain resources and opportunities, it also resulted in exclusion from certain costs and benefits associated with residence in the established communities from which the settlers came. Educational opportunities were limited on the frontier and often were provided for through the church; thus the costs associated with the education of children were low. Consumer goods were limited, a circumstance that encouraged handicraft production. Because population size was limited, few individuals were available for wage labor, so that families relied more upon their own members—hence children were potentially more productive and valuable than they were in the more settled areas of the country.

The Utah settlement was not as the now-predominant myth would have it—the myth that settlement in the Far West was dominated heavily by males. Frontier exploration was often conducted by individualists leading small bands, but settlement tended to fall into two types. Development of mining, lumber, and cattle settlements produced communities dominated by males, while agricultural settlements were typically established by families. There was no one fixed set of stages of settlement as suggested by Turner. Regions varied in the sequence of the development of various types of industries, and therefore the argument that the frontier population was relatively homogeneous, consisting primarily of young males, is incorrect. (See Melbin 1978, p. 7 for a contemporary restatement of the myth.) Agricultural settlements in Utah Territory, and in other regions, consisted of relatively balanced male and female populations, not much different from the population composition found in older, established agricultural communities (Eblen 1965).

Frontier regions varied in the forms of settlement, but they all shared one common feature. The frontier was transitory. Because open productive land was always limited, it was not possible over long periods of time to provide independent farms or ranches for maturing sons. The movement of commercial activities and professionals from the settled areas necessitated the development of formal educational systems to provide the skills that would make children competitive in an increasingly specialized labor market. It is therefore not surprising that Easterlin and his associates, in their study (Easterlin, Alter, and Condron 1978) of American frontier communities in the Middle West and the North Central states during the mid–nineteenth century, indicated that a higher number of children were born to first-generation settlers than to their children's generation.

The relationship between the frontier and fertility should not be treated simply as the consequence of a new set of economic factors allowing for early marriage and large families. Certain classes of early settlers postponed marriage and family, notably men on the move in pursuit of work in trapping, hunting, cattle, lumber, and often mining and railroads. Individuals might not have adjusted their expectations about family size after arriving on the frontier but might have been motivated to join the movement West because they had married early, had had large families, and had sought greater economic opportunities for their children. As economic opportunities declined with increasing population density, according to the Yasuba-Easterlin argument, pro-family, pro-natal individuals might have been encouraged to move again to other developing regions. But by the late 1880s, fewer frontier areas were available. As Turner notes in the first sentences of his paper "The Significance of the Frontier in American History":

> In a recent bulletin of the Superintendent of the Census for 1890 appear these significant words "up to and including 1880 the country had a frontier of settlement, but at present the unsettled area has been so broken into isolated bodies of settlement that there can hardly be said to be a frontier line." (1921, p. 1)

Even within the increasingly restricted frontier, areas remained to be developed throughout the latter part of the nineteenth century, and to a certain extent through the beginning of the twentieth century. Couples entering marriage in the second generation of settlement with high fertility expectations might well have moved into the undeveloped pockets as part of new settlement groups within the region.

For the Latter-day Saints who migrated to Utah, the frontier was more than simply an economic region, an area with accessible agricultural land. Utah represented, of course, an area in which an independent, comprehensive economic system could be developed; but it also represented an area in which at least the active and committed LDS members could pursue a system of religious values, many of which were family- and fertility-specific and in some cases at variance with the prevailing norms and laws of American society generally. Marriage was the expected adult state; rewards accrued to parenthood; and for some years polygyny was practiced in spite of external pressures—social, financial, military, and political.

Any of the advantages associated with frontier settlement disappeared relatively quickly. Within half a century following the LDS pioneers' entry into Salt Lake Valley, high-quality arable land had been developed. The economy had become more tied to the national economic system through the transcontinental railroad. Control by the federal government had enforced the secularization of the political system. Polygyny had been abandoned. Finally, the territory had been admitted into the Union. And, as noted above, the American frontier line had become meaningless, at least in the eyes of the U.S. Superintendent of the Census.

Assuming an "adaptation" argument consistent with the work of Easterlin and others, the implications of the frontier for fertility in general and the fertility of the population of Utah specifically become clear. Given the transitory nature of the comparative economic advantage of the frontier, one would anticipate early marriage, universal marriage, and high fertility for the majority of the first generation of settlers. Active participation in the LDS church would produce rewards such as access to land allocated by ecclesiastical authority, so that even during the early stages of settlement, differences might exist among groups. The closure of the frontier and integration into a national economic system would result in an increasingly widespread need to adjust family size and marriage patterns. Long-term residents would be more likely to perceive changes in opportunities and costs of family formation, while more recent migrants would see the opportunities of the declining frontier as being advantageous relative to those of the areas from which they migrated, the more densely settled urban and increasingly industrial communities of the northeastern region of the United States and of Western Europe.

CONTROLLING FERTILITY ON THE FRONTIER

Frontier settlements occurred over a wide range of time in the United States, and behavioral changes among frontier populations were strongly influenced by temporal events, particularly in the case of childbearing. The women studied in this volume commenced childbearing about 1815, and the women who started their families in Utah Territory would have been born no earlier than 1830. Many had their origins in the New England states, and the population of New England during the first four decades of the nineteenth century had already experienced a major decline in fertility. Thus the women in this study may have already been exposed to communities in which changes in childbearing practices had been initiated.

Early changes in fertility in the United States are attributed primarily to changing marital patterns. This attribution is due to two assumptions. First is the presumed absence of effective contraception:[6] it is assumed that methods of birth control were undeveloped or unknown on the American frontier. Second is the presumed difficulty of following known limitation practices, which made them unacceptable. An early decline in fertility that had been observed in France was largely the result of the practice of coitus interruptus—a demanding and often inefficient technique, which some writers seem to view as having been unacceptable on the American frontier, with its presumed male dominance, vigorous pioneer spirit, and patriarchal authority. The first assumption appears to be based on myth, and the second is simply incorrect. Patterns of fertility change in American society in settled areas shortly after settlement of the frontier repudiate such assumptions. Further, there is evidence that contraceptive technology, although imperfect at this time, was widely known in the nineteenth century (Himes 1963).

Charles Goodyear's 1837 discovery of the vulcanization of rubber lead to widespread production of condoms by midcentury; Robert Dale Owen published a volume in 1831 in which he discussed coitus interruptus, the vaginal sponge, and skin condoms as birth control devices; and Charles Knowltons's 1832 publication, *Fruits of Philosophy, or the Private Companion of Young Married People,* discussed spermicidal douche as a conception-preventing method. In midcentury Frederick Hollik's *Marriage Guide or Natural History of Generation* outlined a rhythm method. His publisher's representative subsequently wrote to him that his work had become "household books, so that not a house, cabin, or miner's camp can be found without for hundreds of miles" (quoted in Reed 1978, p. 12). Reed continues:

> By 1865 various physicians had publicly endorsed withdrawal (coitus interruptus), spermicidal douches, the vaginal diaphragm or pessary, rubber condoms, and periodic abstinence. These birth control methods were effective by nineteenth-century medical standards. Most nineteenth-century birth control advocates intended their advice for married couples who sought only the means to limit their children to a manageable three or four. (1978, p. 6)

The list of possible contraceptives was growing, faster than Reed's summary would indicate. In 1864 Edward Blissfoote developed the "womb veil," the vaginal diaphragm, but three decades earlier Frederick A. White, a German gynecologist, had developed the cervical cap. A paper in the 1864 *Transactions of the National Medical Association* reported the availability of 123 different kinds of pessaries.

The availability of contraceptive devices and the publication of books and tracts discussing their importance and availability may also be demonstrated by the reaction generated. In 1873 Congress passed the

Comstock Act, which treated information on the prevention of conception as obscene and the dissemination of such information as illegal. Subsequently various states passed acts extending the Comstock Act to cover the recommendation or prescription of contraceptives. Such acts remained "on the books" in Connecticut and Massachusetts until the 1960s.

The methods were available (and seemingly widely used if one extrapolates from declining fertility levels); and although they have been described as "imperfect technology," they seem relatively effective. Moreover, these methods were widely used in the United States until the 1960s, when highly effective, non-coitus-related methods became available—the pill and the IUD. In England, methods primitive by modern standards were critical in the twentieth-century decline of fertility. E. Lewis-Faning reports for example that among women married between 1940 and 1947, 43 percent were currently using withdrawal as the method of choice (1949).

The seeming evidence of a homogeneous, natural-fertility population in Western Europe prior to the fertility transition—except in France, where there was, as mentioned, an anomalous decline of fertility owing to the use of coitus interruptus as the major control method—appears to be responsible for the conclusion that birth control devices were unknown, ineffective, and unacceptable until late in the nineteenth century. Yet evidence from a wide range of historical documents and studies of primitive populations confirms the knowledge and use of contraception. *Azl* (coitus interruptus) was recognized by Mohammed, in the Koran, in the seventh century. Linda Gordon has reported that a tenth-century Persian physician, Abu Bekr Muhammed Ibn Zakariya al-Razi, describes methods of abortion that could be used should his prescribed contraceptives fail (1976). She also noted that of the 200 tribal groups for which data were included in the Human Relations Area Files, 125 are reported to have knowledge or evidence of the occurrence of abortion.

That couples on the American frontier could often have controlled fertility, if motivated to do so, therefore seems without question. The population in other regions of the country had initiated fertility limitation; a variety of methods of contraception were known and discussed so widely in professional and lay literature that Congress passed an act, as noted above, to prohibit distribution of information on contraception. Moreover, historical evidence indicates that methods of birth control—mythical, magical, and practical—had been known for centuries among various populations. Techniques per se do not seem to be an innovation but rather part of private, if not public, culture to be adopted at certain times and under certain conditions by certain groups of the population. The evidence presented in this section clearly suggests that attempts to explain the initial absence of rational fertility limitation and the trend to stop childbearing at a smaller number of children need not stand or fall on the question of the availability of modern contraceptive technology. Rather than focusing on *how* fertility was limited, the study is able to focus on the specification of the time, conditions, and selective adoption of fertility limitation among the MHDP population.

SUMMARY

Our study of fertility change on the American frontier complements and extends an increasing body of historical demographic research which seeks through the detailed analysis of individual cases to evaluate a set of "interesting partial hypotheses." It avoids being simply a descriptive analysis of fertility change through our attempt to evaluate two potentially competing or complementary perspectives on historical fertility change, perspectives from which efforts have been made to develop contemporary policy recommendations. Ours is a specifically American study, yet one which deals with a population, a region, and a time admirably suited to evaluate these general theoretical perspectives.

This database is somewhat different from what has been used in many historical demographic studies but consistent with the genealogical files so fruitfully exploited by Knodel. Our analysis plans owe much to the work of Henry, Coale, and Knodel. Building upon the methodological innovations introduced by these investigators, we add two procedures to the analysis of historical patterns of fertility change. First, we focus on the two dimensions of fertility discussed by Norman Ryder: quantum and tempo (1980). Second, we draw upon the work of John Bongaarts and Robert Potter (1983). Our work thus links the specific forms of behavior described by the proximate determinants to changes in two dimensions of fertility: quantum (levels) and tempo (pace). It is with respect to tempo—timing or spacing—that this study extends, in a more rigorous and systematic fashion, the analysis of the presence or absence of fertility limitation beyond the study of age-specific fertility patterns. The available data and the theoretical framework of the adaptation and innovation perspectives provide an exceptionally well-suited environment for this pursuit. Access to detailed individual-level data makes it possible to go beyond previous studies of fertility transitions in

Western Europe. In addition to the analysis of common indicators of natural fertility and the increasing adoption of family limitation—marital age-specific fertility schedules, age at last birth, and Coale and Trussell's indices, we extend the analysis to birth intervals, controlling for the effects of proximate determinants of fertility. We further examine changes and variations in levels, patterns, and timing of childbearing within subcohorts of the population, and examine the geographic patterns of change.

CHAPTER 2

The Context of Changing Fertility

When early cohorts of MHDP women married and began to bear children, around 1815, Utah was largely an unknown region. Spanish explorers had traveled briefly into the area in the eighteenth century, but the famous early trappers and explorers—Peter Skene Ogden, William Ashley, Jedediah Smith, and others—did not enter the territory until after 1825. John C. Fremont did not traverse the area of present-day Utah until his expedition of 1838–45.

A year after the Mormons entered Salt Lake Valley in 1847, the U.S. Senate published an authoritative map of the region which identified Utah as an area just south of the "Great Salt Lake." The term applied more to the presumed Ute Indian territory than to a geographic or political region. Utah, as a territory, was but part of the "Upper California" cited on the Senate's 1848 map; but it secured independent identity as "Utah Territory" in 1850. The Mormon settlers had identified the region as their proposed State of Deseret, but the region and later state would remain as certified by Congress—Utah.

Because Utah emerged as an official regional entity only at midcentury, the earliest groups of women included in this study were born, married, and commenced childbearing elsewhere. Most are bound to Utah by sample definition, however, because on each of the genealogical records in which these earliest women appear—the family-group sheets used in this study[1]—at least one person is listed who was born or died on the Mormon pioneer trail or in Utah. Yet ties to this region of the majority of women included in this study are stronger than this. Nearly two-thirds of the women in the study were born in Utah, and approximately four-fifths of the children were born there. Clearly the majority of the childbearing experiences of MHDP women are linked to experiences within Utah, and it is Utah that provides the context within which most decisions were made regarding marriage and family formation.

Some appreciation for this social and economic context is essential to an interpretation of the trends in fertility reported in this volume. The social context within which individuals are raised and bear children is an important explanatory variable in fertility research, and one of the more comprehensive analyses of World Fertility Survey data emphasizes that its uniqueness rests upon a framework that is contextual, multilevel, and comparative (Entwisle, Mason, and Hermalin 1986). In that spirit, this chapter outlines the context of childbearing of the MHDP women, emphasizing the social and economic systems of Utah as they developed and the religious value system that supported universal marriage and high fertility.

In the following section of this chapter, we outline the processes of migration, dispersion within the region, and population growth generally. Then we describe the socioeconomic changes that have traditionally been associated with declining fertility levels. We conclude the chapter with an examination of the value system that supports high fertility among the Mormons and other religious groups.

MIGRATION, DISPERSION, AND GROWTH

The organized migration between 1846 and 1870 of over 60,000 adherents of the LDS church from the eastern and midwestern United States, as well as from Western Europe, into the unsettled intermountain region marked the beginning of the final frontier experience of the Mormons (Wahlquist 1974). From the time of the church's organization in Fayette, Seneca County, New York, its members had migrated—were often driven—to the fringes of the westerly advancing line of the American frontier. (See figure 2.) A year after founding the church, its leader and founder, Joseph Smith, moved his followers to Kirtland, Geauga County, Ohio. Shortly thereafter he sent a group onward to Missouri to establish new communities. In 1838, seven years after the settlement of Kirtland, Joseph Smith and church members fled armed attacks by local non-Mormon residents and attempted to settle in Far West, Missouri. Within the year, renewed mob violence, legitimated

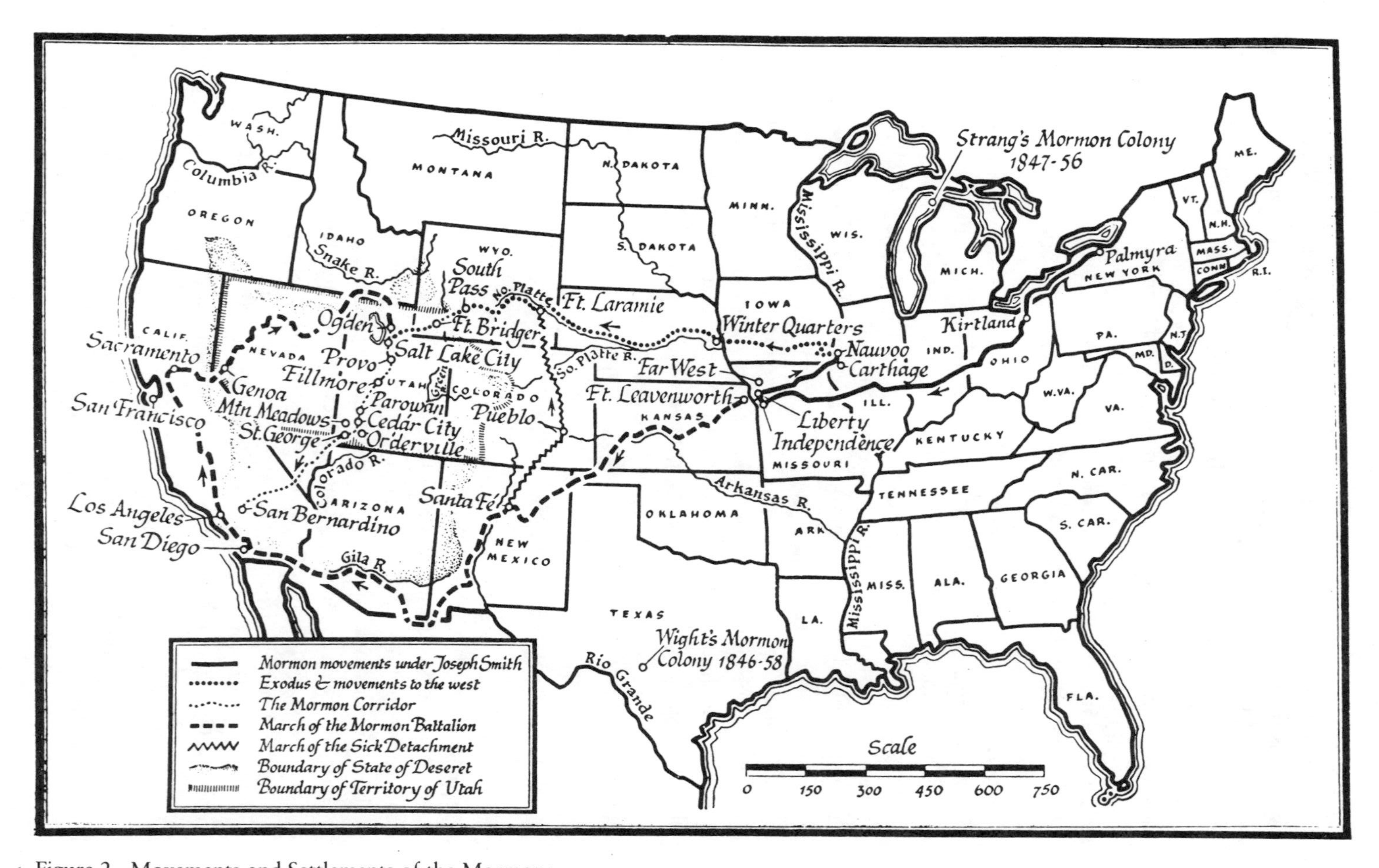

Figure 2. Movements and Settlements of the Mormons
Source: Adapted from William Mulder and A. Russell Mortensen, Among the Mormons (Lincoln: University of Nebraska Press, 1958) p. 58. Used by permission

by Governor Boggs, of Missouri, forced the church's multiplying adherents to Illinois, where they developed a new city, Nauvoo. Less than a decade passed before the "Saints" were driven out again. These migrations were precipitated by local reactions to both religious differences and the relative civil, political, and military autonomy of the Mormon social organization.

Following the assassination of Joseph Smith at Carthage, Illinois, in 1844, the new prophet and president, Brigham Young,[2] led the "Saints" from Nauvoo to Council Bluffs, Iowa, in 1846, using the Iowa site as a staging point for the final movement westward. In the summer of 1847, the first small group of Mormon pioneers entered Salt Lake Valley and established a headquarters to prepare for the migration, which was to accelerate in the next decade.

From the time of the establishment of the first independent community in Kirtland until late in the nineteenth century, the LDS population was continuously involved in frontier colonization,[3] often competing with other settlers. By midcentury they had isolated themselves in virgin territory,[4] and the Salt Lake Valley became the headquarters of the church. From this bastion, church leaders mandated a process of colonization, agricultural development, and commercial and industrial expansion which quickly transformed the region. The expansionist policy pursued by church leaders was successful for several reasons. In the following sections we consider two of the most important: the development of a population supply to fuel expansionism through the church's missionary activities and the ability to order and supervise colonization. Later, this expansion also became hegemonic with the political dominance of the religion asserting itself even within communities less homogenously made up of church members.

DEVELOPING A POPULATION BASE: THE MISSIONARY PROGRAM

Within a year of the founding of the church, the missionary program was formally organized. Its success has depended in part on the fact that ecclesiastical authority rests in the hands of a lay priesthood into which any worthy male may be ordained. From this body, missionaries are selected.[5] The first missionaries worked in the Mid-Atlantic and New England states. Foreign missions were initiated in Canada in 1833, and missionaries were sent to England in 1837. Between 1837 and 1846, 17,849 baptisms were performed in the British Isles. Approximately

4,700 of the early converts migrated to join the brethren in Nauvoo prior to its abandonment in 1846.

As the number of European converts grew, financial arrangements were made by the church to sponsor immigration. The Perpetual Emigration Fund[6] was established by Brigham Young in 1849, and the territorial legislature established the fund in law in the following year. The fund allowed converts in Europe to receive full or partial support for migration to Utah in organized groups.[7] These groups included some families for whom all travel arrangements were made by church representatives but also included families able to support their own travel, in whole or in part. These latter families were able to reduce costs by booking passage on ships contracted to transport sponsored families. Funded migrants to Utah were expected to reimburse the fund for their travel after settling, thus providing a "perpetual source" of funds for other migrants. With support from the fund, 38,000 individuals from the British Isles and 13,000 from Scandinavia and other European countries migrated to Utah between 1846 and 1870.

Coupled with high rates of natural increase, conversion and migration produced a population sufficiently large to fuel the expansion plans of the leaders of the LDS church. Mobilization of these population resources under an economic organization superintended by Brigham Young until his death in 1877 resulted in the development of a society that could survive the competition of the non-Mormons who moved into the area in increasing numbers after the completion in 1869 of the transcontinental rail link in Utah.[8]

ESTABLISHING AN EMPIRE: DISPERSAL OF THE POPULATION

In 1847 the Great Basin region of the Rocky Mountains surrounding present-day Salt Lake City was an area sparsely occupied by native Americans and sketchily mapped by Spanish priests, mountain men, and a few legendary explorers. Settlement in the Great Basin offered a sanctuary and provided an opportunity to establish an independent religious empire. In spite of the dislocations caused by the frequent moves of the church, the assassination of the church's founder, and the subsequent defection by some groups who refused to accept Brigham Young as Joseph Smith's successor, the church moved into Utah with a leader and an organization that could mobilize the church's adherents to spread throughout the area, developing agriculture and industry sufficient to sustain the growing population.

The first Mormon settlement in Utah Territory was the Salt Lake Valley. Within the three or four years between the first arrivals (1847) and the first census (1850, but actually taken in 1851 in the territory), the church had established settlements in what has been described as the Mormon core area (Wahlquist 1981, p. 101). This area consists of the counties along the Wasatch Mountains (or Wasatch "Front") forming a linear settlement pattern from Ogden (Weber County) on the north to Provo (Utah County) on the south. In succeeding decades the settlement continued the predominately north-south expansion: growth was blocked to the west by arid lands and deserts and to the east by mountains. The north-south settlements generally paralleled the mountain range. (See fig. 3.) This allowed access to water runoff from regular stream flows for agricultural irrigation in the valleys. The mountain ranges also provided summer grazing land in the foothills and resources for secondary industries such as lumbering, milling, and quarrying.

The nineteenth-century expansion of the population along the predominately north-south corridor in Utah west of the Wasatch Mountains was the result of two forms of settlement:

> Although there were many variations, Mormon colonization took two basic forms, directed and non-directed. Directed settlements refer to those planned and supervised by Mormon church officials. Exploring parties were often sent out to find valleys with the potential of supporting agricultural communities, then leaders were selected and "called"[9] to direct the colonizing efforts to develop these regions. Participants were sometimes called in public meetings (without warning), but frequently the leader of the colonizing party was authorized to select those families he wished to accompany him to the frontier. In many cases bishops in established communities were assigned the task of selecting a given number of families to participate in a particular colonizing mission. In still other cases a general call for volunteers was issued throughout the region. Many of the dry marginal and submarginal portions of southern Utah, Arizona, and Nevada were founded as directed settlements. . . . Nondirected settlements were those founded by individuals acting without direction from ecclesiastical (or other) authority. Such settlements in Utah have not received as much attention by historians as directed settlements, but they were far more numerous. (Wahlquist 1981, p. 92)

Wayne Wahlquist may be correct in arguing the relative significance of nondirected settlements, but it is also evident that without the man-

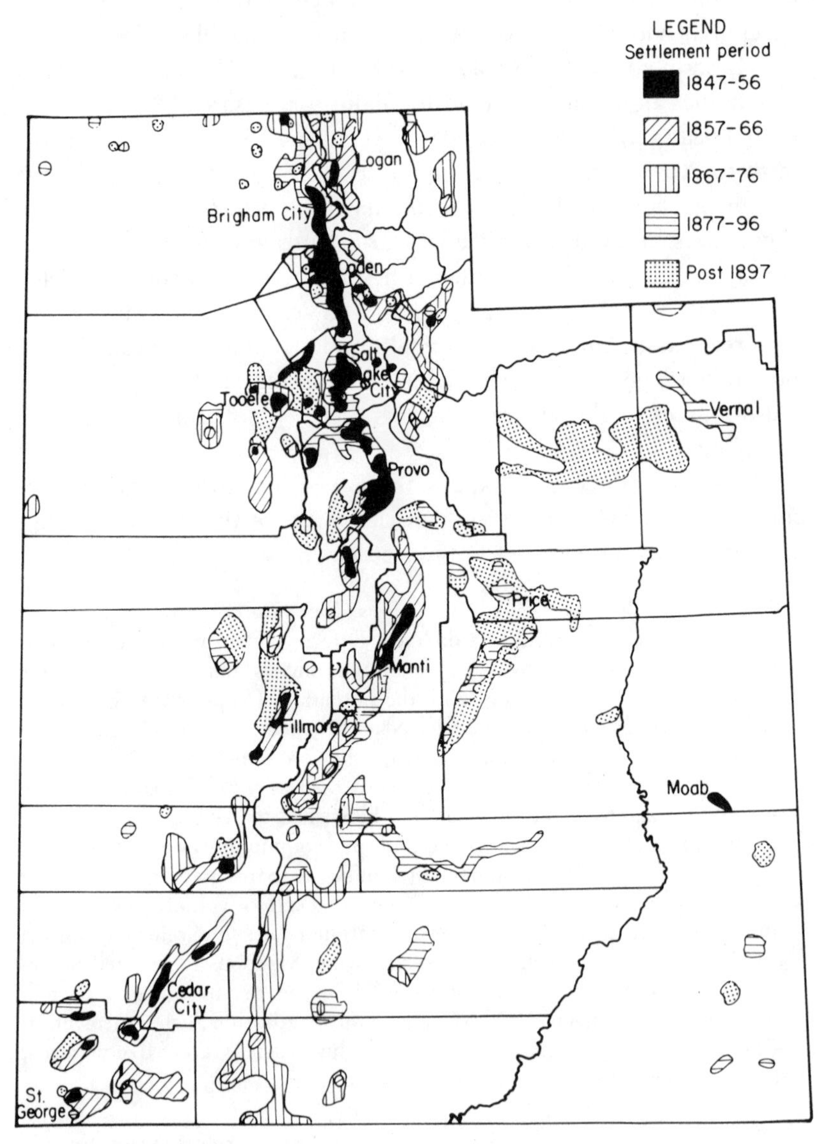

Figure 3. Mormon Expansion by Decade
Source: Wayne L. Wahlquist, ed, *Atlas of Utah* (Provo, Utah: Brigham Young University Press, 1981) p. 90.

dated, directed-settlement program the expansion of the population throughout the region would have been much slower. With such a program, significant Mormon settlements rapidly expanded beyond the boundaries of Utah. As indicated by the map in figure 4, during the last half of the nineteenth century, major Mormon colonies were established in Canada, Mexico, Arizona, Colorado, Idaho, Nevada, New Mexico, and Wyoming.

The linear settlement pattern of close-knit Mormon communities facilitated communication and the distribution of orders, ideas, goods, and economic mandates from the central urban core in Salt Lake Valley to the balance of the state.[10] Families responsive to the "call" to settle outlying areas were obviously committed to accept the dictates of the leaders of the church. Such families, drawn from recently settled areas to establish still others, were exposed to long periods of frontier life. These dual-migration families were perhaps atypical. They were highly committed to the church, and they were willing to move from one frontier area to another. Seemingly, these two characteristics supported large families; for moving provided continuous access to land, and this both allowed sons to be established on their own farms or ranches and enhanced the value of familial labor while lowering the costs of rearing children.

It has been argued that the colonization process produced two types of families. One is characterized by frequent moves during the family-building process; the second type, after initial settlement in the central, more urban counties, remains relatively stable. Some have considered groups of the first type to be dominant:

> The continuing colonizing activity led to a great deal of mobility among the Mormon population of the nineteenth century. A sample study of U.S. agricultural census schedules for three Wasatch Front communities—Brigham City, Kaysville, and Springville—revealed that 75 to 80 percent of the names on those schedules did not recur on succeeding schedules ten years later. (Wahlquist 1981, p. 92; see also May 1977)

Data from our genealogical files may also be used to study mobility or its converse, stability, by comparing the place of birth of children during the entire reproductive span. Such analyses suggest substantial stability, certainly greater than that suggested by Wahlquist. In an analysis of several communities throughout the state, our data indicate that the population of the larger towns—county seats primarily—was generally stable. Among southern Utah towns, 475 per 1,000 residents re-

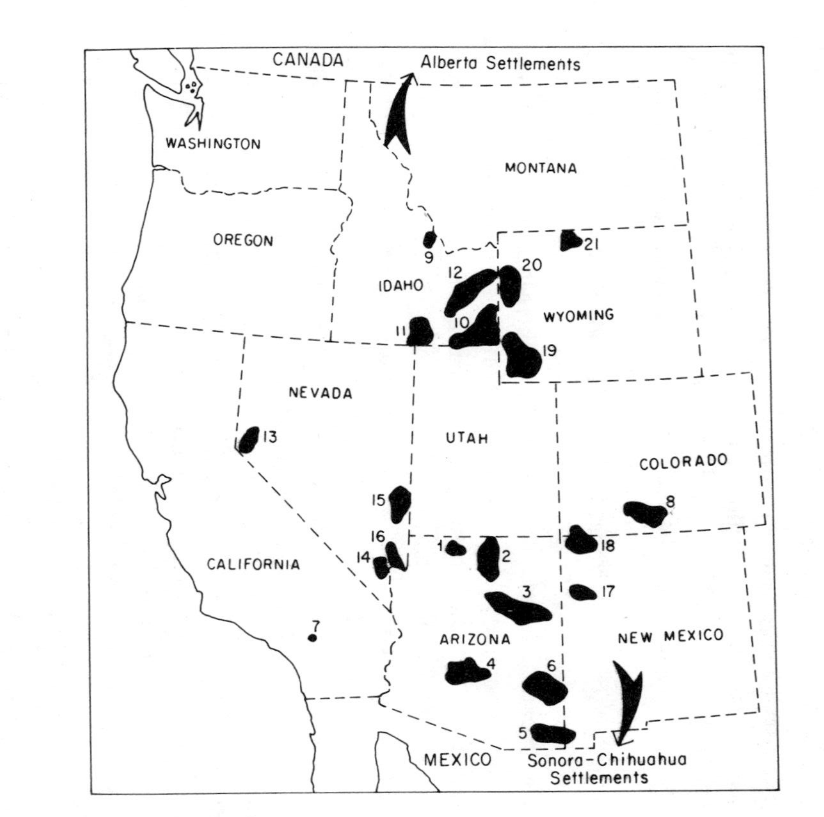

Figure 4. Mormon Expansion beyond Utah, 1849–1900
Source: Wayne L. Wahlquist, ed, *Atlas of Utah* (Provo, Utah: Brigham Young University Press, 1981) p. 92.

mained in the same communities throughout their childbearing years of life. The population in Utah County towns (Lehi and Hyrum) was considerably more stable, and two-thirds of mothers with a first child born in Salt Lake City remained there until the last child's birth (May, Bean, and Skolnick 1986).

Frequent migration is sufficient to bias any analysis of fertility change if such analysis is limited—as it is in many family reconstitution studies—to the current residents of a community or region at a given time or to nonmigrants over time.

In summary, the directed pattern of settlement, which complemented the nondirected settlement process, resulted in a rapid dispersion of the population throughout the state. Not all of the communities established were successful. Water resources in some areas were depleted quickly, and the fragile ecology of selected areas was destroyed by agriculture. The ghost towns of the West are not only mining towns whose ores were quickly extracted but also unsuccessful agricultural settlements. Sometimes the failure of settlements reflected the failure of central planning, as was the case with an aborted attempt to locate a "seaport" at Call's Landing on the Colorado River to the south. A large number of settlements were successful, however, in establishing communities that could absorb a rapidly growing population and generally provide close ties to the central, religiously dominated core settlements.

POPULATION GROWTH IN A FAMILY-BASED SOCIETY

The population size of Utah and its counties, recorded in decennial censuses from 1850 through 1940 is reported in table 1. The terminal date, 1940, is used because it marks the closure of the last decade during which the MHDP population would have borne children.

The initial rates of population growth are unusually high in view of the fact that no rail linkage was provided to the area until the end of the 1860s. Much of the growth during this period is due to pioneer migration, which depended on wagon trains as well as handcart companies.[11] Given the initial difficulty of travel and lack of food resources in the region, early settlements were of course small. It is estimated that 1,853 settlers reached the Salt Lake Valley in the first year, 1847. By 1848 the population had grown to 4,633, and to 7,035 by 1849 (Wahlquist 1974). In the 1850s, 29,000 people were added to the population, and

TABLE 1

POPULATION OF COUNTIES IN UTAH, 1850–1940

County	1850	1860	1870	1880	1890	1900	1910	1920	1930	1940
Beaver	na	785	2,007	3,918	3,340	3,613	4,717	5,139	5,136	5,014
Box Elder	na	1,608	4,855	6,761	7,642	10,009	13,894	18,788	17,810	18,832
Cache	na	2,605	8,229	12,562	15,509	18,139	23,062	26,992	27,424	29,797
Carbon	na	na	na	na	na	5,004	8,624	15,489	17,798	18,459
Daggett	na	na	na	na	na	na	na	400	411	564
Davis	1,134	2,904	4,459	5,279	6,751	7,996	10,191	11,450	14,021	15,784
Duchesne	na	na	na	na	na	na	na	9,093	8,263	8,958
Emery	na	na	na	556	5,076	4,657	6,750	7,411	7,042	7,072
Garfield	na	na	na	na	2,457	3,400	3,660	4,768	4,642	5,253
Grand	na	na	na	na	541	1,149	1,595	1,808	1,813	2,070
Iron	360	1,010	2,277	4,013	2,683	3,546	3,933	5,787	7,227	8,331
Juab	na	672	2,034	3,474	5,582	10,082	10,702	9,871	8,605	7,392
Kane	na	na	1,513	3,085	1,685	1,811	1,652	2,054	2,235	2,561
Millard	na	715	2,753	3,727	4,033	5,678	6,118	9,659	9,945	9,613
Morgan	na	na	1,972	1,783	1,780	2,045	2,467	2,542	2,536	2,611

Piute	na	na	82	1,651	2,842	1,954	1,734	2,770	1,956	2,203
Rich	na	na	1,955	1,263	1,527	1,946	1,883	1,890	1,873	2,028
Salt Lake	6,157	11,295	18,337	31,977	58,457	77,725	131,426	159,282	194,102	211,623
San Juan	na	na	na	204	365	1,023	2,377	3,379	3,496	4,712
Sanpete	365	3,815	6,786	11,557	13,146	16,313	16,704	17,505	16,022	16,063
Sevier	na	na	na	4,457	6,199	8,451	9,776	11,281	11,199	12,112
Summit	na	198	2,512	4,921	7,733	9,439	8,200	7,862	9,527	8,714
Tooele	152	1,008	2,177	4,497	3,700	7,361	7,924	7,965	9,413	9,133
Uintah	na	na	na	799	2,762	6,458	7,050	8,470	9,035	9,898
Utah	2,026	8,248	12,203	17,973	23,768	32,456	37,942	40,792	49,021	57,382
Wasatch	na	na	1,244	2,927	3,595	4,736	8,920	4,625	5,636	5,754
Washington	na	691	3,064	4,235	4,009	4,612	4,123	6,764	7,420	9,269
Wayne	na	na	na	na	na	1,907	1,749	2,097	2,067	2,394
Weber	1,186	3,675	7,858	12,344	22,723	25,239	35,179	43,463	52,172	56,714
TOTAL	11,380	40,273	86,786	143,963	210,779	276,749	373,351	449,396	507,847	550,310

SOURCE: Bureau of Economic and Business Research, *Statistical Abstract of Utah, 1979*. Table 8 (Salt Lake City: University of Utah, 1979).

46,000 were added in the 1860s. Although the numbers increased in the early settlement periods, the rate of increase declined because of the growing population base against which the rate of increase is computed.

From 1850 to 1860 the population expanded by 253 percent, but the growth rate in subsequent decades fell to 115 percent, then to 66 percent. It continued to decline thereafter except for one period of resurgence. From 1890 to 1900 the population increased by only 31 percent, but increased by 35 percent from 1900 to 1910. Prohibition of polygyny in 1890[12] and the economic crises of the 1890s seem to have slowed immigration. In-migration continued to decline after 1910. High rates of natural increase and declining economic opportunities resulted in net out-migration of population at the conclusion of World War I.

The first group of settlers sent to the Salt Lake Valley in 1847 were predominantly male. Their task was to establish a base to receive their families and others. In later years the movement of LDS church members to Utah was essentially a movement of families rather than individuals. The consequence is demonstrated in Utah's population structure, the age-sex distribution of the population. From the earliest periods of settlement, the number of males and females have been closely balanced and the proportion of young children has been high. The resulting age-sex pyramid approximates the type associated with any developing country that is generally closed to migration and that maintains a high fertility rate along with a low or moderately low mortality rate. To illustrate the consequences of family migration and high fertility, the age-sex pyramids for Utah and Arizona are presented in figure 5.

The male-female balance is demonstrated in the graphs of the masculinity ratio (the number of males per 100 females) for Arizona, Idaho, Nevada, Utah, and Wyoming, which is presented by age, for 1870, 1890, and 1910, in figure 6. At all ages, for each of the three census periods, the number of males was closely matched by the number of females in Utah. In each of the other states within the region, however, the adult population was overwhelmingly male. In Wyoming in 1870, there were more than eight males for every female in the age group 40–44. As late as 1910, there were twice as many males as females in each age group over 20 in Wyoming. Even in Idaho, which had LDS settlements in the central and southern parts of the state, males greatly outnumbered females.

Jack Eblen's study (1965) of the sex ratio in agricultural settlements in the nineteenth century finds that a balanced sex ratio was common at the county level across a range of states. This would suggest that in

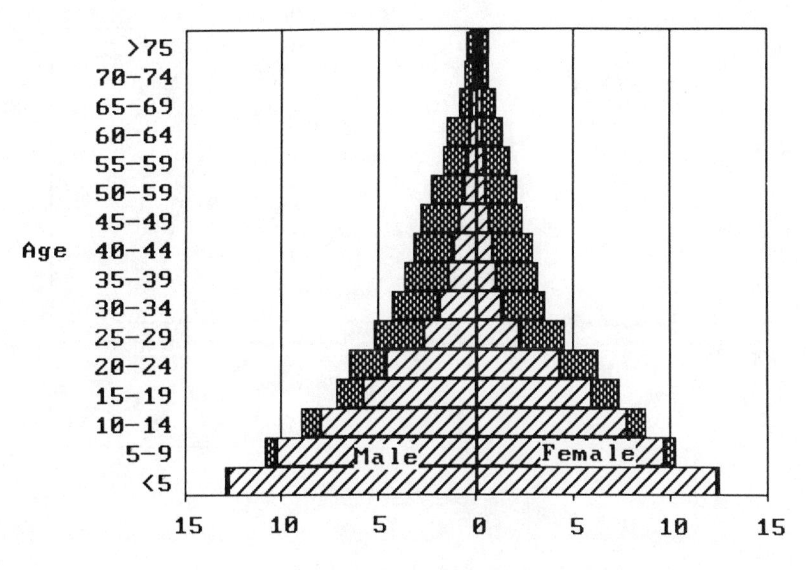

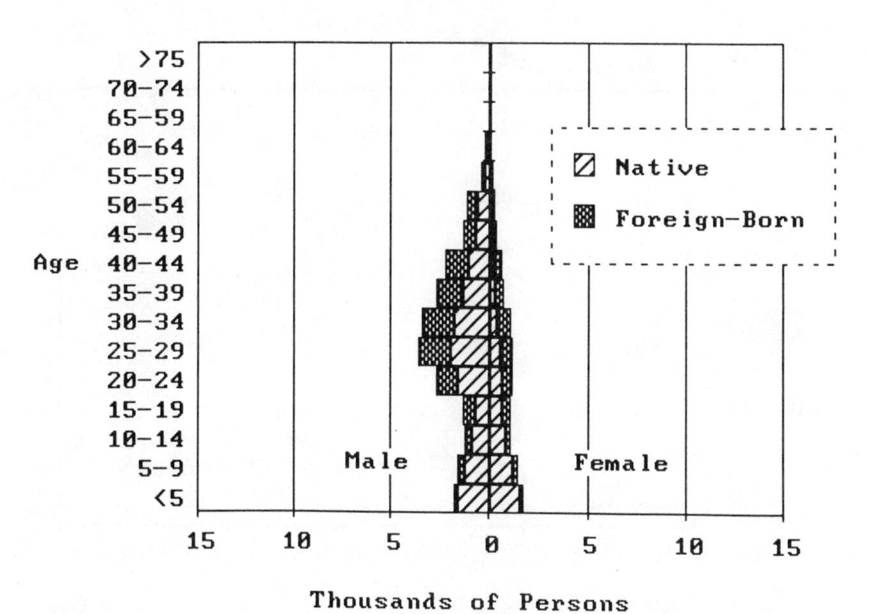

Figure 5. Age-Sex Pyramid for the 1880 White Population

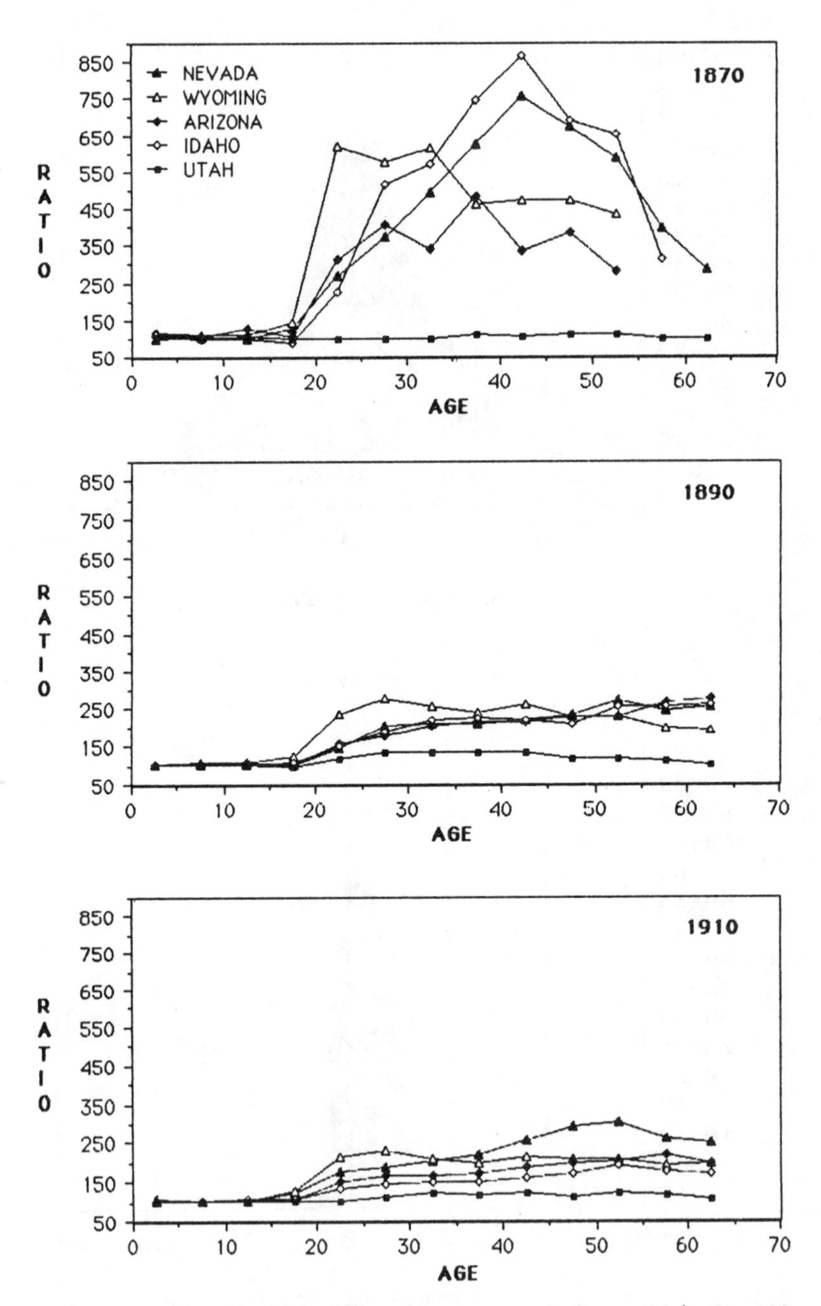

Figure 6. Masculinity Ratio for Selected Intermountain States (Males Per 100 Females)

states other than Utah within the region, the mining and cattle industries distorted the sex ratios. These types of economic activities were pursued in Utah, and Utah became one of the leading mining states in the nation between 1870 and 1880. Nevertheless, at the state level a balanced sex ratio was maintained.

Maintenance of a balanced sex ratio was important because it provided a stable marriage market in which opportunities for marriage were not distorted by the uneven numbers of potential mates. Even though the age and sex distribution was relatively constant, a number of changes were occurring which influenced fertility.

DEVELOPMENT AND ECONOMIC CHANGE: FERTILITY DETERMINANTS

In this section we shall describe a series of changes that may have had an impact on fertility values and decisions in the population. We begin with a discussion of the changing religious composition, which brought the Mormons into contact with alternate value systems. We then examine the processes of protoindustrialization and industrialization, commercialization, urbanization, and educational development—factors usually associated with declining fertility.

CHANGING RELIGIOUS COMPOSITION: THE "GENTILE" INVASION

Sizable non-LDS population groups began to move into Utah within a decade of the initial settlement, changing the religious composition of the territory, exposing the LDS population to secularizing influences, and stimulating the federal government to exercise greater control over Utah, thereby undermining its ecclesiastical authority structure.

In the spring of 1857, President James Buchanan was encouraged to replace Brigham Young, who had been appointed as the first governor of the territory. To ensure acceptance of the new governor, Alfred Cummings, of Georgia and Missouri, Buchanan dispatched a military force to accompany his new appointee. Viewing this as an invasion, LDS settlers harassed the army by burning supply forts and wagon trains, and thus delayed the entry of the army and its camp followers—agents and merchants—until 1858. After Buchanan had granted the Mormons a full pardon for their acts, the Utah expedition of 5,500 soldiers entered the valley, passed through Salt Lake City, and established a base forty miles south of the city. The base, Camp Floyd, was occupied until 1861, when the army was withdrawn for the Civil War (Arrington and Bitton 1979, pp. 167–169). A significant aspect of the military invasion was the creation of a large group of men for whom other religions were important. Catholic services were conducted at Camp Floyd in 1859. Five years later Catholic services were started at Fort Douglas, in Salt Lake City, a new outpost created to provide a military force to protect the pioneers following the trail through Utah to California from hostile Indians. Military officers from Fort Douglas were instrumental in the earliest mining exploration, and in 1866 the growth of mining activities resulted in the first permanent appointment of a Catholic priest in Utah, whose assignment was to serve the mining community. A small Jewish population in Salt Lake City, of approximately fifty people, had sufficient adult males to form a minyan, and Jewish services started in 1864.

Following the establishment of Catholic and Jewish groups, an Episcopal bishop was appointed to serve in Utah in 1867. The Baptists also became active in 1867, Methodists in 1869, Presbyterians in 1870, and the United Church of Christ in 1874.

While dates of the establishment of particular religious groups in Utah are relatively accurate, data on the composition of the state by religion is less complete than one would like. These data are difficult to secure, in spite of the fact that the U.S. Census Bureau was mandated to collect religious data in the 1850, 1860, and 1870 censuses. The Census Bureau also secured religious information by correspondence in 1880 and 1890. By a congressional act of March 6, 1902, the Census Bureau was directed to conduct a special religious census in 1906. The earlier data were not always carefully tabulated and thus are highly suspect, but the last census appears sufficiently reasonable to use as a benchmark to estimate religious composition in 1906.

Assuming a linear rate of population increase between 1900 and 1910, we estimate that the state's population grew from 277,000 in 1900 to 335,000 in 1906. According to the religious census returns there were 151,000 members of the LDS church in 1906. However, individuals were reported as members only if they had been baptized, and that sacrament is limited to those age 8 and over. Those under age 8 in 1900 constituted 24 percent of the population. If one eliminates those under age 8 and calculates the proportion of LDS members for the balance on the basis of the 1906 estimates, one may conclude that 60 percent of the population was LDS. According to the 1880 census, the LDS population was between 85 and 90 percent—85 percent if one

ommencing with the joining-of-the-rails at Promontory and
til the achievement of statehood in 1896, was polarized around
ies, largely separate and disputatious. One of these was the
ormon commonwealth. . . . The other economy was comprised
ndred jerry-built mining districts, populated almost exclusively
mons. . . . The third phase, beginning with statehood and con-
l the outbreak of World War II in Europe, witnessed the begin-
pulation outflow, the commercialization of agriculture, the emer-
"business" sector, the rise of the copper industry, and, above all,
l coalescence of two hostile economies into one. The fourth phase
939. (Arrington and Alexander 1974, pp. 3–4)

DP population would have been influenced by the events of
ree periods. The last cohort of women studied, those born
895 and 1899, typically completed their childbearing by
ich date Arrington uses to mark the beginning of his fourth
economic history. The last epoch is therefore not relevant to
.

ton's description of economic change in Utah is accurate but
certain nuances that are important in the analysis of changing
The description of an agricultural emphasis among the Mor-
ring the first two phases followed by the commercialization of
ure provides a framework within which one may analyze the
in agricultural settlement and development that probably influ-
decisions related to marriage and family formation. The critical
es are represented in table 2, where we present data on the num-
farms, average farm value, and average acreage per farm.

om 1850 to 1870, the number of farms in the state increased by
oximately 500 percent, from slightly less than 1,000 to slightly less
5,000. The value of the individual farms declined, but there was no
ematic change in the size of farm holdings. All were relatively small.
cost of establishing a farm was relatively low, reflecting in part the
trol over land by church authorities. Land could be distributed to
mbers of the church by fiat. As a result of the completion of the rail
k and the introduction of federal control over land distribution, the
st of farm land increased from 1870 to 1920. Much of the increase,
owever, was tied to changing farm size. Value per acre did not increase
ubstantially until 1910. Increasing average farm size was due, in part,
o the fact that the easily irrigated lands were settled and controlled
first; later holdings were essentially in dry-farm areas, thus greater acreage was necessary for farms to be profitable.

discounts the 6,988 people
als who had "left" the chur
century the proportion of th
cantly, from 85 to 60 percen

Religious identification is
1906. However, using LDS rec
of religious composition by cou
ing to Lyon's calculations, 56 pe
in 1920, a further decline from
tion of LDS increases, reaching 7
that the economic conditions tha
from Utah following World War I
LDS to leave Utah. In addition, the
tion affected the changing religious
migration rates for LDS and non-LDS
tion of the population would be identifi
the LDS population was higher.

During any period in the history of
predominately LDS, but the proportion
cant. The presence of a large non-LDS p
population to a different set of values, and p
models and alternate reference groups. The
critical also in stimulating the promulgat
stripped the church of many of its resources, in
of state funds to establish public, secular educa
pressuring the federal government to pass and e
(Papanikolas 1976).[14]

ECONOMIC DEVELOPMENT AND THE DECLINE
OF AGRICULTURE

Economic development in Utah appears to fall i
cific, relatively discrete phases. Leonard Arrington,
writer on Utah economic history, notes that the eco
Utah may be divided into four periods:

> [T]he first began with the arrival of the Mormon pione
> continued until the completion of the transcontinental rail
> featured an isolated but well-organized, relatively self-sufficie
> commonwealth based upon irrigated agriculture, village indu
> sional organized efforts to take advantage of fortuitous wind

TABLE 2

NUMBER, SIZE, AND VALUE OF FARMS IN UTAH, 1850–1940

Year	Number of Farms	Average Value	Average Acreage
1850	926	$1,018	50.6
1860	3,635	850	24.7
1870	4,908	772	30.2
1880	9,452	2,045	69.4
1890	10,517	3,745	125.9
1900	19,387	3,877	212.4
1910	21,676	6,956	156.8
1920	25,662	12,117	196.8
1930	27,159	10,540	206.7
1940	25,411	7,811	287.4

SOURCE: Bureau of Economic and Business Research, University of Utah, "A Statistical Abstract of Utah's Economy: 1964," *Studies in Business and Economics* 24 (3, July 1964), tables 1 and 5.

After 1920, the average value of farms declined, while the average size of farms continued to increase. However, the depression years drove a number of farmers working marginal farms out of the industry. By 1940 there were slightly fewer farms in Utah than in 1920, of lower value but larger in size.

Thus the period up to 1870 is marked by relatively inexpensive farms, modest in size, but with opportunities available for expansion and settlement. The period 1870–1920 is marked by increasing numbers of farms with higher valuations. Opportunities remained but the cost of establishing new farms that were large enough to be profitable increased. After World War I, the decline of markets for agricultural products, compounded in the 1930s by the depression, forced farmers to leave the industry in spite of the declining value of agricultural land. During this period, because the risk involved in farming increased, the proportion of farms that were owner-operated fell. In 1910, 79.3 percent of all farms were operated by owners, but by 1940 only 68.1 percent were worked by owners. Working owners were being replaced by tenants.

PROTOINDUSTRIALIZATION AND COMMERCIALIZATION

According to the observed employment patterns, Utah did not experience what might be described as a normal pattern of "industrialization and modernization." By "the normal process of industrialization and modernization" we mean a decline in extractive industries, accompanied by growth in secondary industries—manufacturing and construction, for example. That change has often been followed by growth in the tertiary sector—services, trade, communication, and transportation. The early onset of industrialization in Utah, however, was strongly influenced by the relative isolation of the community from the central U.S. economy and the frontier tendency toward self-reliance. In turn, understanding industrialization requires an understanding of the more individualistic progress of protoindustrialization in the population and the hegemonic commercialism pursued by those attempting to avoid economic penetration.

The concept of protoindustrialization stems from the work of Franklin Mendels (1972), who suggested that in advance of more generally accepted forms of industrial development (factory-based manufacturing), the transition from agricultural employment to industrial employment involves an intermediate step. This is the extensive development of independent household manufacturing, cottage industries, or small-scale industries that influence values and behavior. Numerous studies have been conducted relating protoindustrialization to demographic changes. Although data to test systematically the relationship between protoindustrialization and population growth are limited, it appears that the expansion of cottage industries, by providing employment in rural areas, encouraged early marriages and larger families (Braun 1978). The concept and the process may be applicable, in a general way, to the case of development in Utah.

From the outset of migration to Utah, the leaders of the LDS religious community were committed to a fully independent economic system, one that would be self-sufficient not only in food production but also in other areas. Reportedly, four days after Brigham Young led his small band into Salt Lake Valley, he said:

> We do not intend to have any trade or commerce with the gentile world . . . for so long as we buy of them we are in a degree dependent upon them. The Kingdom of God cannot rise independent of the gentile nations until we

> produce, manufacture, and make every article of use, convenience, or necessity among our own people. (Quoted in Arrington and Bitton 1979, p. 122)

To judge from the subsequent actions of his people, it seems that Brigham Young was primarily concerned with production rather than distribution. Only in the mid-1860s did he decide that the church should move aggressively into commercial activities. The church was therefore committed to developing local, small-scale industries to meet the basic local needs of the population.

Because many of the American converts were farmers, the church was heavily dependent upon its missionary program in Europe to develop industries. Many of the migrants from England were skilled, nonagricultural workers. This is not unlike early immigrants to the colonies (Bailyn 1986). Arrington and Davis Bitton listed migrants from Liverpool by occupation; the list includes boilermakers, engineers, ironmongers, miners, printers, spinners, weavers, and others. The inclusion of a large number of skilled workers in the pool of European convert-migrants was not by chance. The missionaries were specifically instructed to seek out skilled workers who could develop industries to produce goods required in this isolated kingdom.

Efforts to make communities economically independent are illustrated by the experience in Brigham City, a community sixty miles north of Salt Lake City. In 1854 a group was called to settle this community, originally named Box Elder. The group included a schoolteacher, a mason, carpenters, blacksmiths, shoemakers, and others. In developing a cooperative program, a forerunner of the relatively short-lived communal movement (the United Order), the community started with the construction of a fort, canal, gristmill, and sawmill. In 1866 a tannery was constructed, which later included a shoe manufacturing department that produced goods valued at $700 per week in 1875. In 1870–71 a woolen factory was constructed, and the community's sheep herd was increased from 1,500 to 5,000 to supply the wool. A commercial dairy was established in 1871, which produced fluid milk as well as butter and cheese. The woolen factory was only part of an expanding textile program, which also included a millinery shop. To provide raw materials for this store, the community planted several thousand mulberry trees and began a silk production program. Several young men were sent to southern Utah in 1873 in an abortive attempt to develop a cotton farm. Within twenty years, this relatively small community of

Brigham City became a model of an integrated economic system—agriculturally independent, producing raw materials, converting these into finished products, and disposing of them through a community-owned and -operated cooperative mercantile enterprise (Arrington, Fox, and May 1976, pp. 111–134).

Brigham City might have been more successful than other communities in its industrial and commercial development, but it was not an isolated case. The same pattern of attempts to develop completely self-sufficient communities was found throughout the territory. The experience and skills developed in these communities provided the basis for more extensive, centralized commercial and industrial programs. At the same time, the development of the small-scale, community-based enterprises created a form of protoindustrialization, providing secondary occupations outside of the agricultural sector and the household for both men and women.

As the territorial population expanded, the religious composition changed, economic penetration increased, and the hopes of maintaining an independent colony declined. The church moved aggressively into commercial activities in a bid to retain economic independence:

> The new departure was announced by President Young in 1865 in a call for Mormons to undercut the profiteering of both Gentile and Mormon merchants by setting up their own cooperative merchandising arrangements. The church leadership responded by opening a cooperative store and wholesale marketing operation. Six weeks after the opening of the first cooperative in Salt Lake City, eighty-one cooperative stores had sprung up. (Gottlieb and Wiley 1984, p. 36)

Competitive commercial pressures expanded faster than industrial development. The costs of transporting locally manufactured goods to market from the relatively isolated communities in Utah made goods produced in the state noncompetitive with those mass-produced in eastern factories and shipped by rail. Salt Lake City and Ogden were intermediate to the West Coast cities and Denver; Utah's rail networks made Salt Lake an ideal break-of-bulk point for the transshipment of goods north and south.

The development of commercial activities through cooperative programs and communal industrial activities meant that individuals worked in these activities less than full-time. While maintaining farms, people could work in various agriculturally related enterprises (e.g., textile mills) during the off-season. Consequently many individuals involved in commercial and industrial activities may have been counted in the various censuses as farmers. A substantial number of multiple occupations are recorded in the 1880 manuscript census.

As commercial and industrial activities grew, a decreasing proportion of the labor force was employed in agriculture full-time. As indicated in table 3, the most significant, systematic change occurred among the proportion of workers in agricultural and forestry positions. This class of workers fell from approximately 50 percent in 1850 to less than 20 percent in 1940. Changes in other industrial groups are, in part, less clear because of the relatively significant proportion of "laborers-unspecified" reported in the censuses of 1850 to 1910. In general, however, it appears that although there was slow, modest growth in each of the other sectors, there was no systematic increase in the proportion of workers in manufacturing. Utah has never been a heavy industrial state; as agriculture declined in importance, increasing numbers of jobs were created in trade, transportation and communications, personal and public services, and professional occupations.

URBANIZATION AND EDUCATION

Because of the geographic size of the state of Utah and its relatively small population, density is low; but the simple measure of population density gives a misleading picture of the population distribution of the state. Agricultural settlement tended to take the form of communities from which farmers traveled to outlying fields to work. Later, improved transportation made it easier for farmers and ranchers to reside on their farmlands while retaining relatively easy access to established communities for education, church, and commercial activities. Nevertheless, the population remained clustered in tightly knit nodes, and rapidly became dominated by village and urban settlements. In table 4 the distribution of the population by rural and urban classes is presented. Rural settlements and small, nonurban communities predominated until the end of World War I. After 1920 the population in urban communities became the majority, and that proportion consistently increased thereafter.

The degree of population concentration may be illustrated further by current data. In 1980, twenty-two of the twenty-nine counties in Utah had densities of less than ten persons per square mile. The density of Salt Lake County was 788 per square mile, and four out of every five residents (79 percent) lived in the state's only standard metropolitan statistical area, consisting of Weber, Davis, Salt Lake, Utah, Tooele, and Mor-

TABLE 3

INDUSTRIAL DISTRIBUTION (PERCENTAGES) IN UTAH, 1850–1940

Industrial Group	1850	1860	1870	1880	1890	1900	1910	1920	1930	1940
Agriculture, Forestry	50.7	54.7	48.8	36.8	30.4	34.9	28.4	29.0	24.4	19.4
Mining	0.4	nil	2.7	6.6	5.7	8.3	7.6	6.8	6.2	6.8
Construction	8.1	4.5	5.6	5.2	8.3	4.7	11.7	8.0	9.2	5.4
Manufacturing	15.6	13.8	10.5	12.3	11.5	10.9	11.9	14.5	12.4	11.0
Transportation, Communication	0.4	1.1	5.0	4.9	6.4	6.7	8.9	7.9	8.6	10.5
Trade	2.2	2.4	2.8	5.1	7.2	5.8	9.3	10.3	12.0	19.4
Finance	0.2	0.3	0.1	0.3	2.9	4.3	5.4	7.9	8.7	3.0
Domestic, Personal Service	0.1	3.7	6.1	7.0	9.1	7.8	8.4	7.0	8.3	9.3
Professional Service	2.4	1.4	1.4	2.7	3.9	5.2	6.1	6.7	8.0	8.9
Public Service	0.4	0.4	1.0	1.7	1.8	1.0	2.1	1.9	2.2	4.9
Laborers, Unspecified	19.7	17.4	16.1	17.3	12.8	10.5	*	*	*	*
Industry Not Reported	*	*	*	*	*	*	*	*	*	1.6

SOURCE: Leonard J. Arrington, *The Changing Economic Structure of the Mountain West, 1850–1950* vol. 10, no. 3 (Logan: Utah State University Press, June 1963).

TABLE 4
POPULATION OF UTAH, URBAN AND RURAL, 1850–1940

Census Year	Total Population	Urban and Rural			
		Urban	Rural	Percent Urban	Percent Rural
1850	11,380	—	11,380	—	100.0
1860	40,273	8,236	32,037	20.5	79.5
1870	86,786	15,981	70,805	18.4	81.6
1880	143,963	33,665	110,298	23.4	76.6
1890	210,779	75,155	135,624	35.7	64.3
1900	276,749	105,427	171,332	38.1	61.9
1910	373,351	172,934	200,417	46.3	53.7
1920	499,396	215,584	233,812	48.0	52.0
1930	507,847	266,264	241,583	52.4	47.6
1940	550,310	305,493	244,817	55.5	44.5

SOURCE: U.S. Department of Commerce, Bureau of the Census, *Sixteenth Census of the United States: 1940. Population,* (Washington, D.C.: Superintendent of Publications, 1942), 1:24.

gan counties—the Wasatch Front counties, which were dominated by three cities: Ogden, Salt Lake City, and Provo.

Consistent with the growth in commercial, service, and professional employment was the availability of a relatively well-educated population. Attention was devoted early to education. Investment in education has always been high for the population of Utah, although per-pupil expenditures are relatively low because of the large number of children. Over half of the school-age children were enrolled in school in Utah in 1865 (54 percent). In 1900, 81 percent of the children between 5 and 17 years of age were enrolled in school in Utah, while for the United States the proportion was 72.4. Proportionally more individuals in Utah also continued to higher levels of education. In 1900, 80.9 percent of those 16 and 17 years old were enrolled in school in Utah, but only 57.3 percent of the U.S. population of that age. At the same time, 32.7 percent of the Utah population age 18–20 were enrolled in school, but only 21.4 percent of the U.S. population of that age. In Utah, there was no difference in the proportion of males and females in school. By 1940, the median years of school completed for native whites age 25 and over in Utah was 10.7 years, while the national figure was 8.8 years. Only the native white population 25 and over in Washington, D.C., had a higher level of educational attainment, 12.1 years. Even the foreign-born whites in Utah had completed more years of schooling than the same group in the United States as a whole: 7.9 years versus 7.3.

These levels of educational attainment were achieved even though the LDS church felt for many years that it was necessary to support a completely independent educational system (Arrington and Bitton 1979, p. 253). Church academies and seminaries were set up in most Mormon communities. As late as 1910, half the students in Utah attended church academies instead of public schools. In 1916, the church began to eliminate its noncollege educational system, having reached an agreement with public school officials to recognize educational credit secured by students in church academies and seminaries who transferred to public schools. By 1924 all academies had been closed in Utah, although seminaries for religious instruction were operated by the church in public school buildings during normal school hours. After 1930 the seminaries were moved into separate facilities adjacent to the public schools, and until the early 1980s students continued to have the opportunity to take one religion class at the seminary for regular academic credit during normal school hours. Higher educational facilities, however, continued to be supported by the church, providing an alternative to the state university system, which was established in 1850 with the founding of the University of Utah.

In summary, changes in the structure of the society which would predict a rapid decline in fertility were in place beginning in the latter part of the nineteenth century. These changes include an increasing urban population, exposure to a growing non-LDS community, the increasing availability of alternative consumer goods, declining agricultural opportunities, an increasing proportion of the work force in nonagricultural occupations, and rising levels of educational attainment.[15] At the same time, the majority of the MHDP population was or had been in some measure affiliated with the LDS church, a religious organization widely identified as being pro-family, pro-marriage, and pro-natal. Other religious groups with traditionally high levels of fertility have, in recent years, experienced a decline in fertility. Yet as late as the mid-1980s the population of Utah had a crude birth rate roughly twice the national level, in spite of a significant decline in the average number of children born over the past one hundred years. The relationship between religion and fertility in the case of the LDS may be atypical, and therefore warrants explanation.

RELIGION AND FERTILITY: A COMPARATIVE APPROACH

One of the striking demographic features of the Utah population is its remarkably high level of fertility. Even though fertility has fallen dramatically from very high levels, as detailed in chapter 4, and has paralleled fertility trends in the United States over the course of this century (Spicer and Gustavus 1974), the birth rate in Utah is still higher than the national average and higher than that found in every other state in the Union. The facile explanation is that the high rate of fertility is due to the predominance of the LDS membership in the state and the ideology of the church concerning the family and childbearing. Such an argument is subsumed under what Joseph Chamie identifies as the "particularized theology" proposition (1981, p. 4), also identified as the "particularized ideology" hypothesis. There are alternative explanations that purport to explain observed fertility differences among religious groups more effectively. These alternatives include the "characteristics hypothesis" (see Petersen 1969, p. 538), "the minority group" hypothesis (Goldscheider 1971, p. 297), and the "interaction hypothesis" (Chamie 1981, pp. 9–11). The competing hypotheses are explained in more detail and evaluated in chapter 6. Here we are concerned with providing a more extensive explanation of the basis for proposing that the LDS church has a significant effect on the attitudes and values related to childbearing. In chapter 6 we explore the conditions under which the church appears to influence the behavior of specific groups in Utah.

Thomas O'Dea writes that the basic theology of the LDS church supports interest in high fertility and large families:

> The need to provide earthly bodies for waiting spirits was one of the Mormon justifications of plural marriage, although actually the birth rate per wife was lower for plural than monogamous wives. The result has been a strong preference for large families. (1957, p. 140)

O'Dea's conclusion is based on the fact that the LDS church supports the belief in three states: a pre-earthly existence, an earthly existence, and an afterlife. In the "plan of salvation," the millennium will occur when all worthy spirits from the pre-earthly existence have had an opportunity for an earthly life. Only through birth is this experience possible, and therefore members of the church have a role to play in preparing for the Second Coming. Providing an earthly existence for a large number of souls, having a large number of children, allows the Saints to help in the finalization of God's Great Plan.[16]

Thus there is an overarching theological rationale for high fertility,[17] but the particularized ideology hypothesis must be founded on more solid ground. It must be supported by a set of specifications related to the family-building processes. Moreover, if the basic principles of learning theory are appropriate, translation of a general theological position into a set of normative prescriptions will be effective insofar as (1) the normative prescriptions are exhaustive of the behavioral mechanisms associated with the processes of interest; (2) the normative prescriptions are consistent—devoid of contradictions; (3) the normative prescriptions are expressed in positive rather than negative statements; and (4) there is a set of supporting mechanisms for appropriate behavior—rewards, if you will, rather than punishments.

If one accepts the schematic diagram of the determinants of fertility outlined by Freedman (1961–62) and evaluated by David Yaukey (1969), an adequate sociological explanation must account for two normative structures: norms about family size and norms about the intermediate variables (this is the classification of Davis and Blake 1955, which is subsumed in the Freedman-Yaukey scheme).[18] As noted above, the particular LDS theological interpretation of the "plan of salvation" supports large families—that is, the norms about family size. There is no specification of number, but rather of direction. There is less direct support for norms governing relative or specific family size among other religious groups, although there is support for unconstrained fertility in Islam and Catholicism through the dictate that Allah, or the Lord, will provide. Contrary to Calvin Goldscheider's general rejection of the theological foundation for high fertility, there is, at least among the three religious groups identified, support for a "large," or at least not a limited, number of children.

Consider next the question of whether theological content is related to the second class of norms, norms concerned with intermediate variables directly influencing fertility. For purposes of comparison, in table 5 we have summarized our view of the position of the LDS church, the Catholic church, and Islam regarding Davis and Blake's intermediate variables.

We hypothesize first that the norms related to the mechanisms of childbearing or fertility limitation, specified by the intermediate variables, will be most effective when the normative prescriptions exhaust the range of behavioral mechanisms. Certain intermediate variables are outside the range of individual rational control: involuntary abstinence, involuntary infecundity, and involuntary fetal mortality. Excluding these variables, the LDS church has a position with respect to each of the other variables—with the exception of coital frequency—which can in part be assumed to reflect the more general prescription for large families. The same, however, may be said to be generally true of Catholicism or Islam.

Second, we hypothesize that the position of a church will affect fertility when the normative prescriptions are consistent, or devoid of contradictions. The position of the LDS church is consistently pronatalist, while there are contradictions in Catholicism, namely, the delaying of marriage is legitimized and celibacy institutionalized for certain classes of individuals (priests and nuns). No such contradictions exist within the LDS church or Islam.

Third, we hypothesize that the normative prescriptions will be more effective if expressed in positive rather than negative statements. None of the three religious positions examined avoids negative statements regarding abortion or infanticide. With respect to the use of contraceptives, exclusive of the rhythm method, the Catholic church is strongly negative; the position of Islam is contradictory according to the analysis of various writers; and the position of the LDS church, while negative, is low-key:

> The church shuns open campaigns on the issue of birth control and seems to have taken the position of largely ignoring the question. Yet, despite this tendency not to disturb things, the position of the church is actually quite clear:
>
> "The doctrine that wedded man and woman should not beget children or should limit the number of children born to them is contrary to the spirit of the Great Plan, and is a most erroneous one. Let the waiting spirits come! Let children be born into the earth! Let fatherhood and motherhood be the most honored of all the professions on earth." (O'Dea 1957, pp. 141–142; quotation of LDS doctrine from Widstoe 1915, p. 147)

The position of the LDS church on birth control at the end of the nineteenth century and the beginning of the twentieth century was more negative. Lester Bush confirms that this position has been modified during the past few decades. He notes that in recent years,

> notwithstanding an occasional zealot, questions about birth control practices were not to be (and are not now) a part of the periodic moral evaluations Mormons undergo—for temple recommends, advancement in the priesthood, or when assuming positions of leadership. (1976, p. 28)

TABLE 5

RELIGIOUS NORMATIVE POSITIONS RELATED TO THE INTERMEDIATE FERTILITY VARIABLES

A. Variables governing formation and dissolution of unions	Catholicism	LDS	Islam
1. Age at marriage	Encourages rational delay	Encourages early marriage	Encourages early marriage but allows postponement for economic reasons
2. Permanent celibacy for women	Institutional mechanisms provided; theologically supported	Institutionally disavowed and theologically depreciated	Institutionally disavowed and socially censured
3. Amount of time spent after or between marriages	Divorce illegal and remarriage unsupported. Widow remarriage allowed	Divorce and separation discouraged, but remarriage allowed. Widow remarriage allowed.	Divorce recognized and easy and remarriage supported. Widow remarriage strongly supported.

B. Variables governing exposure to intercourse within unions	Catholicism	LDS	Islam
1. Voluntary abstinence	Strongly approved and held moral	Sexuality strongly supported, but no official position on abstinence	Sexuality strongly supported, but no official position on abstinence
2. Involuntary	Largely biological	Largely biological	Largely biological
3. Coital frequency	Related to B.1; also some discouragement of the recreational function	No official position	No official position, but informal norms are contradictory

TABLE 5 (continued)

C. Variables affecting exposure to conception	Catholicism	LDS	Islam
1. Fecundity and infecundity—involuntary	Largely biological	Largely biological[a]	Largely biological
2. Fecundity and infecundity—voluntary	Theologically illegal	No theological basis, but morally disavowed	Theological position open to question depending on interpretation of certain Hadditheths
3. Use of contraceptives			
a. Mechanical and chemical	Theologically illegal	Generally unsupported by the church authorities	No consistent position or interpretation, but no consistent rejection
b. Other means	Rhythm method approved, but coitus interruptus disavowed	Position similar to that on mechanical and chemical means	Position similar to that on mechanical and chemical means
4. Factors affecting gestation and successful parturition			
a. Foetal mortality—involuntary	Largely biological	Largely biological[b]	Largely biological
b. Fetal mortality—voluntary	Theologically illegal	Immoral in the eyes of the church	No official or informal position, but generally viewed negatively

[a]The positions of all three religions on premarital relations tend to reduce the incidence of sterility due to venereal disease.

[b]Note, however, that high parity levels for each religious group would increase the incidence of foetal loss.

The normative prescriptions of the LDS church are usually couched in positive language, as in the above statement quoted by O'Dea, and there are positive role models in the LDS church. In Catholicism, leadership and authority figures—celibate priests and nuns—provide essentially negative role models for parenthood. In the LDS church, authority is invested in laymen, and the selection and calling of individuals to positions of authority provide strong, positive role models for pronatalist, pro-family values. A content analysis of reports of individuals appointed to positions as stake presidents and their counselors over nine years (1964–66, 1969–71, and 1974–76) indicated that the people selected were married and had an average of 4.1 children, an average education of B.A. or higher, and a modal professional, technical, or managerial occupation.[19] Islamic leaders are also married, but the cloistering of wives makes it difficult to ascertain the degree to which the leaders serve as positive role models.

Finally, we have suggested that normative positions supporting high fertility will be more effective if there is a set of supporting mechanisms for appropriate behavior. Supporting mechanisms may vary but would certainly include reward mechanisms. Within the LDS church such rewards are public, obvious, and frequent, although informal and nonmonetary. Each child is generally named within a month of birth in a public ceremony during one of the regular Sacrament meetings held on the first Sunday of each month. Each child's baptism at age 8 is confirmed in a similar public ceremony. Each male child's appointment to the priesthood and calling to higher levels of rights and responsibilities (ranks) involves his being "set apart" in a public ceremony.[20] These are times when parents receive the accolades of members of the ward or congregation. No similar public ceremonies surrounding repetitive life-cycle events of children are found in Islam or in the Catholic church. In Catholicism naming takes place in a generally semiprivate ceremony in which the parents, godparents, and relatives participate; the ceremonies of confirmation and first communion, although public, are organized around a class or group rather than an individual.[21]

We therefore conclude that the high fertility of the LDS population is at least in part the result of a system of interlocking, mutually supporting norms related to family size and the intermediate fertility variables. Islam approximates this structure, but within the Catholic church there are contradictions (legitimation of celibacy), a lack of support structures (positive role models), and a lack of frequent, informal reward mechanisms.[22]

As a consequence of the LDS normative structures, with their supportive behavioral mechanisms, perhaps the relevant fertility question for the LDS population is not why they have so many children but why they don't have more. The appropriate question is "Why isn't high fertility higher?"

In the case of LDS church members the answer is perhaps found in the social-psychological concept of reference group theory. In the absence of a quantitative specification of the family-size norm, the LDS appear to interpret what is large relative to family size in the resident community. Brian Pitcher, Phillip Kunz, and Evan Peterson (1974), for example, have demonstrated that the family size of Mormons resident in California is lower than the family size of Mormons resident in Utah. But in California, the "reference" groups are the non-Mormon families, neighbors often, with very few if any children. In Utah, the reference groups are again neighbors, but in this case many are also members of the church. What is large is defined by the high fertility of the more prolific LDS church members. And relative to the U.S. population as a whole, LDS fertility might be even higher if the reference-group bench mark, U.S. fertility, were also higher.[23] Certainly when the U.S. fertility rate increased at the end of World War II, LDS fertility also increased, maintaining the gap between LDS and U.S. fertility. Thus the Mormons control births, but with a slightly higher target than other groups in the United States (Heaton and Calkins 1983).

The higher fertility rate of Utah with its LDS population may be explained in reference to religious principles, but it is important not to lose sight of the most interesting feature of fertility in this population. The initial high levels of fertility in the Utah population, largely LDS, in the nineteenth century was similar to the levels found among the New England colonial settlers half a century earlier. Such high levels of fertility have been observed at various times among a variety of first-generation frontier settlers in many parts of the United States. Moreover, after the peak fertility periods, the Utah population followed the same path to reduced fertility observed in other American populations. It is therefore the process of change in patterns of fertility which captures our attention, not the level or the gap.

SUMMARY

Although frontier development was a continuous process extending over a long period for American society as a whole, we argued in chapter 1 that a dominant feature of any specific frontier is its transitory nature. Clearly that fact is demonstrated in the case of Utah. The history of the LDS population began in the New England area, continued through the Midwest, and drew from populations of Europe. The first settlers reached Utah Territory just before midcentury. We have demonstrated in this chapter how the population expanded rapidly, partly from natural increase but also as a consequence of a substantial national and international missionary program. These population resources enabled the LDS church to quickly colonize a vast territory, expanding beyond the boundaries of Utah.

Within the initially colonized areas, the LDS church held sway socially, politically, and economically. Political hegemony came under attack at the end of the first decade of settlement with the appointment of an external governor. The completion of the rail link a decade later opened up the territory to increasing penetration by the national economic system. Within three decades the population dominance of the LDS began to decline and did not begin to increase until after World War II.

In spite of the commitment to the development of an isolated, independent empire, by the last quarter of the nineteenth century changes normally associated with declining fertility had become evident: decreasing agricultural opportunities and increasing urbanization, secularization, commercial development, and educational levels. Throughout the history of Utah, however, the LDS population has continued to maintain a high level of fertility. In the immediately preceding section of this chapter we outlined a detailed explanation for the LDS religious influence on family formation. In many circumstances, investigation of how a religious group is able to maintain relatively high levels of fertility in the face of major social and economic transformations, however, is difficult historically. But the investigation is easier in the case of the Utah population because of its unusual wealth of records. In chapter 3 we describe these records and how they have been organized in a way helpful to the understanding of fertility change on the American frontier.

CHAPTER 3

A Genealogical Approach to Historical Demography

The data used in the MHDP study are different from those normally used in contemporary demographic analysis as well as from the majority of resources employed in a wide range of historical demographic studies. Because of the unique nature of the database, it is important to understand its construction, quality, content, and analytic advantages. The purpose of this chapter is to provide that information.

Familiarity with the MHDP database—which we refer to as "the file" or "the genealogy"—is helpful but not essential to understand the analysis that follows in Part II of this book. Therefore readers interested primarily in the findings may wish to review only sections of this rather detailed methodological chapter. As a guide to such readers, we provide the following outline of chapter 3. The first section, "Developing a Genealogical Database," describes the original records and their conversion into a machine-readable file. The second section, "Quality of the Data," outlines a number of tests used to evaluate the data in terms of completeness and representativeness. The third section, "Characteristics of the Population," describes the composition of the population represented in the constructed file. Three variables are examined: nuptiality or marital characteristics, origin and ethnicity, and religious commitment. This last subsection is particularly important because it details the procedures used to construct an index of religious commitment for further analysis of the relationship between religion and fertility. To place the MHDP database in context, in the fourth section of this chapter, "Genealogies in Historical Demography," we compare our data with those used in a wide range of historical demographic studies. The chapter concludes with a summary of the salient analytic advantages of family genealogical files for demographic analysis.

DEVELOPING A GENEALOGICAL DATABASE

The world's largest collection of nominative records is located in Salt Lake City, Utah. These have been collected and maintained by the Genealogical Society of Utah (GSU hereafter), an organization established and supported by the Church of Jesus Christ of Latter-day Saints. The purpose of the collection is to enable patrons to record their family genealogies, a responsibility assigned to each member of the church for theological reasons. The collection is open, however, to any person interested in genealogical work. Because the function of the collection is to provide the resources to construct family genealogies, there are two major sets of records of primary interest to historical demographers and social historians: nominative records and family group sheets.[1]

Various forms of nominative records are being continuously purchased, copied, or microfilmed. The common feature of these records is information identifying people by name and certain social and demographic characteristics that make it possible to locate an individual uniquely in time and space and within kinship units. Among the records are manuscript censuses, vital statistics, baptismal registers, burial registers, conscription records, taxation data, shipping manifests, and genealogies. The collection program is designed to be universal and comprehensive. The GSU record-gathering efforts are occasionally impeded by government or ecclesiastical authorities who restrict access to records. Such difficulties in securing permission to copy records or to enter a country for the purpose of copying records means that the collection is most extensive for the United States and Western Europe. Some collections are available on Eastern and Southern Europe, selected Latin American countries, and a few locations in Asia, Africa, and Australasia.

Data from the nominative records are utilized to develop family-group sheets, the second major set of records, which are similar to the forms developed independently by Louis Henry for French reconstitution studies (1967). An example of a family-group sheet appears in figure 7. From the family-group sheet, basic demographic data are avail-

HUSBAND JONES, Robert

Born 4 Feb 1838 Place Bolton Lanes, Lncshr, Engl
Chr. Place
Mar 6 May 1863 Place Salt Lake City, S-Lk, Utah
Died 13 Aug 1921 Place
Bur. Place
HUSBAND'S FATHER JONES, George — HUSBAND'S MOTHER WHEELER, Jane
HUSBAND'S OTHER WIVES JOHNSON, Elizabeth

Husband JONES, Robert 1838
Wife DOTY, Harriet
Ward Examiners 1. (18th) C.T.R. 2. N.C.
Stake or Mission

NAME & ADDRESS OF PERSON SUBMITTING SHEET
Blanchard, Sylvia W.
428 I Avenue
Salt Lake City, Utah

RELATION OF ABOVE TO HUSBAND g dau — RELATION OF ABOVE TO WIFE g dau
FOUR GENERATION SHEET FOR FILING ONLY YES [X] NO [ ]
DATE SUBMITTED TO GENEALOGICAL SOCIETY 6 Apr 1978

WIFE DOTY, Harriet

Born 3 Sep 1842 Place Blowich, Lncshr, Engl
Chr. Place
Died 2 June 1923 Place Salt Lake City, S-Lk, Utah
Bur. Place
WIFE'S FATHER DOTY, Raymond — WIFE'S MOTHER WEBB, Nancy
WIFE'S OTHER HUSBANDS

LDS ORDINANCE DATA

	BAPTIZED (Date)	ENDOWED (Date)	SEALED (Date and Temple) WIFE TO HUSBAND
HUSBAND	3 Nov 1853	3 Feb 1866	3 Feb 1866
WIFE	1852	Feb 1866	//////////

SEX M F	CHILDREN List each child (whether living or dead) in order of birth — SURNAME, Given Names	WHEN BORN Day	Month	Year	WHERE BORN Town	County	State or Country	DATE OF FIRST MARRIAGE / TO WHOM	WHEN DIED Day	Month	Year	BAPTIZED (Date)	ENDOWED (Date)	SEALED (Date and Temple) CHILDREN TO PARENTS
1	JONES, Katherine Anne	1	Apr	1865	Nephi	Juab	Utah	— — — —	2	Sep	1871	Child	Child	1 Jun 1950
2	JONES, David Wheeler	29	Dec	1866	Moroni	Snpt	Utah	24 Apr 1895 Bricker, Mary Ann	20	Feb	1931	31 Jan 1877	24 Apr 1895	BIC
3	JONES, Charlotte	29	Sep	1869	"	"	"	21 Apr 1890 Denton, Richard	27	May	1949	Reb. 1 Apr 1890	21 Apr 1890	BIC
4	JONES, Arlene Marie	20	Aug	1871	Salt Lake City	S-Lk	"	— — — —	25	Sep	1872	Child	Child	BIC
5	JONES, Louise Nancy	18	Nov	1873	" " "	"	"	2 Nov 1896 Taylor, John	31	May	1929	7 Jun 1883	2 Nov 1896	BIC
6	JONES, Marilyn	31	Aug	1876	" " "	"	"	31 Jan 1906 McNeil, Joseph	23	Dec	1926	30 Mar 1886	27 Aug 1902	BIC
7	JONES, James Lowell	8	Aug	1878	North Point	S-LK	"	— — — —	8	Aug	1878	Child	Child	BIC
8	JONES, John Lawrence	24	Aug	1879	" "	"	"	— — — —	15	Apr	1880	Child	Child	BIC
9	JONES, Isabel	6	Aug	1881	" "	"	"	— — — —	13	Nov	1904	1 Apr 1890	31 Jan 1906	BIC
10	JONES, Elliot George	6	Nov	1883	Salt Lake City	"	"	30 Aug 1911 Creighton, Cynthia				29 Mar 1893	8 Mar 1905	BIC
11	JONES, Sarah Jane	2	Jul	1886	" " "	"	"	22 June 1910 Anderson, Thomas A.				2 Jul 1894	22 Jun 1910	BIC

SOURCES OF INFORMATION
Personal diary and family records of Robert Jones

OTHER MARRIAGES

NECESSARY EXPLANATIONS

Figure 7. Sample Family-Group Sheet (Fictitious names have been substituted in place of real names.)

able on parents and their children, including date and place of birth, date of death, and place of death (of parents), date of marriage, and relevant religious data. Also provided are the names of the parents of the married couple who serve as the reference individuals (or pivot). Thus the family-group sheets provide information on fertility, mortality, age at marriage, religion, and place of residence at specific points in the life cycle.

Family-group sheets have an advantage of collating information for individuals and their kin on a single form. Over nine million of these family-group sheets were available in 1981, and the number has continued to increase since then.[2] It is from the collection of nine million records that the family-group sheets were selected for the analysis reported in this volume.

SAMPLE SELECTION

In itself, access to the family-group sheets of the GSU would not have sufficed for the present study. Also required were the support resources to select a large, complex sample and develop a machine-readable file—resources generally unavailable for historical demographic research. The demographic analyses of the MHDP database have been made possible through the collaboration of a group of scholars from several disciplines who developed the data file primarily for the purpose of linking the genealogies to a tumor registry for the state of Utah which has been maintained by the Utah Cancer Registry since 1968. Access to this registry, which records all diagnosed cases of cancer in the state, as well as to the GSU records provided the collaborative group an opportunity to study the link between cancer and kinships. The nature of the collaborative effort has been described by Bean, May, and Skolnick (1978), and the projected medical use of the file has been described by Skolnick and others (Skolnick 1980; Williams et al. 1978).

In the present study, to maximize the coverage of the ideal population from the family-group sheets, the sample was defined as all family-group sheets that list at least one member of the family who was born or died on the pioneer trail or in Utah. The selection of the sample involved a review of all family-group sheets in the "Patron" section of the archives in 1975 and 1976; approximately 170,000 family-group sheets were selected. In 1978–1979 an additional 14,417 family-group sheets were added to the sample after a review of the "Main" section. In the time before the second survey, the initial set of family-group sheets was reviewed to identify those that indicated additional wives whose detailed records were not part of the original set. This step identified 14,479 records of the original 170,000 which required updating or correction.

CREATING A MACHINE-READABLE FILE

Information from the family-group sheets was entered onto a computer disk file using a multiterminal data-entry program. Operators using formatted data-entry video terminals keyed information directly from the family-group sheets[3]; there was no initial coding of data by hand before data entry. Four formats appeared on the screen as needed: (1) for parents' names, birth dates, and marriage information; (2) for detailed parents' records; (3) for child's records; and (4) for other marriage records. As part of the input system, names were coded automatically by means of the Russell-Soundex coding method and checked against a name file compiled from previous entries. If the name did not match one in the existing name file, the entry process was blocked until the operator verified the spelling of the current entry or indicated that the new name was to be added to the file. In addition to name checking, later versions of the program range checked for illogical numbers and for chronological order within the family; for example, a mother's birth date could not follow her marriage date.

The data-entry system was interactive and linked individuals at the time of record entry. Specifically, it linked the individual and marriage records within each family-group sheet and linked records across sheets where there was an exact match, creating multigenerational family genealogies. The criteria for linking were very strict, requiring an exact match on last name, first name, birth month, and birth year.[4]

Because of the time required to enter and verify the initial set of 170,000 family-group sheets, the entry of data was organized to create a sample for analysis. Family-group sheets were arranged alphabetically by family name within 20-year birth cohorts, defined by date of the husband's birth. Beginning with the earliest cohort (1800–19), the records of families whose last names started with one of the first three letters of the alphabet were initially entered. Thus the first analysis of the data appeared in 1978, reporting on the fertility experience of 22,382 women married between 1820 and 1920 (Skolnick et al. 1978). The reliability of the procedure adopted is demonstrated by the fact that the values of the variables reported in the 1978 paper are not significantly different from the values derived from subsequent analysis of the complete file.

To store the data, project personnel, Mark Skolnick and Val Arbon, developed what at the time was a unique file-structure but which is now common to many relational database systems (Skolnick et al. 1979). As the data were entered, they were stored in two files: the "Individual" file and the "Marriage" file. The basic family relationships are represented as pointers between the files. To aid programmers, various database interfaces have been used to provide data access that is independent of the physical storage structure. In an effort to consolidate all data access in a single package, GENISYS was developed and released to users in March 1981 (Dintelman et al. 1980). The main feature of the GENISYS Query Language (GQL) is that it enables users to request tabulations that reference data in and across linked records. The major underlying component of GENISYS is its data dictionary, which contains information about all the database files and fields, the queries, and access paths. In addition, a preprocessor allows GQL queries to be embedded in FORTRAN programs. This use of defined links through which complex queries can be formulated allows the data to be manipulated as needed by the specific researcher. The program has been described by Dintelman and Maness (1983).

Many tasks in this collaborative project involve some type of record linking. Before 1984 the record linking was accomplished by developing specific programs and algorithms for each application. A more generalized record-linking system was later completed to take advantage of the capabilities and tools that are part of GENISYS, integrating features available in MERCURE (Chiaramella 1981).

Throughout the processes of data entry and analysis, a variety of verification procedures were implemented. These included computer programs to identify and flag records with logical inconsistencies, machine and manual verification of kinship linkages, and matching of the genealogy with the 1880 manuscript census.

QUALITY OF THE DATA

Every set of demographic data is less than perfect; in most cases events or individuals are underreported. But if the proportion of omitted events is small or random, no significant bias is introduced. Secondary historical-demographic data are often suspect, however, because of presumed biases, culturally or socially determined, introduced into the original records. A classic illustration is found in Chinese clan genealogies, which fail to record female births (Telford 1986).[5] European genealogies are often strongly biased in favor of particular class groups, royalty and other elite classes, although that problem seems to have been avoided in selected *village* genealogies (Knodel 1978).

In view of the possibility of a range of potential errors, a number of tests have been used to evaluate the quality of the MHDP database. A number of the tests involved comparison of parameters of the MHDP records with the theoretical models or empirical findings from studies of other populations. Several of the analyses have been reported in previous publications. For example, Lynch et al. (1985) have examined data on infant mortality and find some underreporting of births that ended in infant deaths before 1870, particularly in rural areas. However, no substantial pattern of sex-preferential reporting of infant deaths was observed, and the underreporting of births ending in infant deaths is too low to affect findings on fertility levels and trends. As another example, Anderton and Bean (1985) compare birth-interval distributions by parity with similar data reported by Knodel (1979) and Henry (1961) and find no difference between the MHDP population and the population included in German genealogies or in studies of the Hutterites. Additional studies investigate maternal mortality (Bardet et al. 1981), widowhood (Mineau 1988), and sterility (Mineau and Anderton 1983).

The results of these studies provide confidence in the quality of the MHDP records, but the studies do indicate certain limitations. First, women who died at the time of the birth of the first child are slightly less likely to be included in the file; second, nulliparous women are less likely to be included;[6] and finally, small families may be slightly underrepresented. The limitations are not significant, and their effect means that our findings have very little bias in the estimates of fertility levels and in detailed fertility analysis.

To further describe the people who are represented in the MHDP data set and to determine the degree to which the MHDP population is representative of the entire population of Utah Territory, we began another project to compare our records to an independent data set for Utah: the 1880 census enumeration forms (manuscript census) of Utah Territory (Bean and Mineau 1984; Mineau, Anderton and Bean 1989). The microfilm copy, provided by the National Archives, was used to create a computerized census file to compare with the MHDP genealogical file. Although the analysis of this comparison is in its initial stages, the information in table 6 provides some insight on the coverage of the

TABLE 6

COMPARISON OF CENSUS RECORDS AND RECORD LINKING RESULTS BY COUNTY FOR UTAH TERRITORY IN 1880 AND FOR WASHINGTON COUNTY BY LOCATIONS

County	Published Census[a]	Computerized Census Records	Census Records Computer-Linked to MHDP data	% Computer Linked	% After Manual Linking
Beaver	3918	3864	1706	44.2	
Box Elder	6761	6777	3974	58.6	
Cache	12562	12562	8699	69.2	
Davis	5279	4924[b]	3879	78.8	88.0
Emery	556	556	345	62.1	
Iron	4013	4034	3128	77.5	
Juab	3474	3477	2245	64.6	
Kane	3085	3092	2474	80.0	90.3
Millard	3727	3721	2698	72.5	
Morgan	1783	1783	1278	71.7	81.5
Piute	1651	1616	911	56.4	
Rich	1263	282[c]	189	67.0	
Salt Lake	31977	31984	15329	47.9	57.3
San Juan	204	204	146	71.6	
Sanpete	11557	11538	7917	68.6	
Sevier	4457	4457	3213	72.1	80.7
Summit	4921	4921	2469	50.2	
Tooele	4497	4496	2376	52.8	

Uintah	799	799	364	45.6	
Utah	17973	17967	12735	70.9	79.4
Wasatch	2927	2928	2182	74.5	
Washington	4235	4140	2369	57.2	66.7
Weber	12344	12632[b]	7543	59.7	
Total	143963	142754[d]	88064	61.7	66.5
		Washington County Locations			
Gunlock	156	156	136	87.2	
Harrisburg; Leeds	334	334	226	67.7	
Hebron	110	80	72	90.0	
Pine Valley	234	234	207	88.5	
Pinto	155	99	99	100.0	
Price City	85	85	84	98.8	
Saint George	1384	1379	1200	87.0	
Santa Clara	194	194	154	79.4	
Silver Reef	1046	1044	141	13.5	
Washington	537	535	444	83.0	
Total	4235	4140	2763	66.7	

a. Source: Bureau of the Census, *Statistics of the Population of the United States at the Tenth Census* (Washington, D.C.: Government Printing Office, 1883), pp. 351–353.

b. The published census placed all of Hooper in Davis County although the microfilm version placed some of the people in Weber County.

c. The microfilm copy was incomplete; it is missing 1000 records in Rich County.

d. Records which were unreadable on the microfilm were not computerized.

resident population of Utah Territory by the genealogies. By means of a computer algorithm designed to link nuclear-family members, 62 percent of the people recorded in the manuscript were linked to individuals in the MHDP data set. Linkage by county ranged from a low of 44 percent to a high of 80 percent.

The algorithm did not include the linking of servants, boarders, and extended kin in the household. In addition, the computer matching underlinked one-person households (which lack many unique identifiers) and female-headed households (for which the mother's maiden name does not appear in census records). To compensate for these deficiencies in the computer linking, additional manual linking has been undertaken for selected counties and locations; the results for seven counties are shown in table 6. To date, less than 1 percent of the computer-produced links have been identified as errors, and manual links have increased computer links by about 9 percent. We estimate that final linking will be about 70 percent statewide.

More detailed studies are underway, but one example of the coverage of the Utah population by the MHDP data set is presented in the bottom panel of table 6—the results of the linking for the ten locations in Washington County listed in the 1880 census. Linkage is very high (about 80 percent or higher) for all but two locations. These two locations contain very high proportions of men who were in mining occupations. These were typically single men who were not LDS and who did not remain in Utah. The coverage of this category of residents was anticipated to be low and does not bias studies of fertility.

GENERAL COVERAGE

In the later part of this chapter and in the remaining chapters, we focus on the marriages and children of women who appear as "wife" on the family-group sheets. However, to present the overall coverage of the MHDP records, we first report on all individuals born between 1800 and 1899.

The date of birth is nearly universally recorded: less than 1 percent of individuals in the computer file are missing the year of birth on the family-group sheets. A few individuals born before 1800 who subsequently experienced the birth of a child or the death of a family member on the pioneer trail or in Utah are listed in the sample family-group sheets. Although their number is small—1,959 cases, or two-tenths of 1 percent of all cases—we decided to exclude them from the study population. The cut-off dates of 1800 and 1899 were selected for several reasons. The period they define covers the range of birth cohorts representing the major changes in fertility and includes those families for whom records were most detailed. The family-group sheets provide more information if the parents were born in the nineteenth century than if they were born in the twentieth century. Comparing these data to Utah State Birth Registration information for 1910, we found that the genealogy represents 69 percent of births in the state; but for 1960 it represents only 28 percent.[7] There appears to be a tendency to complete family-group sheets for families in which one or both parents are deceased; thus more recent sheets are less likely to have been submitted to the GSU, in that most parents are still alive.

SEX RATIOS AT BIRTH

The initial test of the quality of the data reported here follows from Hollingsworth (1976) and examines the sex ratios at birth. Two sets of data are presented in table 7. The three columns headed "Genealogy Individual" include information on all individuals—male and female—appearing in the selected birth cohorts. The next three columns, headed "Those with Parents," list the number of individuals who appear in the file as births to parents who are also part of the genealogy. The distinction may become clearer with an illustration. In one case, a male was born in England in 1803, joined the LDS church in 1840, and moved to Utah in 1850. He, his wife, and children are part of the total genealogy and thus are included in the "Genealogy-Individual" column. His children are repeated in the "Those with Parents" column. Furthermore, because his children form a group of siblings, we can also refer to them as belonging to a "sibship." But because we have no information on the man's parents or his brothers or sisters, he is not included in the "Those with Parents" column and is not part of a sibship as far as the MHDP data set is concerned.

Across the entire set of birth cohorts in the total genealogy, the ratio of males to females at birth is erratic and unusual. The normal sex ratio at birth for a population is between 102 and 106 males per 100 females. There are several patterns evident in table 7 which vary from this. The first, the founder effect, appears in the birth cohorts before 1815, when the sex ratio is well over 106 males per 100 females. This time period represents the birth cohorts of the founders and earliest followers of the LDS church. Among these earliest church members, the husband was

TABLE 7

SEX RATIOS FOR GENEALOGY INDIVIDUALS AND FOR THOSE THAT ENTERED WITH A SIBSHIP, BIRTH COHORTS 1800–04 TO 1895–99

	Genealogy-Individuals			Those with Parents		
Birth Cohort	Males	Females	Sex Ratio[a]	Males	Females	Sex Ratio
1800–04	841	632	133.1	145	136	106.6
1805–09	1,144	1,021	112.0	252	225	112.0
1810–14	1,552	1,389	111.7	375	309	121.4
1815–19	2,042	1,879	108.7	591	493	119.9
1820–24	2,715	2,544	106.7	879	783	112.3
1825–29	3,250	3,098	104.9	1,395	1,209	115.4
1830–34	4,178	3,911	106.8	2,104	1,880	111.9
1835–39	4,559	4,767	95.6	2,708	2,623	103.2
1840–44	5,378	5,726	93.9	3,570	3,571	100.0
1845–49	6,506	6,412	101.5	4,662	4,349	107.2
1850–54	8,353	7,972	104.8	6,245	5,774	108.2
1855–59	10,418	10,235	101.8	8,212	7,775	105.6
1860–64	12,047	12,219	98.6	9,736	9,624	101.2
1865–69	14,018	13,635	102.8	11,647	11,040	105.5
1870–74	15,702	15,477	101.5	13,454	12,834	104.8
1875–79	18,012	17,526	102.8	15,602	14,817	105.3
1880–84	20,516	19,954	102.8	18,058	17,247	104.7
1885–89	22,707	22,262	102.0	20,335	19,670	103.4
1890–94	23,692	23,221	103.2	21,632	20,822	103.9
1895–99	25,231	23,858	105.8	22,857	21,512	106.3
TOTAL	203,131	197,738	102.7	164,459	156,693	105.0

Note: These data omit stillborns.
[a]The sex ratio is the number of males per 100 females.

usually born several years before his wife. This creates an imbalance in the sex ratio of sample family-group sheets because younger wives appear in later cohorts.[8] An additional factor is that the male founders and early male leaders of the church have been more fully recorded in genealogies than their wives and daughters.

The second pattern is the low sex ratios (under 100 males per 100 females) which occur in varying degrees from the 1835–39 birth cohort until the 1860–64 cohort. These are due in part to the excess of females which resulted from the conversion and migration practices of the LDS church and in part to the underrepresentation of single transient men. The sex ratio of the foreign-born population of Utah Territory in the 1860 and 1870 censuses was 96.9 and 94.4 men per 100 women, respectively, and the foreign-born account for about one-third of the population. If European converts who migrated to Utah were slightly more likely to be female, this may also be true of converts from various parts of the United States (but this cannot be discerned from aggregate census figures).

The last three columns of table 7 contain the numbers of males and females in sibships and their sex ratios. These columns focus on that section of the family-group sheet in which the children are listed, eliminating husbands and wives unless they are also members of sibships. This step ameliorates the pattern of low sex ratios; it appears that beginning with the 1835–39 birth cohort there is no consistent pattern that would indicate that males or females are more likely to be included in genealogies. For the earliest cohorts there remains a differential recording of males and females with a slight preference in the recording of males; however, the number of people included in the earliest cohorts is relatively small, a fact that introduces some instability into the results. Nevertheless, the early high sex ratios, in addition to suggesting the founder effect, suggest some preference for recording sons rather than daughters in early generations.

MARRIAGE RECORDS

The founder effect, which seems to be largely responsible for the excessive masculinity ratios among the early cohorts of the total genealogy, is also seen in other records. In table 8 we present information on the proportion of males and females with and without a recorded marriage. For those without a marriage, we distinguish among those who died young, before age 20; those who died after age 20; and those for whom no death date is recorded.

The data presented in table 8 suggest that the proportion of married males and females declined from the first to the midcentury cohorts, and then increased. Among those born after midcentury one would anticipate a rise in the proportion married as mortality conditions improve and a larger proportion of those born survive to the age of marriage.

TABLE 8

DISTRIBUTION (PERCENTAGES) OF FEMALES AND MALES WHO SURVIVED AND MARRIED BY BIRTH COHORT

		No Marriage				
Birth Cohort	N	Died <20	Died 20+	Death Date Missing	Married	Total %
FEMALES						
1800–04	632	1.1	1.7	3.8	93.4	100.0
1805–09	1,021	2.3	0.7	3.3	93.7	100.0
1810–14	1,389	2.0	1.4	3.7	92.9	100.0
1815–19	1,879	2.4	2.3	4.7	90.5	99.9
1820–24	2,544	3.2	2.4	4.5	89.9	100.0
1825–29	3,098	5.0	2.1	5.1	87.8	100.0
1830–34	3,911	7.4	1.7	6.8	84.1	100.0
1835–39	4,767	10.4	1.9	6.2	81.5	100.0
1840–44	5,726	13.2	1.7	6.4	78.7	100.0
1845–49	6,412	15.0	1.7	6.7	76.5	99.9
1850–54	7,972	14.5	2.0	6.1	77.4	100.0
1855–59	10,235	13.1	2.2	4.9	79.9	100.1
1860–64	12,219	16.3	2.0	4.4	77.3	100.0
1865–69	13,635	16.3	2.5	4.3	76.9	100.0
1870–74	15,477	17.3	2.9	3.9	75.8	99.9
1875–79	17,526	16.0	2.8	3.2	78.1	100.1
1880–84	19,954	15.1	2.9	3.1	78.8	99.9
1885–89	22,262	15.6	2.6	3.1	78.7	100.0
1890–94	23,221	14.4	2.5	2.8	80.3	100.0
1895–99	23,858	12.9	2.3	3.2	81.6	100.0
TOTAL	197,738	14.1	2.4	4.0	79.5	100.0
MALES						
1800–04	841	1.3	1.3	4.4	93.0	100.0
1805–09	1,144	1.4	1.6	3.6	93.4	100.0
1810–14	1,552	2.3	2.0	4.8	90.9	100.0
1815–19	2,042	2.9	3.2	4.4	89.5	100.0
1820–24	2,715	3.7	3.3	5.6	87.3	99.9
1825–29	3,250	6.3	4.0	6.6	83.1	100.0

TABLE 8 (continued)

MALES

Birth Cohort	N	No Marriage: Died <20	No Marriage: Died 20+	No Marriage: Death Date Missing	Married	Total %
1830–34	4,178	8.1	3.9	8.3	79.8	100.1
1835–39	4,559	11.6	4.3	8.6	75.4	99.9
1840–44	5,378	15.0	3.9	8.5	72.6	100.0
1845–49	6,506	17.1	4.3	8.8	69.8	100.0
1850–54	8,353	15.8	4.6	7.7	71.9	100.0
1855–59	10,418	15.4	5.2	6.4	73.0	100.0
1860–64	12,047	16.2	5.7	6.1	72.0	100.0
1865–69	14,018	17.4	6.1	5.1	71.4	100.0
1870–74	15,702	19.2	6.4	4.9	69.6	100.1
1875–79	18,012	17.9	6.2	4.3	71.5	99.9
1880–84	20,516	17.1	6.0	3.9	73.0	100.0
1885–89	22,707	17.8	5.7	3.6	72.8	99.9
1890–94	23,962	16.0	5.5	3.5	75.0	100.0
1895–99	25,231	15.5	5.0	3.3	76.2	100.0
TOTAL	203,131	15.8	5.4	4.9	73.9	100.0

The decline from the 1800-04 cohort to midcentury is again simply a founder effect. Migrants to Utah were those who survived and married, although some deaths before or during family migration would be included on genealogy sheets. Family-group sheets on which the head of the family is recorded as having been born in 1800 or later would record no children born before approximately 1815. However, a few children appear in the early cohorts. They are the children of some of the small number of individuals who were themselves born between 1775 and 1799 and who are included in the file because they or a family member experienced an event (birth or death) on the pioneer trail or in Utah. Only some members of this small group would have given birth to children. In the 1800–04 cohort, 19 percent of the individuals are entered as children on their parents' family-group sheets, but for the 1850–54 cohort 74 percent are entered as children on a parent's record.

Thus, in the early cohorts, the decline in the proportion with a marriage record and the rise in the proportion dying before age 20 simply reflect a change in the proportions exposed to risk.

The marital experience of the men and the women in the study population is quite different.[9] As indicated in table 9, nearly 85.7 percent of the women married only once, and the range of percentage variations among cohorts is minimal, from 81.1 to 88.5 percent. Only 76.2 percent of the males married only once, and the range of variation among cohorts is relatively great, from 55.5 to 83.3 percent, with the low figures reflecting selected cohorts of males involved in polygyny.

Although the founder effect is an important feature of a genealogical file, it does not influence the analysis of fertility, which consistently analyzes a set of data defined by the same set of criteria. For example, in table 10 data are presented to demonstrate the degree of completeness in the recording of events affecting the specification of the period of risk of exposure to childbearing within marriages. To simplify the presentation, data are presented in this table for women and their first marriages where this can be accurately specified.

Even though one can identify marriages in the earliest cohort, 1800–04, dates of marriage are available for only three-fourths of the cases. The proportion of first marriages with confirmed marriage dates improves consistently, so that among those born in 1895–99, dates of marriage are missing in less than 2 percent of the cases. Although marriage dates are unknown in a significant proportion of cases in the early cohorts, estimated dates of marriage may be imputed for most of these cases. This imputation is accomplished by subtracting a constant mean interval from the birthdate of the first child.[10]

The period of exposure to the risk of conception and childbirth is defined by age at marriage and age at termination of childbearing, which takes place at the death of the husband or the wife, or at age 45 when both husband and wife survive. Therefore, the columns of table 10 that refer to death dates and "completed family" are important. Death dates are about equally well recorded for males and females. The recording of death dates improves initially, and then for the last cohorts death dates are generally less available. The absence of death dates for the youngest cohort simply reflects that many of these people were still alive at the time the family-group sheets were filed at the GSU, that action had not been taken to record deaths for those individuals, or that deaths had been relatively recent. The presence of information on the wife's or husband's death dates means that between 98.9 and 96.4

TABLE 9

DISTRIBUTION (PERCENTAGES) OF MARRIAGES FOR MALES AND FEMALES, BY BIRTH COHORT

FEMALES

Birth Cohort	N	Number of Marriages							Total %
		1	2	3	4	5	6	>6	
1800–04	418	85.9	12.7	1.4	*[a]	*	*	*	100.0
1805–09	729	83.7	13.3	2.5	0.5	*	*	*	100.0
1810–14	1,015	81.3	15.8	2.3	0.6	*	0.1	*	100.1
1815–19	1,368	81.9	15.0	2.9	0.3	*	*	*	100.1
1820–24	1,838	81.1	15.8	2.4	0.7	*	0.1	*	100.1
1825–29	2,121	81.5	15.0	2.8	0.6	0.1	*	*	100.0
1830–34	2,534	84.1	13.1	2.3	0.4	*	0.1	*	100.0
1835–39	2,913	82.4	14.9	2.3	0.4	*	*	*	100.0
1840–44	3,180	84.7	13.5	1.5	0.3	*	*	*	100.0
1845–49	3,295	85.7	12.0	2.0	0.3	0.1	*	*	100.1
1850–54	4,135	86.4	12.0	1.4	0.1	*	*	*	99.9
1855–59	5,332	88.7	9.7	1.3	0.3	*	*	*	100.0
1860–64	5,998	87.6	10.3	1.9	0.1	*	*	*	99.9
1865–69	6,377	88.5	9.8	1.4	0.3	0.1	*	*	100.1
1870–74	6,800	87.5	10.4	1.7	0.4	0.1	*	*	100.1

TABLE 9 (continued)

Birth Cohort	N	Number of Marriages							Total %
		1	2	3	4	5	6	>6	
FEMALES									
1875–79	7,446	86.8	10.8	2.0	0.3	0.1	*	*	100.0
1880–84	8,071	85.6	11.7	2.2	0.4	*	*	*	99.9
1885–89	8,477	84.4	12.5	2.6	0.4	0.1	*	*	100.0
1890–94	8,513	84.8	12.1	2.8	0.4	*	*	*	100.1
1895–99	8,502	85.3	11.7	2.4	0.4	0.1	*	*	99.9
TOTAL	89,062	85.7	11.8	2.1	0.3	0.1	0.0	0.0	100.0
MALES									
1800–04	635	63.0	21.9	6.8	3.8	2.2	0.6	1.7	100.0
1805–09	881	60.0	20.7	8.3	5.1	3.1	1.0	1.8	100.0
1810–14	1,184	57.2	21.8	10.7	5.7	2.4	1.4	0.8	100.0
1815–19	1,552	55.5	24.6	11.1	5.1	2.2	0.6	0.9	100.0
1820–24	2,026	55.7	27.2	10.3	4.2	2.0	0.3	0.3	100.0
1825–29	2,217	57.9	26.3	10.1	3.5	1.6	0.3	0.3	100.0

1830–34	2,650	59.2	27.1	8.9	3.4	0.8	0.5	0.2	100.1
1835–39	2,614	65.0	23.2	9.0	2.0	0.5	0.2	0.1	100.0
1840–44	2,885	68.1	24.4	5.8	1.3	0.2	0.1	*	99.9
1845–49	3,300	72.2	21.5	5.5	0.7	0.1	*	*	100.0
1850–54	4,323	75.7	20.0	3.7	0.6	*	*	*	100.0
1855–59	5,237	78.0	18.1	3.1	0.7	0.1	*	*	100.0
1860–64	5,806	80.3	16.0	3.0	0.6	0.1	*	*	100.0
1865–69	6,341	80.6	15.9	2.8	0.5	0.1	*	*	99.9
1870–74	6,693	80.5	16.1	2.8	0.5	0.1	*	*	100.0
1875–79	7,167	79.4	17.3	2.7	0.5	0.1	*	*	100.0
1880–84	7,794	79.2	17.6	2.7	0.5	0.1	*	*	100.1
1885–89	8,145	79.1	17.0	3.3	0.5	0.1	*	*	100.0
1890–94	8,491	82.0	15.2	2.4	0.4	0.1	*	*	100.1
1895–99	8,577	83.3	13.2	2.9	0.5	0.1	*	*	100.0
TOTAL	88,518	76.2	18.2	4.1	1.0	0.3	0.1	0.1	100.0

[a] Asterisks indicate that there are no cases or a value of less than 0.1%.

TABLE 10

RECORDING OF DATE INFORMATION FOR WOMAN'S FIRST MARRIAGE, BY WOMAN'S BIRTH COHORT

Birth Cohort	N	First Marriage Date		Wife's Death Date		Full Genealogy on Husband				Incomplete Info. on Husband
						Husband's Death Date		Completed Family		
		% No	% Yes	% No	% Yes	% No	% Yes	% No	% Yes	%
1800–04	418	24.4	75.6	6.2	93.8	4.3	94.3	0.2	98.3	1.4
1805–09	729	25.5	74.5	7.1	92.9	5.2	93.0	0.7	97.5	1.8
1810–14	1,015	22.3	77.7	5.6	94.4	4.3	93.8	0.5	97.6	1.9
1815–19	1,368	23.3	76.7	5.4	94.6	4.1	94.1	0.7	97.4	1.8
1820–24	1,838	23.4	76.6	4.7	95.3	5.2	93.2	0.5	97.8	1.6
1825–29	2,121	22.6	77.4	5.2	94.8	4.3	93.5	0.8	97.0	2.2
1830–34	2,533	18.5	81.5	3.8	96.2	3.6	95.1	0.4	98.3	1.3
1835–39	2,910	17.7	82.3	4.5	95.5	2.6	95.7	0.4	97.9	1.7
1840–44	3,178	14.9	85.1	3.0	97.0	2.7	95.7	0.4	97.9	1.7
1845–49	3,288	13.4	86.6	2.6	97.4	2.6	96.0	0.4	98.2	1.4

1850–54	4,108	11.1	88.9	2.3	97.7	2.5	96.0	0.2	98.3	1.4
1855–59	5,283	9.1	90.9	1.8	98.2	2.1	97.1	0.2	98.9	0.9
1860–64	5,923	8.0	92.0	2.0	98.0	2.1	96.6	0.3	98.4	1.3
1865–69	6,313	6.0	94.0	1.8	98.2	1.5	97.4	0.0	98.8	1.1
1870–74	6,751	4.9	95.1	3.1	96.9	1.9	96.6	0.3	98.2	1.5
1875–79	7,376	3.7	96.3	8.0	92.0	3.1	95.2	0.5	97.9	1.7
1880–84	8,006	3.2	96.8	15.3	84.7	6.1	91.8	1.5	96.4	2.1
1885–89	8,414	2.2	97.8	25.7	74.3	11.4	86.7	4.8	93.4	1.9
1890–94	8,455	1.9	98.1	39.1	60.9	19.0	79.0	9.2	88.7	2.1
1895–99	8,457	1.6	98.4	55.6	44.4	28.9	68.7	18.0	79.6	2.4
TOTAL	88,484	7.7	92.3	15.2	84.8	7.9	90.4	3.4	94.9	1.7

Note: Table includes women who entered the genealogy as wives. For the 14 percent of women who had more than one marriage, their marriages were ordered by date to identify the first marriage (if marriage date or children's birth dates were present). Marriages for which dates were absent and could not be estimated were not used as first marriages. Therefore the percentage of first marriages with dates is slightly high.

Note: The women included in this table appear as a "wife" on the family group sheet (see Figure 7).

percent of the families may be considered to be "closed" or "completed" if the wife was born before 1885; that is, we can precisely identify the end of the childbearing years of the marriage.

QUALITY OF THE DATA: A SUMMARY ASSESSMENT

The numerous tests that have been made to evaluate the quality of the MHDP data have identified certain limitations. In some cases imputation procedures may be used to estimate missing events, and in other cases the number of missing events seems to be relatively small, producing no significant bias. Given the time period covered and the scope of the MHDP data, the extensive tests of completeness indicate a generally high quality of data. The completeness of the records is seemingly due to three factors. First, the massive file of nominative records provides unusual opportunities for researchers—often family members—to identify family members and the events of their lives in multiple record sets that may be cross-checked for accuracy. Second, the training programs provided by GSU professional staff members for those family members filling out family-group sheets were seemingly effective. Third, and finally, the fact that professional genealogists check family-group sheets at the time of filing makes it possible to identify records with significant gaps or inconsistencies; such sheets are then returned for further work to the people submitting them.[11]

In this section of the chapter, we have summarized selected steps used in the evaluation of the records analyzed in the study. Our review of the records leads us to recognize certain gaps in the file, but none of sufficient magnitude or importance to substantially alter any of the analyses. Taking into account that not all family records are equally complete, we have run a series of preliminary tests on the file in each analysis to identify cases with missing pieces of information. Where appropriate, such cases have been dropped from the analysis if the number is sufficiently small and if the elimination of cases introduces no systematic bias. As a consequence of this procedure, however, the number of cases reported in selected tables will vary slightly.

The information contained in this section describes the size and quality of the database. The information is derived from a single set of records—family-group sheets—compiled under the authority of the LDS church. These records are not simply of high quality but also cover a population that is remarkably diverse. As will be seen in Part II of this volume, recognition of this heterogeneity is important to understanding the variations in patterns of fertility change and control. To illustrate the point further and at the same time to expand our investigation of data quality, in the following section we present data on the composition of the population represented in the database.

CHARACTERISTICS OF THE POPULATION

In this section a brief summary of critical characteristics of the population is given. Three characteristics of the population are examined: type of marriage or nuptiality, origin and ethnicity, and religious affiliation and commitment.

NUPTIALITY

Evidence presented above indicates that most women who survived to the age of 20 eventually married, a fact that documents the pro-family values of this population (Bean et al. 1987). The patterns of marriage are quite diverse and vary across the cohorts studied in this volume. For the analysis of nuptiality patterns, the wife is used as the focal point; and the complete marriage record of the husband in each of her marriages is examined. Ten categories are identified which distinguish variation in number of marriages, types of marriages, and marital disruptions. These categories are as follows, identified additionally by the mnemonic in the tabular presentation.

1. ONEONE. Once-married couple. The woman had only one husband and the husband had only this wife.
2. ONEFRS. Once-married woman, first wife. The wife had only one marriage, and she was the first wife of her husband, who married one or more additional women following this woman's death or divorce.
3. ONEHOR. Once-married woman, higher order. The wife had one marriage, and her husband had one or more previous marriages.
4. ONELAP. Once-married woman, overlapping events. This is a category in which the data clearly indicate that the wife was married once, that it was the first marriage for her husband, and that he remarried while the woman was still alive. The date of termination of the marriage is not specified; that is, the life span of the wife in question overlapped the husband's marriage to a second wife. However, there is

no indication of polygyny, although the possibility, for this population, does exist.

5. ONEAMB. Once-married woman, unspecified or ambiguous order. The data indicate that the wife had only one marriage and that the husband had two or more, but the absence of marriage dates makes it impossible to determine wife order.

6. ONEPLG. Once-married woman, polygynous husband.

7. TWOCFM. Woman married two or more times, monogamous husbands, complete fertility history. The wife was married more than once. All husbands were monogamous, although any may have had additional sequential marriages. All events are recorded; thus fertility history is complete.

8. TWOCFP. Woman married two or more times, one or more polygynous husbands, complete fertility history. This group differs from TWOCFM only in that at least one of the woman's husbands practiced polygyny.

9. TWOINM. This category is the same as TWOCFM except that selected dates or events are missing from the records, so that the fertility history is incomplete.

10. TWOINP. This category is the same as TWOCFP except that selected dates or events are missing from the records, so that the fertility history is incomplete.

The distribution of marriage types is presented in table 11. The dominant form of marriage is expectedly the single marriage or once-married form (ONEONE), with approximately two-thirds of the women falling into this category. The proportion, however, declined among the early cohorts as the practice of polygyny increased. Then ONEONE marriages increased as polygyny declined and life expectancy increased. A significant proportion of the women married two or more times, 13.1 percent overall.

Four categories indicate data deficiencies: ONELAP, ONEAMB, TWOINM, and TWOINP. In the first cohort, a quarter of the women fall into these four categories, although the majority of these are women whose marriage records make it difficult to ascertain the time when a specific marriage began or ended even though all of the births to the woman are recorded. Fertility histories are incomplete for 9.5 percent of the women in the first cohort and 8.2 percent in the last cohort. In the last cohort, only 3.7 percent of the women with one marriage cannot be properly ordered with respect to their husbands' marriage histories.

As reported elsewhere, the age patterns of fertility of women classified according to the above nuptiality scheme are similar, and variations in completed fertility (fertility levels) are essentially due to variations in length of exposure to the risk of conception (Bean et al. 1987). Moreover, an extensive analysis of the fertility of polygynous women indicates similarities in age patterns of fertility, with differences in completed family size largely explained by wife order.

ORIGIN AND ETHNICITY

The LDS church has often been described as the epitome of a native American religion, yet it is evident that the growth of the church and the Utah community depended to a large extent on a successful missionary program, which attracted large numbers of converts from Europe (see chap. 2). The importance of the missionary program is reflected in the ethnicity and origin of the MHDP population, particularly in the earliest cohorts, as reported in table 12.

Until midcentury the majority of the MHDP population was born in Europe, with the largest group born in Great Britain and the next largest in the Scandinavian countries of Denmark, Norway, and Sweden. Among the cohorts born in the last half of the nineteenth century, those born in Utah Territory increasingly dominate the population, so that by 1895–99 nine of ten were born in Utah. The drastic reduction in the proportion of foreign-born among the last cohorts reflects a number of factors beyond the simple increase in the number of births in Utah: the federal government confiscated and outlawed the Perpetual Emigration Fund, which had supported the migration of converts from Europe; immigration laws came into effect early in the twentieth century that made it more difficult for individuals to enter the United States; World War I intruded on the process of migration at a time when members of the last cohorts would have been at the most common age of migration—young adulthood; and because of the restriction on migration the LDS church stressed the building of institutions in Europe and elsewhere in the United States.

One of the more interesting features of the data set is the care given to the identification of place of birth. Overall, only 1 percent of the married women are missing the record of an identifiable place of birth.

Identification of the place of birth of one individual in itself, of

TABLE 11

DISTRIBUTION (PERCENTAGES) OF MARRIAGE TYPES FOR EVER-MARRIED WOMEN, BY WOMAN'S BIRTH COHORT

		One Marriage–86.9%						>One Marriage—13.1%				
Birth Cohort	N	ONE ONE	ONE FRS	ONE HOR	ONE LAP	ONE AMB	ONE PLG	TWO CFM	TWO CFP	TWO INM	TWO INP	Total %
1800–04	408	52.7	8.3	5.6	4.2	9.3	6.4	2.5	1.5	8.8	0.7	100.0
1805–10	721	45.8	6.8	4.7	6.4	10.0	10.5	4.9	0.7	8.9	1.4	100.1
1810–14	997	45.3	7.6	3.4	3.4	11.1	11.0	3.6	2.6	9.6	2.2	99.8
1815–19	1,340	43.4	6.6	3.7	5.4	9.2	14.9	3.7	1.3	9.5	2.4	100.1
1820–24	1,808	39.0	6.7	5.7	4.7	9.2	16.1	3.7	2.2	10.3	2.4	100.0
1825–29	2,081	39.8	6.3	5.6	3.9	9.1	17.7	2.9	2.7	8.9	3.0	99.9
1830–34	2,481	38.0	5.7	6.5	2.5	9.3	22.8	4.0	2.7	5.8	2.8	100.1
1835–39	2,818	39.1	5.0	7.0	2.1	7.6	23.1	3.3	3.1	6.8	3.1	100.2
1840–44	3,087	44.0	5.5	7.8	1.4	7.4	20.1	3.3	2.7	5.4	2.4	100.0
1845–49	3,187	48.6	6.0	7.1	1.1	6.4	18.6	3.1	1.3	5.8	2.0	100.0
1850–54	4,002	52.8	6.3	6.3	1.1	6.8	14.6	3.8	1.4	5.7	1.1	99.9

1855–59	5,206	59.2	6.9	6.1	0.8	6.3	10.3	3.9	0.8	5.0	0.9	100.2
1860–64	5,789	63.1	7.5	5.3	0.6	5.8	7.0	3.5	0.5	6.2	0.5	100.0
1865–69	6,209	65.9	7.4	6.0	0.7	5.7	4.0	3.6	0.2	6.0	0.5	100.0
1870–74	6,614	67.0	7.9	5.5	0.7	6.4	1.4	4.5	0.2	6.4	0.1	100.1
1875–79	7,250	67.2	8.7	5.3	0.6	5.6	0.8	4.2	*[a]	7.4	0.1	99.9
1880–84	7,846	66.8	9.2	4.6	0.7	5.0	0.5	4.9	*	8.2	0.1	100.0
1885–89	8,221	65.4	9.3	5.0	0.6	5.1	0.2	6.1	*	8.1	*	99.8
1890–94	8,331	66.4	9.2	5.0	0.6	4.4	*	5.8	*	8.6	*	100.0
1895–99	8,325	70.2	7.3	4.7	0.4	3.3	*	5.8	*	8.2	*	99.9
Total %		60.3	7.7	5.5	1.1	5.9	6.3	4.5	0.7	7.2	0.7	99.9
Total N	86,721	52,308	6,665	4,756	978	5,139	5,481	3,884	597	6276	637	

Note: The percentage of women with two or more marriages and incomplete information decreases in cohorts 1830–59 because these have been verified more fully.

[a] Asterisks indicate that there are no cases or a value of less than 0.1%.

TABLE 12

DISTRIBUTION (PERCENTAGES) OF WOMAN'S BIRTH PLACE BY WOMAN'S BIRTH COHORT

Birth Cohort	N	(1)	(2)	(3)	(4)	(5)	(6)	(7)	(8)	No Match	No Place	Total %
1800–04	418	12.7	47.4	3.1	22.7	6.0	1.7	*	3.8	1.0	1.7	100.1
1805–09	729	14.0	41.4	2.1	25.4	9.5	2.1	*	2.6	0.5	2.5	100.1
1810–14	1,015	16.4	46.9	1.5	19.1	7.3	2.9	*	2.5	0.9	2.6	100.1
1815–19	1,368	18.8	48.0	1.3	17.8	4.7	4.3	*	2.3	0.8	2.0	100.0
1820–24	1,838	24.0	46.1	2.4	12.1	4.4	4.5	*	3.8	0.7	2.0	100.0
1825–29	2,121	22.9	46.7	2.6	11.9	3.5	6.4	*	3.3	1.0	1.8	100.1
1830–34	2,533	22.0	45.0	3.6	10.2	3.0	9.1	0.1	3.8	1.0	2.1	99.9
1835–39	2,910	23.9	41.6	4.1	8.4	2.8	11.8	*	4.7	1.0	1.8	100.1
1840–44	3,178	23.7	41.6	3.6	4.7	1.9	17.6	0.1	3.6	1.3	2.0	100.1
1845–49	3,288	23.4	39.1	3.6	2.4	1.2	19.9	5.3	2.2	1.2	1.6	99.9
1850–54	4,108	21.7	30.4	2.9	2.1	1.2	9.0	27.6	2.1	1.4	1.7	100.1
1855–59	5,283	16.3	19.9	3.0	2.4	1.0	4.0	48.9	1.9	1.4	1.1	99.9
1860–64	5,923	13.6	14.9	2.8	1.0	1.0	2.5	60.5	1.7	1.0	1.0	100.0

1865–69	6,313	9.6	10.9	3.3	1.0	1.0	1.6	69.3	1.3	0.9	1.0	100.0
1870–74	6,751	7.2	8.0	3.2	0.9	1.2	1.8	73.8	1.7	1.2	1.0	100.0
1875–79	7,376	6.1	5.7	3.2	0.6	1.0	1.6	78.3	1.5	1.3	0.8	100.1
1880–84	8,006	4.2	4.3	2.5	0.3	0.9	1.4	82.8	1.6	1.2	0.6	99.8
1885–59	8,414	3.0	3.1	2.0	0.4	0.8	1.2	85.8	1.9	1.2	0.6	100.0
1890–94	8,455	2.0	1.8	1.6	0.3	0.7	1.3	87.9	2.7	1.0	0.7	100.0
1895–99	8,457	1.2	1.4	1.5	0.4	0.7	1.1	90.1	2.0	1.0	0.5	99.9
TOTAL	88,484	10.4	16.0	2.6	2.8	1.5	4.1	58.2	2.2	1.1	1.1	100.0

Note: This table includes women who have entered the genealogy as wives.
(1) Scandinavia: Finland, Norway, Sweden, and Denmark
(2) Great Britain: England, Wales, Scotland, Ireland, and Channel Islands
(3) Other European: Switzerland, Germany, Netherlands, Belgium, France, and Luxembourg
(4) Eastern U.S.: Maine, New Hampshire, Vermont, Massachusetts, Rhode Island, Connecticut, New York, New Jersey, and Pennsylvania
(5) Mid-Atlantic states: Delaware, Maryland, West Virginia, Virginia, Kentucky, Tennessee, North Carolina, and South Carolina
(6) Trail States: Ohio, Missouri, Illinois, Iowa, Nebraska, and Indiana
(7) Territory: Utah, Idaho, Colorado, Nevada, Arizona, Wyoming, and New Mexico
(8) Other: includes other U.S. states, Canada, and Mexico

TABLE 13

DISTRIBUTION (PERCENTAGES) OF WOMAN'S BAPTISM AND ENDOWMENT INFORMATION, BY WOMAN'S BIRTH COHORT

Birth Cohort	N	Woman's Death Date Recorded					No Death Date Recorded				Total
		(1)	(2)	(3)	(4)	(5)	(6)	(7)	(8)	(9)	%
1800–04	418	44.5	13.2	10.3	18.2	2.9	4.5	*	0.5	6.0	100.1
1805–09	729	50.8	10.0	10.8	15.8	1.6	5.1	*	1.0	4.9	100.0
1810–14	1,015	53.8	11.0	9.3	13.5	1.3	4.0	0.2	0.6	6.3	100.0
1815–19	1,368	57.4	10.5	8.6	10.6	1.7	3.6	0.1	0.8	6.9	100.2
1820–24	1,838	59.5	10.0	7.7	9.5	1.4	3.3	0.2	0.3	8.1	100.0
1825–29	2,121	61.1	8.8	7.9	8.4	1.3	3.2	0.3	0.5	8.5	100.0
1830–34	2,533	68.7	7.6	5.4	6.5	1.1	2.2	*	0.3	8.2	100.0
1835–39	2,910	69.5	6.9	5.6	5.8	1.0	3.2	0.1	0.3	7.6	100.0
1840–44	3,178	70.3	6.6	6.4	6.0	1.1	1.9	*	0.2	7.5	100.0
1845–49	3,288	71.0	6.1	7.0	5.7	0.7	1.4	0.1	0.3	7.7	100.0
1850–54	4,108	71.9	5.9	7.1	5.9	0.8	1.3	0.1	0.1	6.9	100.0
1855–59	5,283	71.1	7.6	6.6	5.3	0.8	1.0	0.1	0.1	7.4	100.0

1860–64	5,923	69.9	9.2	5.8	5.6	0.6	0.9	0.2	0.1	7.7	100.0
1865–69	6,313	71.6	9.7	4.2	5.3	0.6	1.0	0.1	0.1	7.4	100.0
1870–74	6,751	69.4	12.2	3.6	4.6	0.6	2.2	0.2	0.1	7.1	100.0
1875–79	7,376	68.0	11.6	2.9	3.7	0.4	6.0	0.5	0.4	6.5	100.0
1880–84	8,006	64.0	10.8	2.1	2.6	0.3	12.4	1.0	0.4	6.4	100.0
1885–89	8,414	56.7	9.4	1.5	1.6	0.3	21.0	2.2	0.5	6.9	100.1
1890–94	8,455	46.8	8.3	1.0	1.2	0.2	32.3	3.7	0.5	6.0	100.0
1895–99	8,457	34.5	6.4	0.8	0.7	*	46.3	5.8	0.6	4.9	100.0
TOTAL	88,484	61.5	9.0	4.0	4.3	0.6	12.2	1.3	0.3	6.8	100.0

Note: This table includes women who entered the genealogy as wives.

(1) Baptism and endowment before death
(2) Baptism before death
(3) Endowment before death
(4) Baptism and endowment after death
(5) Baptism or endowment after death
(6) Baptism and endowment
(7) Baptism only
(8) Endowment only
(9) No Baptism and no endowment

course, fails to identify the degree to which individuals may have been influenced by the particular sociocultural conditions of the community of birth. A better indicator of the impact of such conditions, however, is captured by the analysis of a combination of locations—mother's place of birth and place of birth of each child—for married women bearing children. This type of analysis is presented in further detail in chapter 5.

RELIGIOUS AFFILIATION

Data available from the family-group sheet make it possible to distinguish between those who were members of the LDS church and those who were not, and to specify the level and timing of commitment to the LDS church among the former group. The information presented in this section will be best understood in conjunction with the family-group sheet displayed in figure 7. The right-hand side of the sheet provides "LDS Ordinance Data," that is, information on two religious events: baptism and endowment. Baptism occurs no earlier than age 8 for children and may be later for converts. Endowment occurs before an individual goes on a mission, at the time of a "temple" marriage, or later for converts or reactivated members of the LDS church.[12] Under LDS church doctrine, an individual may become associated with the LDS faith after death; baptism and endowment are performed by a living proxy. Children whose parents were married in a temple ceremony are identified by the notation "BIC" (born in the covenant). If these children die young, baptism or endowment need not be performed by proxy because such children are permanently attached to parents who are "sealed" to each other for eternity. For purposes of this study we regard the absence of information indicating baptism—a prerequisite to endowment—before death as evidence that the individual was not a member of the LDS church.

Religious affiliation data are presented in table 13 for ever-married females used in the fertility analysis. Of those who were born between 1805 and 1889, over 50 percent (column 1) are recorded as having been both baptized and endowed during their lifetime. Although the timing of these events is not detailed by the data presented, one can assume that they occurred at older ages for the earlier cohorts made up of converts and at younger ages for the later cohorts born into LDS families living in Utah. In the 1800–04 cohort, both events occurred after death (columns 4–8) for 26.6 percent of the women; this proportion decreases to and remains at about 10 percent from 1835 to 1869. The cohorts from 1880 to 1899 increasingly lack recorded death dates, as discussed earlier.

The lack of baptism and endowment dates does not necessarily result from recording or record-entry errors. In column 9 of table 13, the data indicate women who probably did not have an affiliation with the LDS church although another family member or relative did. Of course, there is the possibility that information on baptism and endowment may be lacking simply because it was not recorded, not because the events never occurred. Nevertheless, the data presented in columns 3 and 8 indicate inconsistencies in the record, because endowment can occur only after baptism. Other information, such as that presented in columns 2 and 7, indicates only partial affiliation with the LDS church. These women were baptized but never endowed. The religious index, discussed in chapter 6, uses information for both husband and wife together to minimize the appearance of partial or no affiliation due to recording or input errors.

GENEALOGIES IN HISTORICAL DEMOGRAPHY

At the beginning of this chapter we indicated that the MHDP database is different from types of data used in contemporary demographic analysis as well as from a large number of data sets used in historical demographic analysis. In this section we illustrate the differences to explicitly identify the analytical advantages of the database employed in this study.

The types of records used in historical demographic analysis, their strengths and limitations, have been described in a number of important publications. One of the earliest is Hollingsworth's *Historical Demography* (1969), and one of the more recent is Willigan and Lynch's *Sources and Methods of Historical Demography* (1982). Given these excellent sources it is not necessary to discuss these issues here. It is, however, important to identify the major differences between the database used in this study and the records used in other major studies.

The MHDP database was not constructed for historical demographic analysis but was originally conceived as a file of linked family genealogies from which pedigrees could be abstracted and linked to medical records for a range of genetic epidemiology studies (Bean, May, and Skolnick 1978). As construction proceeded, however, a series of historical-demographic goals emerged which focused on the need to understand the process of a fertility transition, with particular emphasis on the timing of fertility change, the geographic loci of fertility change, and the mechanisms involved in the shift from high, uncontrolled fertility to moderate, relatively controlled fertility. Two of these goals—specification of time and geographic loci—are similar to those that guided the Princeton European Fertility Project, as described by the project's director, Ansley J. Coale:

> Surprisingly enough . . . there has not been a systematic compilation and comparison of the statistical records of various European populations to provide a thorough documentation of these changes and a possible basis for their explanation. We have begun a project along these lines at Princeton. The decline of fertility in each of the provinces of Europe will be recorded from the time in each province when marital fertility was essentially constant[13] until it reached a minimum or until the present if it is still declining. (Coale 1969, pp. 3–4)

The significance of the Princeton European Fertility Project has been evidenced in an invaluable series of papers and monographs including studies of Portugal, Italy, Germany, France, Belgium, and Russia (Livi Bacci 1971, 1977; Knodel 1974; van de Walle 1974; Lesthaeghe 1977; Coale, Anderson, and Härm 1979).[14] Through its extensive set of publications, the project has made major methodological as well as substantive contributions to our understanding of the fertility transition. Nevertheless, the study was unable to document in detail the underlying behavioral changes involved in the transition from high to low fertility. Thus some writers have argued that understanding of fertility transitions may require different types of data than those employed in the Princeton European Fertility Project. M. Livi Bacci (1977, p. 289) concluded that "further research on the aggregate level is not likely to add to the general picture of fertility decline," and Michael Haines, in his review of the European Fertility Project, suggested:

> The project has so far concentrated on geographic units, but the real test of the demographic transition will come at the micro- or family level, where individual tastes, perceptions of costs and benefits, income and wealth circumstances, contraceptive capability, and institutional and social constraints come into play. (1978, p. 170)

Efforts to move below the level of aggregate analysis and address the critical issues outlined by Haines are widespread and involve the construction of individual and family data files. Typical of the constructed data files are the series of reconstitutions of French villages developed under the direction of Louis Henry (Henry and Fleury 1958), the reconstructions of English parishes developed by the Cambridge group (Wrigley 1983), and the reconstruction of the Quebec population under the direction of Jacques Légaré (Légaré, Lavoie, and Charbonneau 1972). The English data have been employed to great advantage by Chris Wilson (1984), who has moved beyond the macrolevel description of demographic levels and trends in England (Wrigley and Schofield 1981) to the analysis of behavioral changes.

An alternative to using constructed individual- and family-level records is to use genealogies, written records of families, their members, and their vital events.[15] Perhaps the most important illustration of the use of genealogies is the extensive work of Knodel, who has abstracted and analyzed genealogies from fourteen German villages (1975, 1979).

Although most historical studies of fertility levels and change in the United States also rely upon aggregate-level data, there are a number of important examples of efforts to "reconstruct" family or community populations that yield individual-level data or to use available genealogies (Condran and Seaman 1979; Temkin-Greener and Swedlund 1978; Kantrow 1980; Logue 1985; and Byers 1982).

Clearly one way of approaching historical-demographic data sets is by level of analysis. On the one hand, there are aggregate-level studies; these are best represented by the Princeton European Fertility Project, which has documented the time and locus of fertility change in Europe and demonstrated the importance of two "revolutions"—a nuptiality revolution and a contraceptive revolution. On the other hand, there are individual-level record sets, which have two benefits that are missed by aggregate analyses. First, one can group the records into meaningful social and economic categories and thus expose significant variations that may be masked by the arbitrary aggregation created by reports on distinctive political or geographic entities. Second, individual-level data are essential to infer behavioral changes and to evaluate the relative importance of the proximate determinants of fertility.

One hopes to find further specification of the mechanisms and causes of fertility change through the use of individual-level data. A number of studies using family- or individual-level data have made important contributions in this area, but often the records possess certain limitations. First, many of the studies deal with a population that is relatively homogeneous, so that it is impossible to determine whether the characteristics of the population have any effect on its members' demographic behavior. Ideally, to evaluate the effect of social, economic, and cultural differences, the data should cover a heterogeneous population. Second, many of the data sets refer to brief time periods, thereby making it impossible to ascertain whether the observed phenomenon is the continuation of a previous pattern or the beginning of a new pattern of demographic behavior. To understand fertility transitions, the data set must cover a time period of sufficient length to embrace both the period of presumably high, uncontrolled fertility and the initiation of the subsequent period of decline. Third, a number of studies focus only on events recorded in a particular community, and therefore migrants are lost to observation for some period during their life course. To avoid this, the sample must cover a region or population in such a way that it is possible to study the behavior of individuals across their life course independently of a set of observations for specific communities. Individual records that are community-based, village genealogies, for example, by definition exclude those segments of the population who move into or out of the community. This constraint is important for two reasons. First, it makes it impossible to ascertain differences between the way stable residents behave and the way migrants behave; and second, it makes it impossible to study the relationship between migration and demographic behavior. Finally, individual records, regardless of other strengths, are of minimal utility if the number of cases is so small as to yield statistically unreliable results.

In summary, there are analytical advantages to having access to a historical body of data which (1) contains records of individuals and families, (2) covers a heterogeneous population, (3) covers a period of time of sufficient length to document significant demographic changes, (4) identifies individuals by residence but is not limited to observations within a specific community, and (5) is large enough to yield statistically reliable results.

It is the fact that all five of these features are to be found in the MHDP database which distinguishes it from many other historical demographic projects. The advantages of this type of database may be described briefly here, although they become explicit in the analysis presented in Part II.

First, the use of individual-level data makes it possible to ascertain whether aggregate-level indicators of natural fertility are consistent with the behavior of subcohorts of the population. Second, individual-level data covering the entire life course of individuals provide the opportunity to examine the independent and interactive effects of age at marriage, marriage type, birth spacing, and age at last birth on completed family size. Third, the heterogeneity of the population makes it possible to investigate the effects of religion, residence, and migration on fertility levels, variations, and changes. Regarding fertility changes, multiple strategies leading to controlled fertility can be taken into account; modifications in age at marriage, modifications in spacing patterns, and changes in age at last birth. Finally, by using a series of events and places associated with each individual rather than the registration of events occurring at a given place, it is possible to examine explicitly the hypothesis of geographic diffusion of innovative fertility control.[16]

SUMMARY

In Part II of this volume, we provide evidence on a population that settled and developed one region of the American frontier. This population, dominated by a particular religion, has traditionally been identified as a high-fertility population. Regardless of the actual or presumed normative influence of the religion upon marriage and family formation, the dominant church, the Church of Jesus Christ of Latter-day Saints, is noteworthy for its commitment to family records. Access to these records, which are maintained by the Genealogical Society of Utah, has made it possible to develop a set of linked individual records. The MHDP database makes it possible to investigate not simply the presumed normative influences on fertility but also a set of more general hypotheses that relate to fertility transitions and underlie resolving the question of the adoption of innovative fertility behavior versus the adaptation of fertility behavior to changing environmental, economic, and social conditions. Consequently we argue that the advantage of the MHDP database lies not in its documentation of an interesting case study but its potential for the evaluation of general demographic propositions. To a large extent, this chapter has been designed to provide justification for that argument.

In the first section the development of the database was outlined. The database became available because of a unique record repository, the GSU, and the combined efforts of a number of investigators to develop a file that could be used for medical research but that also provided exceptional opportunities for demographic analysis. In this section we also briefly described the steps taken to create a computer-based file for the analysis of genealogical records.

In the second section of this chapter, we discussed a variety of the procedures used to ensure that the quality of the data set and the constructed database warranted exhaustive examination of fertility change in this frontier population. In addition to the internal evaluation of the data, using procedures normally involved in the analysis of genealogies and family reconstitutions, the external evaluation involving comparisons with other data sources and the linkage of the 1880 manuscript census to the genealogy enhanced our confidence in the quality of the data set. Although we have identified certain limitations in the records included in the database, none of these are significant enough to effect the results of the projected analysis. However, the strengths and limitations are carefully documented so that the reader may make independent judgments when reviewing the arguments developed.

In the third section we have presented basic descriptive data covering nuptiality, ethnicity, and religion to support the argument outlined in chapter 1 that the population is diverse and thus provides the opportunity to examine in some detail the consequences of changes in population composition for the significant shift in levels of fertility to be described in the following chapter.

In the fourth section we demonstrated that the database addresses a number of the critiques of historical-demographic studies that rely on aggregate-level data. One advantage of the MHDP database is its use of individual-level data, although this advantage is far from unique—a wide range of other historical-demographic studies make use of similar levels of analysis. However, in comparison to data used in many other studies, the MHDP data set has certain other advantages: its large size, the heterogeneity of the population it covers, its linkage of place to individual records rather than individuals to community records, its coverage of events occurring over the entire life course of individuals, and its capability of supporting cohort analyses over a period of more than one hundred years of childbearing, during which the fertility of successive cohorts rises and then declines. Chapter 4 begins with the documentation of that rise and decline in overall fertility. In subsequent chapters we use the individual life-course records to test general propositions outlined in chapter 1.

PART II

Results: Multilevel Tests of Adaptation and Innovation

CHAPTER 4

Fertility and Nuptiality

In this frontier population the "average" woman born between 1825 and 1829 married at age 23 and gave birth to seven children. Women born twenty years later married at age 20 and gave birth to eight children, and those born between 1895 and 1899 married at age 22 and gave birth to five children. There was a 14 percent increase in the mean number of children ever born, followed by a decrease of 43 percent. This illustration summarizes in rough approximations the broad outlines of fertility change among MHDP women, but the "average" experience obscures important differences in marital and childbearing experiences across the 125 years of childbearing represented by the study population.

Before exploring the subcohort variations in fertility, we provide in this chapter a summary of the trends in levels of fertility for the population as a whole and demonstrate the commonality of fertility trends within groups experiencing different marital histories. One characteristic of marriage which is critically important because of the relationship between age and fecundability is age at marriage, and this variable is retained in subsequent analysis. Therefore, this chapter also examines the importance of age at marriage on fertility levels and trends: that is, we examine fertility trends within marriage classes controlling for age at marriage.

Before proceeding with the analysis of changing fertility behavior, an initial comment on analytical strategies needs to be made. Changes in fertility may be indexed in different formats, any one of which could have been used in this study because the accessible data provide nearly complete marital and reproductive histories for a sequence of birth cohorts of women. Three of these formats are period rates, birth cohort rates, and marriage cohort rates. A number of publications deal with the relative advantages and disadvantages of these three analytical formats. (See, for example, Barclay 1958; Henry 1976; Ryder 1956.) To explicate further the relative advantages and disadvantages of these strategies, additional detail is provided in the appendix of this volume, along with data to enable researchers using less extensive forms of historical-demographic data to compare their analyses for other populations with the MHDP population. In this chapter we simply provide a comparison of patterns of fertility change derived from these three approaches.

After a comparison of these rates, we will consistently use data organized by birth cohorts. As Barclay (1958, p. 183) has indicated, "The gain of precision by measuring fertility in this way appears to be enormous." The birth cohort format enables one, for example, to analyze the probability that women who have had a birth of a given order will have an additional birth within a specified period or duration of marriage. We are also encouraged not to adopt additional analytical strategies but to use birth cohort rates alone, because other measures of fertility provide similar types of information.

GENERAL FERTILITY TRENDS

Summary measures of period, birth cohort, and marriage cohort rates derived from the fertility experience of women born in the nineteenth century are presented in table 14. The MTFR (marital total-fertility rate) is the sum of the marital age-specific fertility rates across all ages. CEB (children ever born)—or completed fertility—is the mean number of live births to women at the time they end their childbearing years of life, are widowed, or die. Both of these measures are indices of completed fertility, for synthetic and true cohorts, respectively. Computed for periods, the MTFR summarizes the lifetime marital fertility expected for women who experience the age-specific rates—marriage, fertility, and mortality—common to a specific period. The measure is thus most sensitive to historical conditions prevailing at a specific time. When calculated for birth cohorts, both measures—MTFR and CEB—are sensitive to a common sequence of historical events experienced at

TABLE 14

SUMMARY FERTILITY INDICES FOR EVER-MARRIED WOMEN BORN BETWEEN 1800 AND 1899, BASED ON PERIOD, BIRTH COHORT, AND MARRIAGE COHORT MEASURES

Period Rates		Birth Cohort Rates			Marriage Cohort Rates		
Date of Observation	MTFR[a]	Date of Birth	CEB[b]	MTFR	Date of Marriage	CEB	MTFR
		1800–04	7.1	10.5			
		1805–09	7.1	10.7			
		1810–14	6.8	10.7			
		1815–19	7.0	10.7			
		1820–24	6.8	10.5			
		1825–29	7.2	10.8			
		1830–34	7.5	11.1			
		1835–39	7.9	11.1			
		1840–44	8.2	11.1	1840–44	7.3	10.5
1845–49	10.3	1845–49	8.2	11.1	1845–49	7.4	10.5
1850–54	10.8	1850–54	8.2	11.0	1850–54	7.7	11.1
1855–59	10.9	1855–59	8.1	10.9	1855–59	8.0	11.0
1860–64	11.2	1860–64	7.7	10.6	1860–64	8.0	11.3
1865–69	11.2	1865–69	7.4	10.4	1865–69	8.1	11.0
1870–74	11.4	1870–74	7.0	10.1	1870–74	8.3	11.1
1875–79	11.3	1875–79	6.5	9.8	1875–79	8.2	10.8
1880–84	11.3	1880–84	6.2	9.5	1880–84	7.7	10.6
1885–89	11.2	1885–89	5.7	8.9	1885–89	7.4	10.4
1890–94	10.8	1890–94	5.2	8.5	1890–94	7.0	10.1
1895–99	10.6	1895–99	4.7	7.7	1895–99	6.7	9.9
1900–04	10.4				1900–04	6.3	9.5
1905–09	10.3				1905–09	5.8	9.0
1910–14	9.7				1910–14	5.4	8.5
1915–19	9.2				1915–19	4.8	8.0

Note: This table includes only women who married before age 45 and have complete fertility histories.

[a]Marital total-fertility rate

[b]Children ever-born

similar ages, while the same measures computed for marriage cohorts are sensitive to a common sequence of events experienced at specific marriage durations beginning from a common time of marriage. The MTFR is, however, insensitive to variations in duration of exposure to childbearing because the measure presumes that all women commence and end childbearing at the same time in spite of variation in age at marriage, variation in age at death, and changes in marital status. The CEB measure summarizes the exact individual childbearing experience.

The three forms of fertility measures—period, birth cohort, and marriage cohort—are presented in table 14 for all ever-married women.[1] The general changes in childbearing are consistent regardless of the measures or indices, MTFR or CEB: an initial rise in fertility is followed by a systematic decline in levels. This pattern suggests an increasing degree of fertility control. Period rates may be computed beginning with the 1845–49 interval because it is only at this time, when the first cohort of women born in 1800–04 reached ages 45–49, that we have observations for women across the entire range of childbearing years, ages 15–49. The last observation period is 1915–19, since this is the last period when we have a young cohort entering the normal initial age of marriage; that is, the women born in 1895–99 were then ages 15–20. After 1919, the observations of very young women are censored. The last observation period therefore includes women who began childbearing during the five-year period that includes World War I, but also includes women who commenced childbearing as early as 1880.

The period MTFR index increases from 10.3 in 1845–49 to a peak of 11.4 in 1870–74 and then declines consistently to 9.2 in 1915–19. The relatively modest decline reflects the fact that women most likely to control fertility in subsequent years were in the early years of childbearing in 1915–19. Clearly the pace of decline accelerated. The data indicate a decline in the period MTFR of 19 percent from 1870–74 to 1915–19, but the first 10 percent decline took thirty-five years and the second 10 percent was achieved in ten years.

The increasing pace of the decline is more evident in the changes in MTFR calculated for birth cohorts, listed in the central section of table 14. After an initial increase, the birth-cohort MTFR fell from a peak of 11.1 for the 1830–49 birth cohorts to 7.7 for the 1895–99 birth cohort, who would not have completed childbearing until approximately the end of the 1930s. These women experienced certain periods of childbearing risk in the depression years, when fertility rates became exceptionally low throughout the United States. The birth-cohort MTFR fell by

31 percent, with two-thirds of the decline (20 percent) occurring among the 1875–99 birth cohorts of women.

The magnitude of the overall decline suggested by changes in the birth-cohort MTFR is consistent with the decline in CEB for birth cohorts. The four birth cohorts from 1840–59 completed their childbearing with roughly the same number of children ever born (8.2, 8.2, 8.2, and 8.1). Subsequent cohorts completed their childbearing with increasingly fewer children, ending with 4.7 children born to the 1895–99 birth cohort, an overall decline of 43 percent. Two-thirds of the decline occurred among the last five cohorts.

Among the marriage cohorts, changes in fertility are similar to those of the birth cohorts, with a lag of about twenty years. The MTFR exceeds 11.0 among the marrriage cohorts of 1850–74 and then declines by 29 percent, from the high of 11.3 to the low of 8.0. CEB peaks at 8.0–8.3 and declines by 42 percent to the CEB of 4.8 for the 1915–19 marriage cohort.

The consistent, significantly higher values of MTFRs relative to CEBs are a function of the MTFR index's assumption that all women maintain the same pace of childbearing as women who marry at the earliest age and the same pace as those women who survive and persist in childbearing to age 49. The CEB index reflects the actual childbearing experience of women over exactly the period of exposure to the risk of childbearing. In addition, the consistent pattern of gradual change reflected in the period rates does not evidence historically specific disruptions in the gradual processes of fertility control. Demonstrating the insensitivity of aggregate indices to such effects supports the strategy of focusing upon cumulative patterns of social change used in our analysis.

The very high period-summary measures (MTFRs) are not unusual. Marital total-fertility rates exceeding 11 are typical of populations observed in many developing societies today. For example, the MTFR in Libya in 1973 was 11.2 (El Faedy and Bean 1987). Among historical Western populations, similarly high MTFRs have been reported. Henry, in his seminal article "Some Data on Natural Fertility" (1961), reports age-specific legitimate-fertility rates, ages 20–24 through 45–49, for thirteen "natural fertility" populations. Partial total-fertility rates (excluding women aged 15–19) for these groups range between 10.9 and 6.2. The highest, 10.9, is for a contemporary population, the Hutterites. The partial MTFR for the 1870–74 MHDP birth cohort reported in table 14 is 8.9, and this rate is exceeded in Henry's data by eighteenth-century French Canadians (10.8), Hutterites married before 1921 (9.8), and seventeenth-century bourgeoisie of Geneva (9.4). The partial rate of the 1870–74 cohort is equal to that of Norway in 1899–1900, 5 percent higher than that of Denmark in 1890–1900, 9 percent higher than that of Sweden in 1896–1900, and 8 percent higher than that of the population of the Anthracite mining counties of Pennsylvania in 1846–50. However, it is 53 percent higher than that of the total U.S. white population of 1895–99 (Tolnay, Graham, and Guest 1982, p. 135). Thus the high MTFRs observed among the married MHDP women—when there was seemingly no major effort to limit fertility—are similar to rates found in a number of European populations before the fertility decline and similar to high-fertility U.S. populations for which comparable data are available during early periods of the nineteenth century. The period levels of fertility are notable only in comparison to late nineteenth-century U.S. fertility levels, but by that time large segments of the U.S. population had already adopted fertility limitation practices.

Comparison of the MTFR and CEB measures indicates that the CEB measure is preferable because it more adequately describes the changing behavior of individual women. MTFR overestimates the magnitude of fertility change during a period of rapid population decline. During the peak period of fertility the MTFR is 35 percent higher than CEB but 64 percent higher for the relatively low fertility 1895–99 birth cohort.

NUPTIALITY AND FERTILITY

In chapter 3 we described the variations in marital experience among the MHDP women. In this section, we first examine the variations in fertility levels and changes among groups experiencing different types and sequences of marriage and then examine the effects of age at marriage on fertility.

In the analysis that follows we use the marital categories described in chapter 3, the subsection "Nuptiality," although selected groups are excluded.[2] The differences in childbearing experience of this population of ever-married women reflect differing marital and survival experiences. The relevant data are initially presented in table 15 and figure 8. For the total (all cohorts), fertility is highest for the polygynous wives (ONEPLG), 7.7 children. That figure is misleading, however, because the majority of their fertility experiences occurred during a natural-fertility period. In addition, we have argued elsewhere that the computation of average fertility rates aggregating all polygynous women fails to identify variations in fertility among polygynous wives. When fertility

TABLE 15

MEAN CHILDREN EVER BORN (CEB) BY WOMAN'S MARRIAGE TYPE AND BIRTH COHORT

Birth Cohort	ONEONE (1) mean	ONEFRS (2) mean	ONEHOR (3) mean	ONEAMB (4) mean	ONEPLG (5) mean	TWOCFM (6) mean
1800–04	7.3	(7.0)[a]	(6.6)	(6.6)	(6.0)	*[b]
1805–09	7.4	(6.3)	(5.0)	6.9	6.9	(7.8)
1810–14	7.2	5.5	(4.0)	6.6	6.6	(6.7)
1815–19	7.4	5.5	(5.4)	6.5	6.9	(7.2)
1820–24	7.3	5.0	4.7	6.2	7.0	8.2
1825–29	7.6	5.5	6.0	7.1	7.2	7.3
1830–34	7.9	5.4	6.3	7.2	7.8	7.9
1835–39	8.3	5.8	7.0	6.9	8.2	8.4
1840–44	8.7	6.2	6.9	7.3	8.2	8.8
1845–49	8.7	6.4	6.9	7.3	8.3	9.1
1850–54	8.6	6.6	6.9	7.3	8.1	8.6
1855–59	8.5	6.6	7.0	7.9	7.7	8.2
1860–64	8.1	6.2	6.1	7.3	7.5	8.2
1865–69	7.6	5.9	6.3	7.0	7.4	7.4
1870–74	7.2	5.6	5.9	6.8	7.2	7.3
1875–79	6.7	5.4	5.6	6.1	6.3	6.9
1880–84	6.4	5.4	4.9	5.8	(7.2)	6.2
1885–89	5.9	4.8	4.8	5.6	*	5.8
1890–94	5.4	4.6	4.3	4.8	*	5.4
1895–99	4.9	4.1	3.9	4.5	*	4.7
TOTAL	6.8	5.4	5.7	6.5	7.7	6.7

Note: This table includes only women who married before age 45.
[a]Parentheses indicate fewer than 50 cases.
[b]Asterisks indicate fewer than 20 cases.
ONEONE: Once-married couple
ONEFRS: Once-married, first wife
ONEHOR: Once-married, higher-order wife
ONEAMB: Once-married, ambiguous order
ONEPLG: Once-married, polygynous husband
TWOCFM: More than one marriage, complete fertility history, monogamous husbands

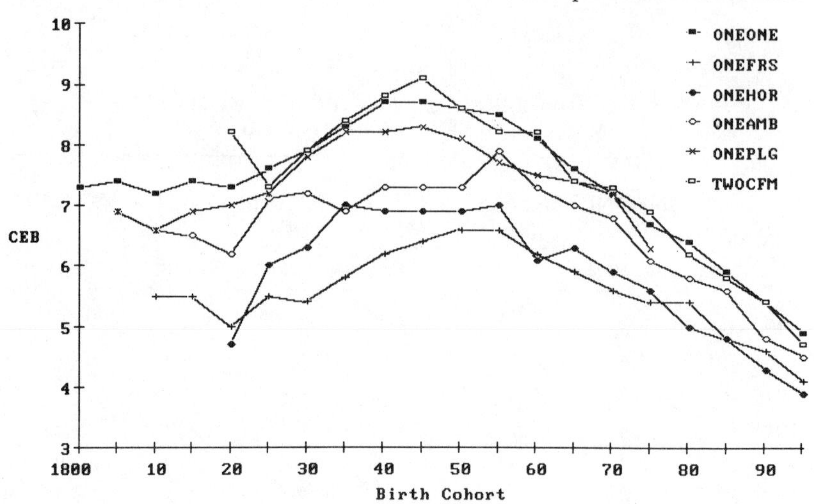

Figure 8. Mean Children Ever Born (CEB) by Woman's Marriage Type and Birth Cohort (for Women Who Married before Age 45)

of polygynous wives is specified by wife order, first wives have higher average fertility than second and later wives. First-order polygynous wives have higher fertility than once-married wives, but higher-order polygynous wives have lower fertility than once-married wives. (See Bean and Mineau 1986.)

Excluding the polygyny anomaly, higher fertility is associated with marital stability among women with one marriage. Fertility is highest among once-married couples (ONEONE); fertility is lower in every category marked by instability in the marriage experience—divorce, widowhood, and remarriage. The relative positions of the groups shift only slightly over the twenty cohorts, but of particular interest is the relatively low fertility among women who are first wives (ONEFRS). Most of the women in this group died relatively young; thus when these women died their husbands were also relatively young and opted for second marriages. The observed differences may simply reflect the fact that differential survival rates produced variations in years of exposure to risk of childbearing. However, those women with two or more marriages (TWOCFM) approximate the fertility levels of once-married couples. For those women who experienced a marital disruption followed by remarriage during the childbearing years, the interruption was not extreme in its effects on completed fertility.

The evidence available suggests that changes in survival rates may be a major factor in the change in the proportion of once-married women, as discussed in chapter 3, as well as a major factor in accounting for variation in fertility by marriage type and cohort. To control for the effect of differences in survival rates, we have separated the ever-married women by marriage type into two categories. The first group had marriages that remained intact—the couple survived—until the women reached age 45, approximately the end of the childbearing years of life. The second group had marriages terminated by death or divorce before the women reached age 45. We consider only the first marriage of women who married more than once. The couple-survival rates of the earliest cohorts are somewhat artificial. All marriage and fertility experiences before 1847 occurred outside Utah Territory. In some first marriages, one spouse may have died before or during migration; thus, it is the events that occurred after remarriage that took place in Utah.

We present data for these two groups in table 16: wife's age at marriage, husband's age at marriage, and CEB for selected birth cohorts. The data enable us to evaluate the effect of variations in proportions of couples surviving as well as the effect of variations in age at marriage and marital disruption, although the latter relates to a single category. Consider first the mean age at marriage by marriage type. For couples in which both spouses survived until the wife was age 45, once-married wives (ONEONE) and single-married first wives (ONEFRS) had approximately the same mean age at marriage, 21.4 and 21.8 years. Single-marriage higher-order wives (ONEHOR) married somewhat later (25.6 years). Some proportion of higher-order wives fall into the ONEAMB group because of incomplete records; therefore the group had a slightly higher mean age at marriage (22.2 years) than ONEONEs and ONEFRSs. Polygynous wives married young (20.8), although the mean age at marriage of their husbands was nearly ten years greater (30.2). Of course part of that substantial age difference reflects the fact that polygynous wives in this category were married once and the mean was for first marriages. The mean for the polygynous husbands includes second and higher-order marriages that occurred at older ages. Women whose first marriage ended in divorce or widowhood and who remarried were consistently younger at the time of the first marriage (19.7 years). Among couples who were once-married or who included a higher-order wife who did not survive until she reached 45, wives had generally younger mean ages at marriage and husbands had older mean ages at marriage. This reflects greater age differences in a larger number of these couples—young women marrying older men.

Excluding women with more than one marriage, the fertility differ-

TABLE 16

MEAN AGE AT MARRIAGE FOR WIVES (AMW) AND HUSBANDS (AMH) AND MEAN CHILDREN EVER BORN (CEB), BY MARRIAGE TYPE AND SURVIVAL FOR SELECTED BIRTH COHORTS OF WOMEN

ONCE-MARRIED COUPLES (ONEONE)

Birth Cohort	Couple Survived until Wife Age 45				Couple Did Not Survive		
	%	AMW	AMH	CEB	AMW	AMH	CEB
1815–19	86.7	22.9	25.5	7.5	21.2	24.5	6.9
1830–34	88.5	22.5	25.6	8.0	22.4	28.2	6.4
1845–49	85.9	20.6	25.2	9.0	19.7	26.4	7.1
1860–64	88.8	20.5	24.5	8.2	20.0	25.5	6.5
1875–79	89.5	21.6	25.6	6.8	21.1	26.1	5.8
1890–94	92.1	21.8	24.8	5.4	21.3	25.8	4.7
TOTAL	89.6	21.4	25.0	6.9	20.7	26.0	5.9

FIRST WIVES (ONEFRS)

Birth Cohort	%	AMW	AMH	CEB	AMW	AMH	CEB
1815–19	26.1	(24.2	23.2	7.2)[a]	21.8	24.1	4.7
1830–34	28.9	(21.5	22.9	8.2)	22.5	23.8	4.3
1845–49	29.8	20.6	22.9	8.8	20.1	24.3	5.3

1860–64	31.9	20.2	22.6	8.5	19.9	23.1	5.2
1875–79	40.3	22.5	24.0	6.7	21.0	24.5	4.5
1890–94	45.5	21.7	23.6	5.5	21.1	23.8	3.9
Total	38.2	21.8	23.5	6.8	20.8	23.9	4.6

HIGHER-ORDER WIVES (ONEHOR)

Birth Cohort	%	AMW	AMH	CEB	AMW	AMH	CEB
1815–19	77.8	(28.5	35.6	5.8)	*	*	*
1830–34	72.7	27.1	37.8	6.5	(22.8	40.5	6.0)
1845–49	68.5	23.8	38.8	7.5	22.4	41.5	5.7
1860–64	75.5	24.5	36.9	6.4	22.6	39.1	4.8
1875–79	80.2	26.1	36.0	5.9	23.0	36.1	4.7
1890–94	89.2	27.2	36.7	4.3	23.7	33.4	4.0
Total	78.4	25.6	36.8	5.9	23.0	38.8	4.9

TABLE 16 (continued)

AMBIGUOUS ORDER (ONEAMB)

Birth Cohort	Couple Survived until Wife Age 45				Couple Did Not Survive		
	%	AMW	AMH	CEB	AMW	AMH	CEB
1815–19	76.0	23.3	25.9	6.6	(22.4	27.2	4.3)
1830–34	74.8	23.2	28.1	7.6	22.4	28.8	4.9
1845–49	66.8	21.0	27.1	8.1	20.2	27.5	5.1
1860–64	66.4	20.8	26.4	8.2	19.7	26.7	5.5
1875–79	64.4	22.1	25.8	6.5	20.9	25.3	5.3
1890–94	66.3	22.5	26.0	4.9	21.3	25.6	4.6
Total	67.1	22.2	26.7	6.9	20.7	26.2	5.3

POLYGYNOUS WIVES (ONEPLG)

Birth Cohort	%	AMW	AMH	CEB	AMW	AMH	CEB
1815–19	72.9	23.4	26.5	7.4	23.0	26.1	5.4
1830–34	77.7	22.1	30.1	8.2	21.2	31.9	6.2
1845–49	72.8	19.4	30.6	8.9	19.1	33.6	6.4

1860–64	75.6	19.9	30.8	8.1	19.9	34.1	5.6
1875–79	64.9	(22.0	30.4	7.1)	(23.4	38.7	4.8)
1890–94	*	*	*	*	*	*	*
Total	75.3	20.8	30.2	8.3	20.1	32.5	5.9

WIFE MARRIED MORE THAN ONCE (TWOCFM)—HER FIRST MARRIAGE

Birth Cohort	%	AMW	AMH	CEB	AMW	AMH	CEB
1815–19	40.0	(20.4	24.1	7.4)	(22.5	26.0	3.9)
1830–34	25.3	(20.5	26.2	6.4)	21.2	27.2	3.9
1845–49	33.3	(19.1	26.1	8.2)	19.4	26.7	3.4
1860–64	53.2	18.4	25.2	7.3	18.9	25.8	4.4
1875–79	64.9	19.6	25.6	6.6	20.5	26.1	4.4
1890–94	56.5	20.2	25.1	5.3	20.7	24.5	3.5
Total	54.5	19.7	25.2	6.2	20.4	26.2	3.8

Note: Table includes only women who married before age 45.
[a]Parentheses indicate fewer than 50 cases.
[b]Asterisks indicate fewer than 20 cases.

ences are generally consistent with the differences in age at marriage: the lower the age at marriage the higher the fertility level. The lowest fertility for all nonsurviving couples is observed for first marriages of remarried women (3.8 children) and first wives of remarried husbands (4.6 children). These families experienced the early death of a spouse and then remarriage of the surviving spouse, who thus had the possibility of more children.

Differences in the probability of a couple's surviving through the age of childbearing are integral to the definition of the marriage types. If widowhood or divorce occurred early, it is likely that either males or females remarried, and of course later marital disruption is less likely to be followed by remarriage. Thus 89.6 percent of the once-married couples survived until the wife reached age 45, compared to 38.2 percent for the single-marriage first wives (ONEFRS), 78.4 percent for the single-marriage higher-order wives (ONEHOR), 67.1 percent for the ambiguous category (ONEAMB), and 54.5 percent for the wives with two or more marriages (TWOCFM).

If we control for couple survival, the once-married women and the single-marriage first wives share the same type of marital experience up to the end of the childbearing years of life. This is reflected in the fact that these two groups have basically the same CEB. The trends in CEB for the cohorts from 1830–34 onward are the same for women with one marriage: a slight increase followed by a systematic decline. Indeed, for the cohorts which evidenced fertility control (1860–99), the downward trends are consistent for all groups, survivors and nonsurvivors alike.

The importance of couple survival through the childbearing years is illustrated by one additional comparison—between those whose marriages did survive until the wives reached age 45 with those whose marriages did not survive. These two groups' differences in CEB decline from the peak-fertility cohorts to the lowest-fertility cohorts. Those whose marriages did not survive until the wives reached age 45 were likely to experience widowhood (the dominant reason for marital termination) much later in life if they were in the more recent, rather than the earlier, cohorts. This demonstrates the effect of variations in periods of exposure.

The analysis provides strong supporting evidence for the assumption that during periods of generally uncontrolled fertility and during periods when the initial adoption of fertility limitation occurred, variations in periods of exposure due to differences in age at marriage, survival, and marital disruption account for fertility variations by marriage experience or type. This observation applies not only to monogamous marriages; exposure variables also account for much of the difference in fertility found among polygynous wives when specified by wife order (Bean and Mineau 1986). A more definitive test of the importance of couple survival is made through the examination of marital age-specific fertility rates by type of marriage. In this case the age-specific fertility rates are computed with births by women's age and cohort as the numerator and women's years of exposure to risk (by age and cohort) as the denominator. We thus control for the times of entry into and exit from a marital union as well as for marital disruption.

The marital age-specific fertility patterns by cohort are presented in figure 9 for selected birth cohorts. During the peak childbearing years of life, with minor exceptions, women in different marriage categories bear children at the same pace and adopt fertility limitation at the same time. This conclusion may seem trivial, but the implications are important. For example, the ONEHOR group, which had relatively low fertility when measured by CEB, were simply exposed to the risk of conception for a shorter period of time because of a somewhat later age at marriage and seemingly because their husbands were much older at the time of the marriage. However, during the years of marital exposure, this group bears children at about the same pace as other married women if age at marriage and couple survival are controlled.

The analysis of fertility by marriage types indicates a high degree of commonality in terms of fertility behavior. Certainly, there are differences in completed family size, with larger families found among the women who were in stable marital unions, other things being equal. Aside from variations in levels, which are essentially attributable to differences in length of exposure to the risk of conception within a marital union, the behavioral patterns of fertility change are consistent across all marriage types, and the pace of childbearing within periods of marital exposure to the risk of conception is remarkably similar.

AGE AT MARRIAGE AND FERTILITY

In his initial formulation of the concept of natural fertility, Henry suggested that the fertility of such populations was independent of age at marriage (1961, p. 82). The results of an increasing number of historical-demographic studies led Henry to modify that proposition. Among populations in which age at marriage is relatively uniform and invariant over time, no errors of interpretation arise as a consequence of

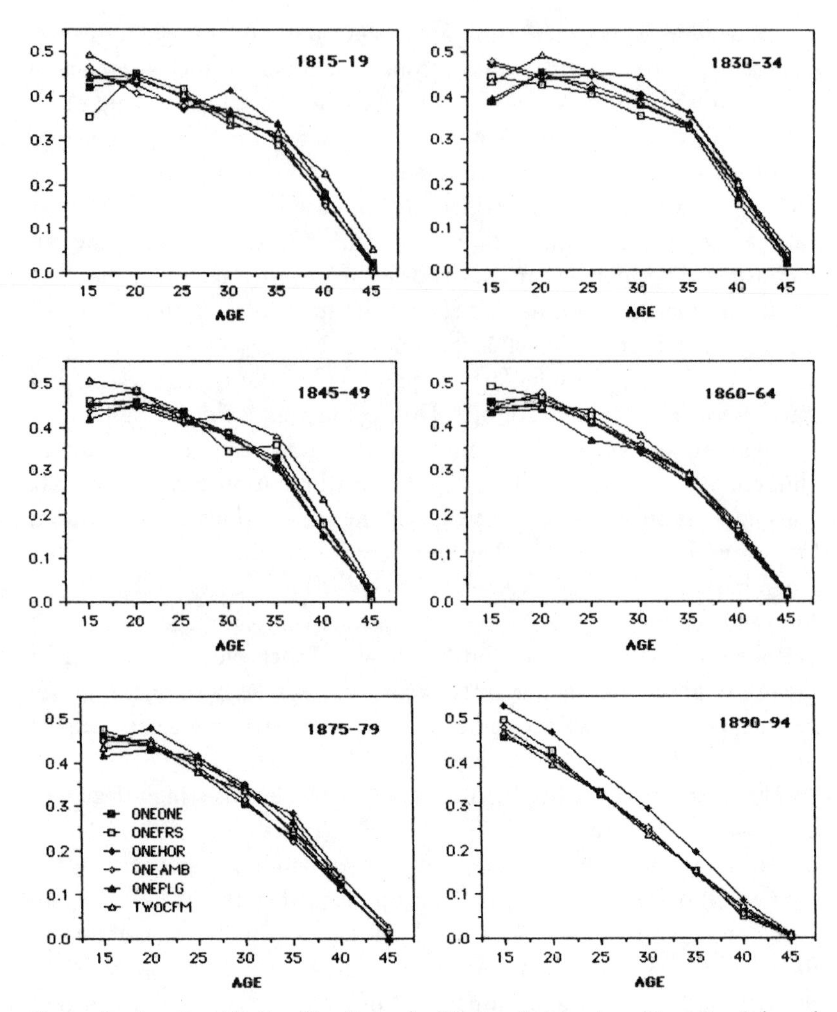

Figure 9. Age-Specific Fertility Rates by Woman's Marriage Type For Selected Birth Cohorts

not examining the relationship between age at marriage and fertility. For our MHDP population, however, there is considerable variance within and between cohorts of women (Mineau, Bean, and Skolnick 1979). Such variance is summarized by data presented in table 17, which reports mean age at first marriage, its standard deviation, and the proportions married before age 20, at ages 20–24, and at age 25 or older for ever-married women by five-year birth cohorts for 1800–99. The mean age at first marriage drops to a low of 20.1 for the cohorts

TABLE 17

MEAN AGE AT FIRST MARRIAGE AND PROPORTIONS MARRIED WITHIN SELECTED AGE GROUPS, BY BIRTH COHORT

Birth Cohort	Mean Age at First Marriage	N	Standard Deviation	Proportions Married in Ages			
				<20 %	20–24 %	25+ %	Total %
1800–04	23.4	355	5.5	30.1	40.3	29.6	100.0
1805–09	22.7	601	5.1	31.9	40.9	27.1	99.9
1810–14	23.5	837	5.5	29.0	39.8	31.2	100.0
1815–19	23.0	1,131	5.2	31.9	39.0	29.1	100.0
1820–24	23.4	1,497	5.2	28.3	39.9	31.8	100.0
1825–29	23.0	1,743	5.0	30.7	40.4	28.9	100.0
1830–34	22.4	2,181	4.8	35.1	40.9	24.0	100.0
1835–39	21.3	2,448	4.7	48.4	32.0	19.6	100.0
1840–44	20.6	2,738	4.6	51.5	33.0	15.6	100.1
1845–49	20.3	2,863	4.2	56.4	32.4	11.2	100.0
1850–54	20.1	3,633	4.1	58.2	30.6	11.2	100.0
1855–59	20.2	4,796	3.7	55.9	33.9	10.2	100.0
1860–64	20.4	5,294	3.8	53.3	36.8	10.0	100.1
1865–69	20.8	5,719	3.9	48.6	39.2	12.2	100.0
1870–74	21.2	6,090	4.0	43.9	41.2	14.9	100.0
1875–79	21.6	6,580	3.9	38.3	45.2	16.5	100.0
1880–84	21.7	7,089	3.9	37.5	47.0	15.6	100.1
1885–89	21.6	7,464	3.8	38.3	46.4	15.3	100.0
1890–94	21.9	7,497	3.9	34.7	48.7	16.5	99.9
1895–99	21.7	7,530	3.9	37.3	47.9	14.8	100.0
TOTAL	21.4	78,086	4.2	42.7	41.5	15.7	99.9

Note: Table includes only first marriages of ever-married women who married by age 45 and have complete fertility histories.

born at midcentury and thereafter increases to 21.9 for the 1890–94 cohort. These differences are described graphically in figure 10. From the 1800–04 birth cohort to the 1850–54 cohort there is a substantial increase in the proportion of women who married before age 20. This increase is balanced by a moderate decrease in the proportion of women who married between 20 and 25, as well as by a substantial decrease in

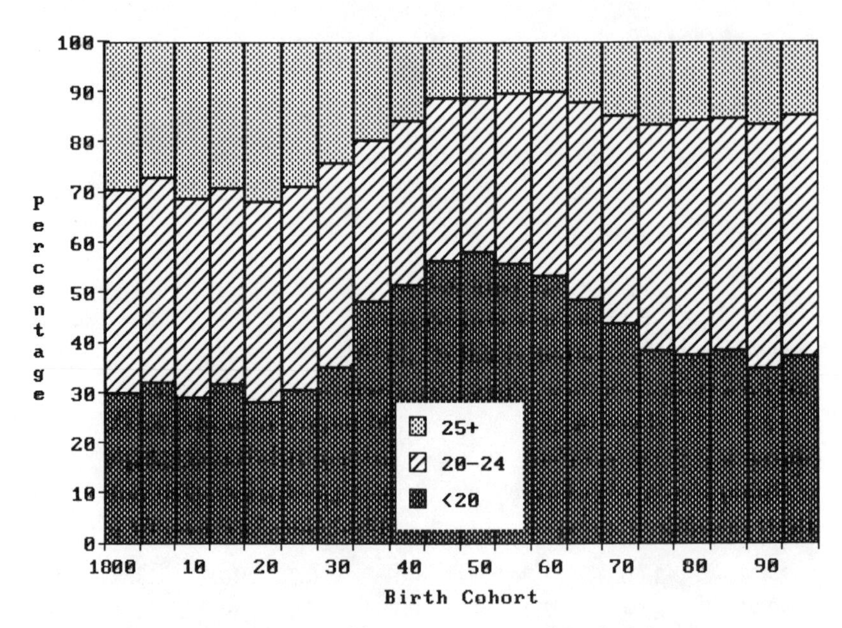

Figure 10. Proportions Married by Age Groups and Birth Cohorts

the proportion of women who married after age 25. From the 1850–54 cohort through the 1875–79 cohort there is a decrease in the proportion of women who married young, which is accounted for primarily by an increasing proportion who delayed marriage until ages 20–24. From 1875–79 on, the distribution remains relatively constant.

Changing patterns of marriage are important factors in the fertility shifts that occurred among the nineteenth-century MHDP cohorts of married women, but changes in age at marriage are insufficient to explain the fertility trends. The overall fertility trends in figure 11 are consistent across the three age-at-marriage groups. Regardless of age at marriage, there is an initial rise followed by a subsequent decline in fertility. For example, if we average the number of children ever born for the first four birth cohorts (1800–19) and the midcentury birth cohorts (1840–59), we see that the women born in midcentury had approximately one more birth (1.19) than women born shortly after the turn of the century. The increase was about one-half child (0.4) for women married before age 20, one-fourth (.24) for women married between ages 20 and 24, and less than one child (.70) for women married after age 25. The fact that the fertility level increased more for the total population than for any of the individual age-at-marriage groups reflects the significant compositional shifts in the proportion married at selected ages, reported in figure 10.

The changes in mean age at marriage and proportions married in selected age groups are insufficient to account for the dramatic shifts in

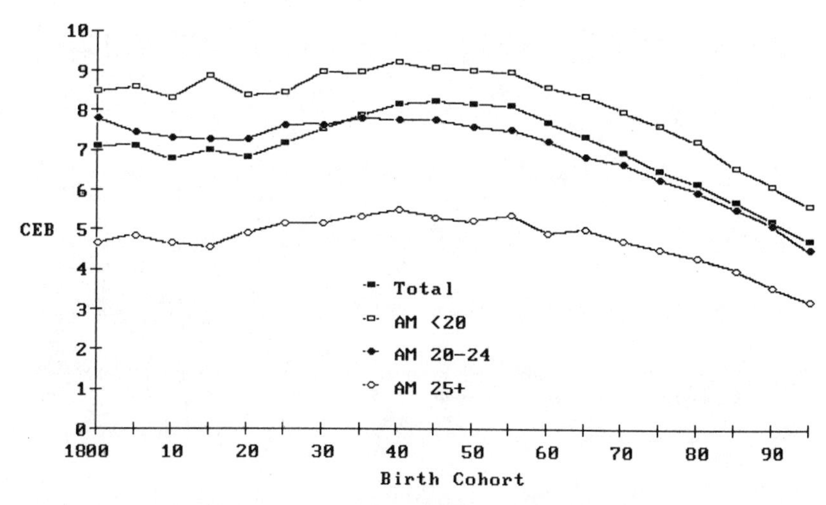

Figure 11. Mean Children Ever Born (CEB) by Age at Marriage (AM) by Birth Cohort

overall fertility. Given the relationship between age at marriage and duration of childbearing, a change in fertility behavior would have a different impact within age-of-marriage groups even without changes in age at marriage. Thus at least some portion of the variation in fertility removed through controlling for age at marriage within cohorts may, in fact, be causally attributable to changes in fertility over time rather than to changing age at marriage.[3]

A decline in the mean age at marriage results in increased periods of exposure to the risk of childbearing, and an increase in mean age at marriage reduces the period of exposure. If the desired number of children is constant, however, adjustments could be made to offset the increase or decrease in overall length of exposure by exercising control over the timing of births. Data presented in figure 12 indicate that such changes are present in the study population. For every birth cohort, the higher the age at marriage, the later the mean age at last birth. Within each of the three groups defined by age at marriage—less than 20, 20–24, and 25 and older—there is essentially no increase in age at last birth across cohorts marked by rising and peak fertility levels.

Changes in the time spent at risk of childbearing largely reflect shifts in proportions of women married at specific ages. The data on age at first and last birth for the three age-at-marriage groups indicate that during the period of the rise in completed family size, the ages at first and last birth are remarkably consistent. The most dramatic change in age-related fertility data is the decline in age at last birth associated with

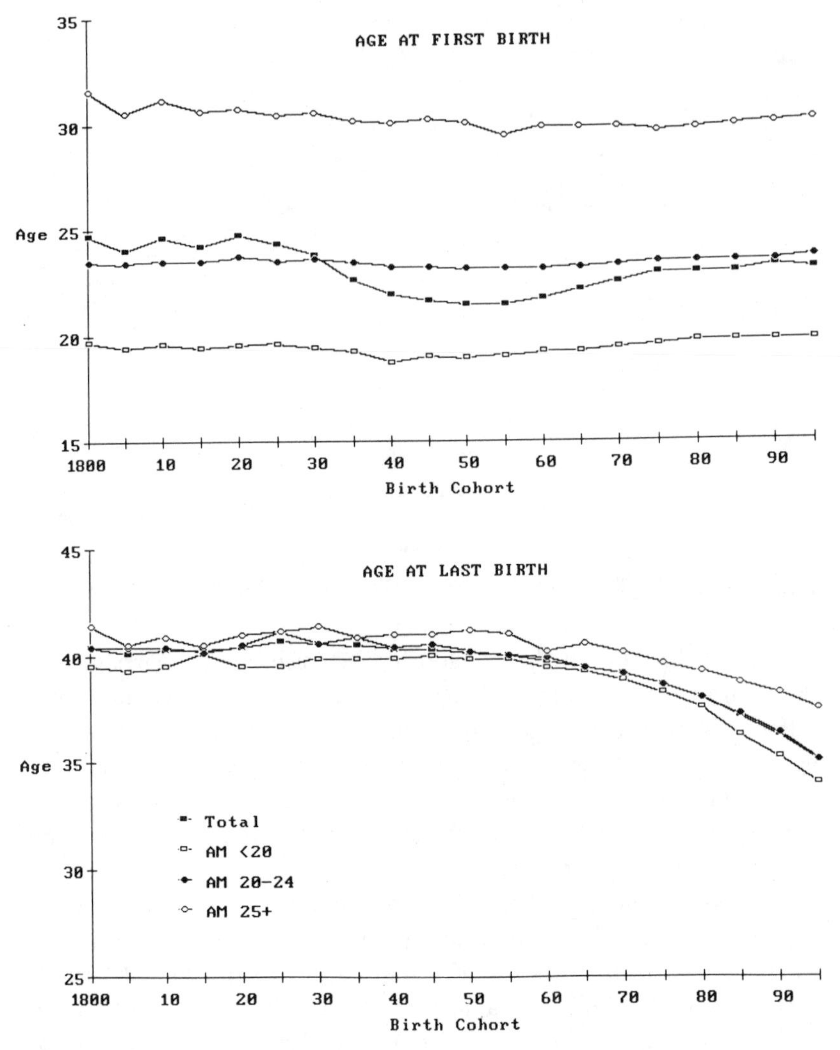

Figure 12. Age at First Birth (AFB) and at Last Birth (ALB) by Age at Marriage (AM) and Birth Cohort

the decline in fertility during the last half of the nineteenth century. The decline in the mean age at last birth is slightly more than five years for all women, nearly six years for women married before age 20, slightly more than five years for women married between the ages of 20 and 24, and less than four years for women married after age 25.

Data presented above suggest three distinct phases in this population's fertility experience. Each phase was in part associated with differing nuptiality behavior. Completed family size of ever-married women born before the middle of the century was lower than the completed family size of those born in midcentury. This early group was dominated by women who differed from later cohorts in several ways. The initial cohorts of women were born in the more settled areas of the eastern United States or Europe. The earliest cohorts completed their childbearing before the migration to the new, intermountain frontier area, and those women associated with the early LDS groups experienced all or most of their childbearing during a period of frequent migration and settlement of new areas, often within regions quite hostile to this new religious group. Women born between 1820 and 1830 who migrated to the frontier would have completed their childbearing during the most difficult times of settlement, periods marked by colonization of isolated communities sustained by limited resources. Mean age at marriage was also highest among these early cohorts. Many women emigrated from areas that had similarly high ages at marriage. In addition, the migration process itself may have affected age at marriage.

The women with the highest levels of fertility represent the second period and were born around the time of initial settlement in the West. They commenced their childbearing after the organized dispersal of the population, a process which by the 1870s had created the communities that would constitute the essential structure of the state for the next several decades. When these women commenced childbearing, the territory was homogeneous, essentially an LDS state, and the distribution of land was largely controlled by ecclesiastical authorities, a circumstance that created economic opportunities for the faithful. The population continued to be fueled by migrants from the East and Europe, but with each passing year the population became more dominated by frontier-born men and women. These groups married early and commenced childbearing early. The data presented indicate that age at marriage was important in the initial rise of fertility.

The third period is notable for the steady decline in the size of completed families among those cohorts born after midcentury. This trend is also associated with changes in nuptiality. The age at marriage increased, and the proportion of women married before age 20 fell from over one-half of those born at midcentury to almost one-third of those born in the last years of the nineteenth century. Control of fertility within marriages is also evident in the third period.

Changes in age at marriage and proportions married at selected ages thus suggest that nuptiality is an important determinant of fertility levels in this population. Again, to clarify the effect of such changes upon the fertility of women at different ages we employ the age-specific fertil-

TABLE 18

MARITAL AGE-SPECIFIC FERTILITY RATES AND MARITAL TOTAL-FERTILITY RATES BY AGE AT MARRIAGE, FOR SELECTED BIRTH COHORTS OF EVER-MARRIED WOMEN

Birth Cohort and Age at Marriage	Age at Birth of Children							
	15–19	20–24	25–29	30–34	35–39	40–44	45–49	Total
1815–19								
Total	.434	.439	.401	.361	.308	.175	.024	10.7
<20	.434	.423	.377	.354	.314	.163	.019	(4.2)[a]
20–24		.462	.402	.360	.309	.190	.029	(4.4)
>25			.453	.370	.302	.170	.023	(4.3)
1830–34								
Total	.407	.453	.431	.384	.331	.182	.026	11.1
<20	.407	.444	.409	.376	.312	.163	.018	(4.3)
20–24		.467	.439	.378	.334	.190	.028	(4.6)
>25			.474	.408	.350	.195	.035	(4.9)
1845–49								
Total	.444	.458	.427	.383	.321	.171	.021	11.1
<20	.444	.454	.408	.368	.305	.166	.020	(4.3)
20–24		.471	.445	.394	.329	.177	.021	(4.6)
>25			.512	.426	.371	.176	.026	(5.0)
1860–64								
Total	.458	.462	.404	.351	.275	.152	.018	10.6
<20	.458	.454	.388	.339	.268	.149	.018	(3.9)
20–24		.480	.420	.355	.277	.157	.019	(4.0)
>25			.449	.398	.302	.152	.017	(4.3)
1875–79								
Total	.462	.442	.383	.311	.235	.118	.014	9.8
<20	.462	.434	.358	.300	.225	.115	.013	(3.3)
20–24		.454	.390	.304	.229	.117	.013	(3.3)
>25			.452	.360	.272	.129	.016	(3.9)

TABLE 18 (continued)

Birth Cohort and Age at Marriage	Age at Birth of Children							Total
	15–19	20–24	25–29	30–34	35–39	40–44	45–49	
1890–94								
Total	.467	.419	.334	.246	.155	.065	.007	8.5
<20	.466	.400	.304	.223	.135	.059	.006	(2.1)
20–24		.441	.344	.243	.151	.065	.006	(2.3)
>25			.401	.308	.205	.079	.008	(3.0)

[a]Figures in parentheses represent partial marital total-fertility rates: the summation of age-specific rates × 5 for ages 30–49.

ity rates, within age-at-marriage classes. These data are presented in table 18 for selected birth cohorts; the trends are fully captured by the data presented and are consistent with the CEB measures presented previously. The marital total-fertility rate (MTFR) increases from the earliest to the midcentury cohorts and then declines. The peak MTFR was achieved by the 1830–49 birth cohorts but dropped to 10.6 for the 1860–64 cohort. The decline again cannot be explained only by changing nuptiality patterns. Age-specific fertility rates at ages 15–19 and 20–24 are slightly higher for the 1860–64 cohort relative to the 1845–49 cohort. The lower 1860–64 MTFR is due to lower age-specific fertility rates for the age groups 25 and older.

An important feature of the data presented in table 18 for the cohorts born in 1845–49 and after is that with the exception of the youngest age group (15–19), the age-specific fertility rates decline in each age group, systematically and consistently. The innovation-diffusion explanation of the adoption of fertility limitation would predict that fertility control is parity-dependent, and thus that the decline in age-specific fertility rates would initially appear among the older, higher-parity women. In partial support of that argument, it is evident from the data presented in table 18 that the proportionate decline is greater at older ages. However, the pattern of change appears to be more complex than one would anticipate from the innovation-diffusion perspective. Seemingly some proportion of women in every age group in each successive cohort after the 1845–49 cohort had fewer births, for the age-specific fertility rates declined in each age group and within each age-at-marriage category. (See Endnote at the end of this chapter.)

To describe more precisely the changes that occurred in childbearing at older ages, partial MTFRs for each age-at-marriage group are also presented in table 18. These represent the summation of the age-specific rates after age 30.[4] Women married at younger ages have fewer children in the later years of childbearing than women married later; their pace of childbearing after age 30 is slower than that of women married at later ages. Not only are the partial marital total-fertility rates directly related to age at marriage, but within each five-year age group—given one or two exceptions among the first birth cohorts—the fertility rate is directly related to age at marriage. Thus there is a strong relationship between age at marriage and fertility behavior which cannot be explained simply in terms of the years of marital exposure to the risk of conception (Mineau and Trussell 1982).

No single explanation can be provided for the relationship between age at marriage and fertility. Several plausible explanations may be posited, however. These include the possibility of reduced coital frequency associated with duration of marriage and increased subfecundity associated with parity, as well as the adoption of some limited form of parity-dependent family limitation. If the latter condition is present, then the applicability of the concept of "natural fertility" to the population must be questioned.

NATURAL FERTILITY OR CONTROLLED FERTILITY?

In chapter 1 Henry's concept of "natural fertility" was discussed. As indicated in that chapter, two common methods of ascertaining the presence of natural fertility are the examination of marital age-specific fertility curves and the calculation of Coale and Trussell's M and m values, where M is a scale or level index and m represents the degree of departure from model natural-fertility schedules. Coale and Trussell also provide a goodness-of-fit measure, the mean square error (MSE), which has an intuitive interpretation. A mean square error of zero is interpreted as a "good fit"; a value of 0.005 as a "mediocre fit"; and a value of 0.01 and higher a "terrible fit" (Coale and Trussell 1978). To estimate the presence of and departure from natural-fertility patterns both indices are presented below.

Figure 13 presents a graph of marital age-specific fertility rates

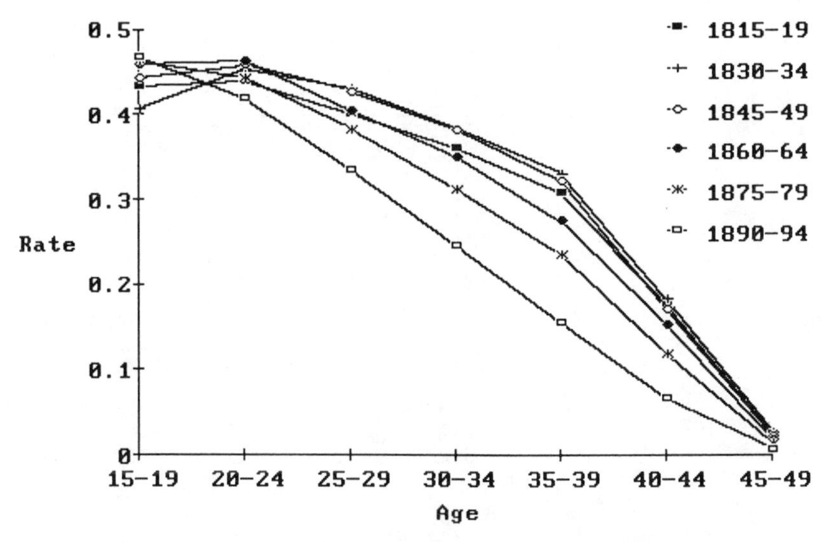

Figure 13. Marital Age-Specific Fertility Rates for Selected Birth Cohorts

selected birth cohorts: 1815–19, 1830–34, 1845–49, 1860–64, 1875–79, and 1890–94. The curves presented in figure 13 reflect the predicted convex shape of the curves Henry has associated with natural fertility among the early and midcentury birth cohorts. The 1875–79 and 1890–94 curves indicate movement in a direction that would ultimately produce a concave curve, which is presumed to indicate the adoption of fertility limitation. Although the shape of the curves is similar among the first several cohorts, levels do vary, indicating the rise and then subsequent decline in fertility.

In table 19 we present the Coale and Trussell M and m values and the MSEs for each of the twenty five-year birth cohorts. For each cohort the MSE test indicates a better than "mediocre" fit between the observed and predicted values. However, it is somewhat difficult to interpret the findings. Among the birth cohorts of 1800–04 through 1845–49 the m values are negative, and fluctuate somewhat. In general one would assume all of these cohorts represent natural-fertility schedules. As indicated previously, increasing values of m would suggest increasing adoption of fertility limitation. Although the m values for the 1835–39 through the 1850–54 birth cohorts are negative or zero, the value of m begins to increase slowly but systematically through the 1855–59 birth cohort. Among the cohorts after 1855–59, the magnitude of m increases more rapidly. However, an m value of .2 or greater, which has been interpreted as the level at which one can be relatively certain fertility control has begun to emerge, is found only from the 1875–79

TABLE 19

COALE AND TRUSSELL'S INDICES OF NATURAL FERTILITY BY MOTHER'S BIRTH COHORT, 1800–04 TO 1895–99

Birth Cohort	*M*	*m*	MSE	Birth Cohort	*M*	*m*	MSE
1800–04	0.930	−0.064	0.0006	1850–54	0.975	0.000	0.0006
1805–09	0.969	0.008	0.0010	1855–59	0.977	0.021	0.0012
1810–14	0.942	−0.041	0.0026	1860–64	0.969	0.080	0.0014
1815–19	0.920	−0.062	0.0013	1865–69	0.952	0.097	0.0007
1820–24	0.895	−0.122	0.0007	1870–74	0.953	0.156	0.0003
1825–59	0.932	−0.103	0.0007	1875–79	0.944	0.224	0.0005
1830–34	0.971	−0.065	0.0006	1880–84	0.941	0.313	0.0006
1835–39	0.962	−0.072	0.0005	1885–89	0.913	0.443	0.0006
1840–44	0.976	−0.041	0.0002	1890–94	0.917	0.603	0.0002
1845–49	0.984	−0.017	0.0002	1895–99	0.883	0.797	0.0003

Note: Mean square error (MSE), *m*, and *M* are based on marital age-specific fertility rates, using ages 20–24 . . . 45–49 and regressed over ages 20–24 . . . 40–44. Ages 15–19 are not used in calculating *m*.

birth cohort and among those born later. The results of the analysis therefore indicate that over time we are assured that the population has shifted from a natural-fertility schedule to schedules marked by increasing levels of control. However, it is difficult to determine from either the graphic analysis or the analysis of Coale and Trussell's *M* and *m* values precisely when control begins to emerge. The inability to clearly identify the initiation of the shift from uncontrolled to increasingly controlled fertility suggests that the lack of precision in either of these two methods may also make it difficult to identify the presence of some subclasses that control fertility even during periods of presumed natural fertility.

While graphs and Coale and Trussell procedures have been widely utilized to identify the presence of natural fertility schedules and the adoption of parity-dependent family limitation, our initial analysis suggests that these procedures are somewhat imprecise. These aggregate measures may well mask internal variations, and it is difficult to determine with precision when the systematic adoption of parity-dependent family limitation is initiated, and by what subgroups of the population studied. Consequently, we shall extend the analysis substantively and methodologically below. We examine patterns of childbearing among subcohorts of the population, and extend the analysis through the explicit examination of birth-spacing patterns. These analyses are presented in chapters 6 and 7.

SUMMARY

Census-based studies of fertility in the United States have identified the Utah population as unusual. Studies by Yasuba (1962) and others (Forster and Tucker 1972) have noted that in the last half of the nineteenth century the fertility ratios for Utah were among the very highest of all states and territories. Among the volumes based upon the 1920 census, Warren Thompson's represents one of the earliest general analysis of differential fertility in the United States (1931). Failing to find systematic fertility differences by rural-urban status in Utah of the order of magnitude observed elsewhere in the United States, Thompson simply attributed the phenomenon to the large LDS population in the state. Currently the high level of fertility in Utah marks the population of the state as unique. Consequently, the casual observer tends to draw a simplistic demographic picture of this population. The dominant features of that simplistic portrait are early marriage, high fertility, and a historical background of polygyny during the nineteenth century.

The data we have presented in this chapter confirm only part of that picture. Certainly, the cohort fertility of the Utah population was high, at least during the early and middle decades of the nineteenth century. A highly select group—women married before the age of 20 who lived in monogamous unions that remained intact until the women passed out of the childbearing years of life—had a number of children roughly equal to that observed for the Hutterite population.

There was an initial rise in fertility during the settlement of the frontier followed relatively quickly by a systematic decline. Nuptiality was important in accounting for the increase. Because of divorce, widowhood, and polygyny among the earliest cohorts, only four out of ten women married once and had a husband who married only once. Among women born at the end of the century, seven out of ten were similarly situated. Access to frontier opportunities produced an initial decline in the mean age at marriage and a slight increase in the age at last birth; and while these changes are important in the initial rise in marital fertility, they are insufficient to account fully for the increase in completed fertility.

As the frontier disappeared with widespread colonization, urban settlement increased, there was a shift toward nonagricultural activities, and non-LDS populations grew. Concomitantly, age at marriage increased, age at last birth declined, and fertility dropped dramatically. Using now-standard indicators of natural fertility, one can show that the data support the argument that at the aggregate level the population of women born during the first five decades of the nineteenth century did not practice parity-dependent birth control. Subsequent cohorts of women evidenced increasing control over fertility.

Fertility was certainly high among women in Utah who were born in the nineteenth century, but it might have been higher in the absence of marital disruptions due to divorce, widowhood, and polygyny. While nuptiality variables produce a form of differentiation which affects fertility, the population was also marked by variations in other characteristics. The population of frontier settlements came from many areas of the United States as well as various nations of Europe. Settlement was in diverse communities: some were completely and continuously agricultural, and others quickly became substantial urban settlements. Most of the population was affiliated with the LDS church. However, substantial numbers never joined the church or joined late in life, and some people who joined were not strongly committed to the church, its values and beliefs. In the next chapter we turn to a more detailed analysis of the composition of the population—its origin, settlement patterns, and religious commitments—to investigate further variations in fertility behavior.

ENDNOTE

Sorting out the multitude of changes appearing in table 18 is difficult. A simple graphic illustration will confirm the argument that the pattern of change in age-specific fertility rates (ASFRs) suggested by the innovation-diffusion perspective is not evident among the MHDP data. We will compare ASFRs across cohorts by age at marriage. Relative to the ASFR within age-at-marriage groups for the earlier cohort, we will use minus (−) to indicate a decline of ten points or more, plus (+) to indicate an increase of ten points or more, and zero (0) to indicate a change of ten or fewer points. Eliminating the oldest and youngest groups, consistent with the procedure often used in the calculation of Coale and Trussell's *m* and *M* values, and listing the changes by sign only, the innovation-diffusion position would suggest the following pattern of change within each age-at-marriage group:

	Age				
Cohort	20–24	25–29	30–34	35–39	40–44
1845–49	+	+	+	+	0/−
1860–64	+/0	+/0	+/0	0/−	−
1875–79	0	0	−	−	−
1890–94	0	−	−	−	−

The pattern suggests an initial decline among the older (and higher-parity women), spreading in each later period to younger groups of women. The observed pattern for women married before age 20 is:

	Age				
Cohort	20–24	25–29	30–34	35–39	40–44
1845–49	+	0	0	0	0
1860–64	0	−	−	−	−
1875–79	−	−	−	−	−
1890–94	−	−	−	−	−

It is the pattern of changes to the left of the diagonal line which is particularly critical if diffusion to young age-groups is to be demonstrated. Fifty percent of the predicted changes are in error. For the women married at ages 20–24, 50 percent of the predictions are in error, as is the case for women married at age 25 or later.

CHAPTER 5

Subcultural Variations I

Migrant Assimilation of Fertility Norms

The largely common adoption of the Mormon religion, shared migration experiences, and residence in interdependent settlements in the narrow habitable range bordering the Wasatch Mountains of Utah would seem to form a homogeneous setting for fertility during the first years of Utah's colonization. Nonetheless, significant social and cultural differences were present among groups settling this frontier area.

The original Utah frontier settlers were unified under the charismatic leadership of the early LDS church authorities and a shared minority-group psychology (Ericksen 1922). Later immigrants arrived during the breakdown of traditional patterns, a time marked by increasing bureaucratic rationalization of church authority and the birth of a secular state (O'Dea 1957). While initial settlers faced an arduous migration to an unknown destination, late immigrants often received assistance from the Perpetual Emigration Fund, traveled established transcontinental railroad routes, and joined relatives already settled in the Salt Lake Valley. As discussed in chapter 2, within a relatively short period the independent empire established under ecclesiastical authority was invaded by federal authorities, who established a military base in the core settlement of Salt Lake. Although church leaders were initially able to exercise a great deal of control over the settlement and development of the region, economic development attracted growing numbers of non-LDS settlers, creating further subdivisions within the population and introducing disparate values and ideologies into the community.[1]

Immigrants, for example the Irish, often initiated political movements, openly supporting a secular rather than religiously dominated local government (Papanikolas 1976). Immigrant groups and religious splinter groups also dominated several of the more isolated and outlying settlements (Hatch 1982; O'Dea 1957). The nearly constant stream of immigrants fueled the growth of the central or core settlements at the same time that non-core settlements expanded to account for over one-fourth of the state's population (Wahlquist 1977). However, the large and growing central settlement, subject to greater cultural penetration from external U.S. society through the transcontinental railroad (1869), distinctly contrasted with more isolated, outlying settlements. Thus, despite widespread participation in the general culture, the MHDP data capture a diverse and distinctively formative picture of a population in social transition.[2]

To account for the changes in fertility behavior documented in the previous chapter, we must go beyond the analysis of aggregate population patterns to address the compositional changes in the population over the course of the fertility transition and examine the extent to which subcultural groups or strata of the population influenced fertility behavior. This is particularly important for a population with both the dramatic fertility transition and the degree of emergent stratification witnessed in the Utah population. These simultaneous processes of change parallel the fertility and industrial transformations in Europe which have attracted much interest among social historians.

We begin our study of internal variations of fertility change by addressing the effects of four principal dimensions of stratification and social change on fertility behavior. Two of these dimensions are discussed in this chapter and two in the next. In the present chapter we look first at ethnicity across cohorts by defining ethnic or cultural groups of frontier immigrants according to place of birth. Second, we highlight when—that is, at what phase in their life course—these migrants arrived on the western frontier. These data clarify the processes of assimilation to a set of common fertility norms. To be more precise, we are interested in the degree to which migrant populations are acculturated as evidenced by the acceptance of a particular set of family-formation norms. Acculturation is mirrored by the degree of assimilation into a common behavior pattern of childbearing and family formation.

In chapter 6, a third dimension, commitment to or affiliation with the prevailing LDS church, and a fourth dimension, residence in the central settlement areas of the state as a proxy for urbanization, are examined. Focusing on changes in religious commitment and residential differences allows us to evaluate the significance of the concepts of secularization and urbanization. Thus chapters 5 and 6 investigate fertility change through the methodological strategy of successive decomposition. In the analysis of the origins of migrants, the decomposition variables are those which reflect the declining importance of subgroup cultural values as migrant populations assimilate a set of common cultural values. In the analysis of secularization and urbanization, the selected variables emphasize the declining significance of religious influences and the increasing emphasis of new secular influences.[3]

ORIGINS OF THE POPULATION

As indicated in chapter 2, the historical Utah population primarily originated in the eastern United States, Great Britain, and Scandinavia. Initial Mormon settlements were established in 1831 in Kirtland, Ohio, by migrants from New York State and expanded to western Missouri later that year. LDS missions in Great Britain began in 1837 and produced converts who made up the first group of foreign migrants to join Mormon colonies in the Midwest. Successful missionary activities in Denmark in the 1850s and in Sweden somewhat later increased the numbers of Scandinavian migrants joining the newly established colonies in the Utah Territory.

The variations in origin generated by differentially timed missionary activities are evident in table 20. This table uses data on women married between ages 10 and 44 who have complete fertility histories. Only 1 percent of women have no birthplace recorded in these genealogical records.

Prior to the establishment of Utah Territory in 1847, the birthplace of most married women was Europe: 59.0 percent for the 1800–09 birth cohort, 67.2 percent for 1810–19, 72.8 percent for 1820–29, and 70.0 percent for 1830–39. Over 40 percent of women in all of these early cohorts were from Great Britain. However, one-fourth to one-third of the people in the early cohorts were from the eastern United States and Canada, and this group includes the founders of the Mormon church. The 1830–39 and 1840–49 cohorts show the effects of migration: 10 to 18 percent of women were born in trail states, and they were among the first children born in Mormon settlements. After the migra-

TABLE 20

DISTRIBUTION (PERCENTAGES) OF WOMEN'S PLACE OF BIRTH, FOR EVER-MARRIED WOMEN BY BIRTH COHORT

Birth Cohort	N	Great Britain	North Europe	Canada, United States	Trail States	Terri- tory	Utah	None	Other
1800–09	999	43.4	15.6	35.9	2.2	*	*	2.0	0.8
1810–19	2,045	48.0	19.2	26.1	3.8	*	*	2.2	0.7
1820–29	3,396	47.7	25.1	19.1	5.5	*	*	1.7	0.9
1830–39	4,787	43.8	26.2	16.5	10.6	0.1	*	1.9	1.0
1840–49	5,778	40.8	26.9	7.9	18.7	0.2	2.5	1.7	1.2
1850–59	8,610	24.7	21.2	5.3	6.2	0.4	39.5	1.3	1.4
1860–69	11,192	12.8	14.4	3.5	1.9	1.8	63.6	1.0	1.0
1870–79	12,849	6.8	9.9	3.2	1.7	2.8	73.5	0.9	1.2
1880–09	14,696	3.7	5.9	2.7	1.3	6.3	78.2	0.6	1.3
1890–99	15,171	1.6	3.2	2.5	1.1	8.7	80.4	0.6	1.8
TOTAL %	100.0	16.0	12.9	6.1	4.0	3.6	55.1	1.0	1.3
TOTAL N	79,523	12,702	10,282	4,821	3,192	2,869	43,800	825	1,032

Note: Table includes only first marriages of women who married at ages 10 through 44 and who have complete fertility histories.

Great Britain: England, Wales, Scotland, Ireland, and Channel Islands

Northern Europe: Finland, Norway, Sweden, Denmark, Switzerland, Germany, Netherlands, Belgium, France, and Luxembourg

Canada and United States:

a. Canada
b. Most cases are in Maine, New Hampshire, Vermont, Massachusetts, Rhode Island, Connecticut, New York, New Jersey, and Pennsylvania
c. Next in frequency are Delaware, Maryland, West Virginia, Virginia Kentucky, Tennessee, North Carolina, and South Carolina
d. Included but accounting for only several percent are Michigan, Minnesota, Wisconsin, Alabama, Mississippi, Georgia, Louisiana, Arkansas, Texas, Montana, Kansas, and California

Trail States: Ohio, Missouri, Illinois, Iowa, Nebraska, and Indiana

Territory: Idaho, Colorado, Nevada, Arizona, Wyoming, and New Mexico

Other: A place name was recorded but did not match any of the above. In the last two cohorts there were 136 births in Mexico.

TABLE 21
U.S. NATIVE AND FOREIGN-BORN IN UTAH TERRITORY, 1870 AND 1880

	1870 Census			1880 Census		
	U.S. Native	Foreign-born		U.S. Native	Foreign-born	
Age	N	N	%	N	N	%
<5	16,347	319	1.9	25,106	369	1.4
5–9	12,495	1,055	7.8	19,908	1,164	5.5
10–14	9,505	2,062	17.8	15,720	2,015	11.4
15–19	4,973	3,071	38.2	11,618	2,953	20.3
20–24	2,889	3,466	54.5	8,921	3,914	30.5
25–29	2,128	3,421	61.6	4,910	4,797	49.4
30–34	1,708	3,282	65.8	3,214	4,676	59.3
35–39	1,452	3,105	68.1	2,359	4,522	65.7
40–44	1,099	2,661	70.8	1,999	4,090	67.2
45–49	775	2,332	75.1	1,514	3,673	70.8
50–54	719	1,947	73.0	1,092	3,324	75.3
55–59	566	1,267	69.1	748	2,662	78.1
60–64	496	1,044	67.8	659	2,239	77.3
65–69	281	600	68.1	476	1,424	74.9
70–74	175	394	69.2	381	855	69.2
75+	183	225	55.1	333	788	70.3
Unknown	1	1		0	0	
TOTAL	55,792	30,252	35.2	98,958	43,465	30.5
Sex Ratio	107.1	94.4		109.2	100.9	

SOURCE: *Census of the United States,* 1872:624–645, and vol. 30, 632–633

tion of Mormons to the West, this pattern changed. Of women born in 1850–59, only 39.9 percent were born in western territorial states, but of those born in 1890–99, a large majority, 89.1 percent, were born in Utah (80.4 percent) or the adjacent states and territories (8.7 percent).

The genealogical data are consistent with the censuses for 1870 and 1880 reported in table 21. Over 30 percent of the territory's total population recorded in both censuses was foreign-born. The percentage of adults who were foreign-born was much higher because most of the children are classified as native-born. In 1870, 67.9 percent of individu-

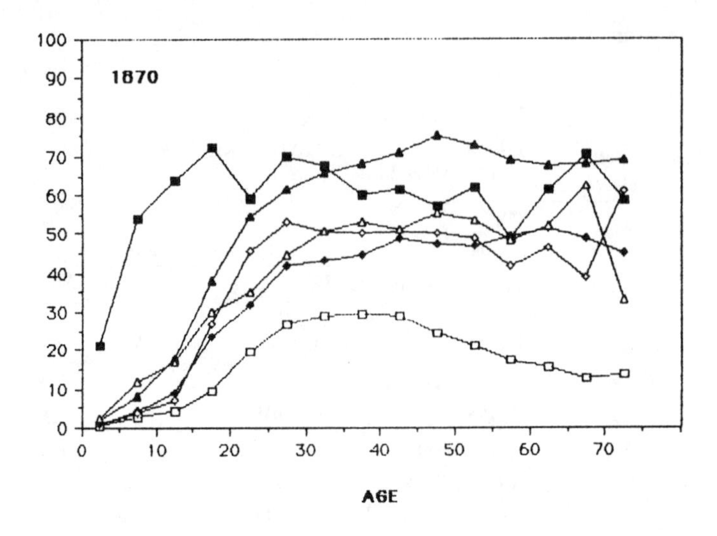

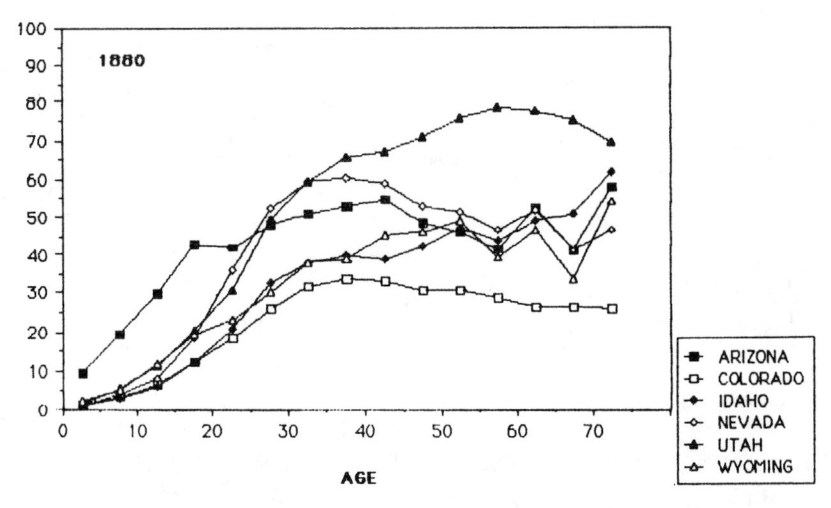

Figure 14. Proportion of Foreign-Born for Selected Intermountain States

als age 25 and over were foreign-born; by 1880 the proportion had decreased to 65.1 percent. Relative to the populations of other western states, Utah's population in 1870 and 1880 generally contained a significantly greater proportion of foreign-born.

In figure 14 the proportion of foreign-born for six western territories, by age, is reported in two panels representing 1870 and 1880. The somewhat higher proportion of selected ages of foreign-born in Arizona is in part a reflection of the tie between Arizona and Mexican territories, as well as the very small population of Arizona—only 3,803 persons in 1870—as compared to a Utah population of 55,792. In 1880 the proportion of foreign-born residents in Nevada was similar to the proportion in Utah for ages up to 30, but the proportion of foreign-born in Utah was significantly higher for most older ages (in the final age group the numbers are so small as to be somewhat unreliable).

The data reflected in figure 14 confirm, however, the importance of foreign migrants in Utah. The rapid growth of Utah Territory was due not only to high fertility but also to large numbers of converts emigrating from Europe. While this society may have been homogeneous with respect to general religious affiliation, it was heterogeneous with respect to the backgrounds of the adults.

ETHNICITY AND FERTILITY

There have been extensive studies of the relationship between ethnicity or origin and fertility among nineteenth-century American populations (Hareven and Vinovskis 1978; Temkin-Greener and Swedlund 1978). Studies of twentieth-century changes in the fertility of the foreign-born have noted the centrality of immigration to the explanation of changing American fertility levels (Easterlin 1961). American studies of fertility in the last half of the nineteenth century found that foreign-born women exhibited higher fertility levels than native-born women. Using 1880 census data, Tamara Hareven and Maris Vinovskis studied five Massachusetts towns in which the foreign-born were mainly Irish and Canadian and found that both groups had substantially higher fertility than the native-born in urban as well as rural communities (1978). Jerry Wilcox and Hilda Golden also observed higher fertility among Irish and French Canadians as compared to natives of western Massachusetts and commented that the native population in 1880 experienced low fertility (1982). On the basis of such evidence, Andorka (1978, p. 289) suggested that in advanced societies "migrant couples partly retain the fertility of their original environment and partly adapt themselves to the fertility usual at their destination; in consequence, they have an intermediate fertility between that of the place of origin and that of the destination." This statement reflects an assumption that fertility is higher in the place of origin than in the place of destination. Our data do not support these conclusions fully.

As indicated in table 22, one finds fairly consistent fertility differences among migrant subgroups for cohorts born in the first half of

TABLE 22

MEAN AGE AT MARRIAGE (AM) AND MEAN CHILDREN EVER BORN (CEB), BY MOTHER'S BIRTHPLACE AND BIRTH COHORT

Birth Cohort	Total		Great Britain		Northern Europe		Canada, United States		Trail States		Territory		Utah	
	AM	CEB	AM	CEB	AM	CEB	AM	CEB	AM	CEB	AM	CEB	AM	CEB
1800–09	23.1	7.0	23.6	6.8	25.3	6.2	21.5	7.5	21.2	7.8	*[a]	*	*	*
1810–19	23.3	6.7	23.2	6.9	26.2	5.6	21.5	7.0	20.9	7.6	*	*	*	*
1820–29	23.3	6.7	23.0	7.0	26.3	5.7	20.7	7.4	20.7	7.0	*	*	*	*
1830–39	21.9	7.4	21.9	7.6	25.1	6.3	18.9	8.3	18.7	8.1	*	*	*	*
1840–49	20.6	7.9	20.3	8.1	23.0	7.2	19.2	8.1	18.1	8.6	*	*	18.8	7.8
1850–59	20.2	7.9	20.3	8.0	22.0	7.3	20.2	7.6	19.3	8.0	19.6	8.3	19.3	8.3
1860–69	20.6	7.4	20.8	7.4	22.2	7.2	20.3	7.2	20.0	7.0	20.3	7.4	20.3	7.5
1870–79	21.5	6.7	21.8	6.4	22.7	6.5	21.4	6.5	21.0	6.3	20.9	7.0	21.3	6.7
1880–89	21.7	5.9	22.9	5.4	22.9	5.8	21.1	6.1	21.5	5.0	21.2	6.1	21.6	5.9
1890–99	21.8	4.9	23.0	4.8	23.0	5.1	21.5	5.0	21.1	4.8	21.7	5.3	21.8	4.9
TOTAL	21.4	6.6	21.6	7.3	23.3	6.6	20.5	7.2	19.3	7.6	21.3	6.0	21.2	6.2

Note: Table includes only first marriages of women who married at ages 10 through 44 and have complete fertility histories.
[a]Asterisks indicate fewer than 20 cases.

the nineteenth century. Among the earliest cohorts, American-born women had higher fertility than European-born women. Among these European-born women, the migrants from Great Britain had higher fertility than the Scandinavians (the major group from Northern Europe). For the 1840–79 cohorts, the women born on the frontier had the highest fertility. In the 1840s, these women were born in the states along the Mormon pioneer trail. By the 1850s and 1860s, these women were born in Utah Territory. Beginning with the birth cohorts of the 1860s, the fertility differences among origin groups converged, suggesting assimilation to a common pattern of fertility and nuptiality.

Studies that report higher fertility among the foreign-born than among the native-born have usually examined American native populations resident in older, settled communities in which fertility had been reduced substantially since the beginning of the nineteenth century. Our analysis, in contrast, compares foreign-born populations with American-born populations migrating to the frontier or born on the frontier. These American migrant or frontier-born populations had levels of fertility higher than those observed in the older, established northeastern region of the United States. Thus the observation that the foreign-born have higher fertility than the native-born cannot be accepted as a general truism. Most European populations, with the exception of the French, initiated fertility limitation within marriage after the U.S. population as a whole, although completed fertility might have been lower in the European populations because of a higher age at marriage. As a result, if European migrant populations imported the fertility values of their places of origin, one might expect that they had higher fertility than the dominant nonfrontier native population, which had already adopted fertility limitation.

Much of the difference in family size among origin groups before midcentury was the result of differences in age at marriage. For example, the mean age at marriage for groups of women born in the United States was less than age 22; and for the 1830–69 cohorts, the mean was age 20.3 or less. These American women, most of whom migrated to the West, experienced marriage at very young ages. In the early cohorts the European-born women had much higher ages at marriage; the Scandinavian women married on average after age 25, and those from Great Britain after age 23. The age at marriage of the earliest cohorts is a reflection of variations in the marriage patterns of their places of origin.[4]

EXPOSURE TO THE FRONTIER AND FERTILITY

The marriage pattern in the frontier society was dramatically different from that described by John Hajnal (1965) as the "European pattern." The establishment of new households met few obstacles and in fact was encouraged as the Mormons expanded into new settlements. The marriage patterns among populations in older, settled areas such as New England could be viewed as somewhat more complex. Young adults who remained in the East may have had more limited economic opportunities than those willing to resettle, and this would have affected both timing of marriage and fertility. For example, on the basis of their study of the native-born population in western Massachusetts, Wilcox and Golden suggested, "By 1880, the natives who were unwilling to migrate westward probably accepted fertility limitation in some form" (1982, pp. 274–275).

Individuals from Europe or New England who migrated in their youth with their parents, or as young adults, would have been exposed to a very different set of societal norms regarding age at marriage and would have had access to different opportunities to create new households. However, access to unexploited land declined relatively rapidly. Wahlquist (1981, p. 93) commented that Mormon expansion in Utah was at its peak from 1847 to 1876. From 1877 to 1896 there was still some expansion in Utah, but there were even more intensive colonization efforts in surrounding states by polygynists seeking to escape persecution as well as prosecution. Thus by 1896 the colonization era was drawing to a close. Those couples married on the frontier through the 1880s and 1890s could expect adequate opportunities to establish new families and households. Those who married later would have had fewer opportunities in the agricultural regions but more opportunities in the nonagricultural regions, where costs of household establishment and expansion might have been higher. The period when a family arrived on the frontier should, therefore, be related to fertility through marital timing and household formation.

Another factor that may influence the relationship between migration and nuptiality is the availability of potential mates after migration. Diverse ethnic groups may or may not intermarry readily; ethnic diversity can be a barrier in defining acceptable mates (Blau 1977). Anderton (1986*a*), in his study of assimilation in Utah Territory, examined intermarriage among couples who married only once for the marriage cohorts of 1860 through 1910. Intermarriage was high between the native Utah population and those from other parts of the United States but even higher between the native Utah population and those from the British group. This fact indicates the importance of spouses from outside the territory and the use of proselytizing to recruit women into the marriage market. Anderton demonstrated that within the central settlement areas intermarriage was most likely among the earlier marriage-cohorts, that intermarriage produced a common age-at-marriage norm, and that the assimilation observed was real assimilation into a common cultural group.[5]

Although marriage is a critical variable and we are able to evaluate the effect of age at marriage, place of marriage may be important as well. Unfortunately, place of marriage is not well recorded in the genealogical data. Birthplace is much better recorded, but birthplace does not indicate residence at marriage. Some women married near their birthplaces while others migrated to frontier communities as young girls with their families and married in Utah Territory. Thus to understand more fully the differences in age at marriage and fertility among these groups requires knowledge of when each woman or family migrated.

Most research on migration does not indicate whether marriage occurred before or after migration, but more importantly such research does not show whether children were born before or after the migration. However, several studies have been able to infer such information. Easterlin, George Alter, and Gretchen Condran, in their study of sixteen northern states using the 1860 manuscript census, stated, "Among households with head born out-of-state, the proportion with any children born outside the state provides a *minimum* estimate of those who migrated as adults" (1978, p. 44). A contemporary study of Melbourne by Elwood Carlson (1985), using a 1971 sample, provided detailed data on husband's and wife's births, marriage, children, and year of migration to Australia. Carlson found no migration effect on immigrants who arrived as children, but for those migrating after age 15 there was either an impact on age at marriage or a short-term impact on the timing of the next birth. Thus we may anticipate that individuals and families in the MHDP population followed life courses that differed according to when migration occurred; so it is important to examine information on immigrant arrivals if these differential impacts on nuptiality and fertility are to be observed.

In order to assess the way in which the frontier experience influenced age at marriage and family size, we need to establish the time at which the individuals arrived in Utah Territory. Given the nature of the data, we can identify the location of demographic events but not the exact time of migration. The demographic events that bracketed arrival in Utah are the birth of the woman, the birth of the first child, the births of subsequent children, and the deaths of the woman and her spouse. As indicated in chapter 4, date of marriage is missing in about 30 percent of cases prior to the 1835 birth cohort, but recording improves over time. Place of marriage is even less well recorded, but the records show the same pattern of improvement over time. For these and other reasons place of marriage will not be used in this analysis.[6] Consequently in table 23 we classify women by selected life-cycle events that occurred in Utah.

Among the cohorts born in the first half of the nineteenth century, three patterns predominate but shift in importance. First, in the first two cohorts the most common group of women were born out-of-state, bore all their children out-of state, but died in Utah (column 3 in table 23). (In this analysis, those born out-of-state include those who were foreign-born and those born in other parts of the United States.) These women migrated to Utah as adults past their childbearing years. They constitute 68.8 percent of the 1800–09 cohort and gradually decline to 9.3 percent of the 1840–49 cohort. Second, women who were born out-of-state but who gave birth to one or more children in Utah (column 2) constitute only 7.6 percent of the earliest cohort but increase to 86.5 percent of the 1840–49 cohort. If their first child was not born in Utah, these women came to Utah as adults during their childbearing years (see table 25). If their first child was born in Utah, these women could have migrated as children, young unmarried adults, or young married but childless adults. Third, some women experienced no demographic event in Utah—they even died elsewhere—but are included because their husbands died in Utah. This last group declines from 15.4 percent of the 1800–09 cohort to 1.2 percent of the 1840–49 cohort. The last two columns of table 23 are residual categories constituting about 1 percent of the birth cohorts of 1800 to 1849. These categories include those women whose places of death were unrecorded but whose husbands died in Utah, and those women who experienced no demographic event in Utah but whose husbands were born in Utah. In general, the first two cohorts had few or none of their children in Utah; their marriage and fertility histories represent those of other regions or countries. The children of these women arrived in Utah at younger ages; some were able to

TABLE 23

DISTRIBUTION (PERCENTAGES) OF TIMING OF UTAH EVENTS

			Wife Born Out-of-State				
				Children Born Out-of-State			
Birth Cohort	N	Wife born in Utah (1)	Some Children Born in Utah (2)	Wife Died in Utah (3)	Husband Died in Utah (4)	Husband Died in Utah (5)	Husband Born in Utah (6)
1800–09	963	*	7.6	68.8	15.4	8.1	*
1810–19	1,960	*	32.4	50.4	12.4	4.7	*
1820–29	3,279	*	56.7	32.5	7.5	3.2	*
1830–39	4,626	*	79.8	15.8	2.9	1.5	*
1840–49	5,628	2.5	86.5	9.3	1.2	0.4	*
1850–59	8,451	40.0	54.2	4.6	0.9	0.2	0.1
1860–69	11,035	64.2	31.2	3.7	0.5	0.1	0.4
1870–79	12,663	74.2	22.4	2.5	0.4	0.1	0.5
1880–89	14,430	78.7	18.7	1.1	0.1	0.2	1.1
1890–99	14,806	80.8	17.1	0.4	0.0	0.2	1.5
Total %	100.0	55.7	35.0	6.8	1.3	0.6	0.6
Total N	77,841	43,328	27,207	5,307	1,043	470	486

Note: Table includes only first marriages of women who married at ages 10 through 44 and have complete fertility histories; omits women with no birthplace recorded, zero parity, and no Utah event for them or their first marriages

(1) Wife born in Utah
(2) Wife born out-of-state, one or more children born in Utah
(3) Wife born out-of-state, children born out-of-state, wife died in Utah
(4) Wife born out-of-state, children born out-of-state, wife died out-of-state, husband died in Utah
(5) Wife born out-of-state, children born out-of-state, wife's place of death not recorded, husband died in Utah
(6) Wife born out-of-state, children born out-of-state, wife died out-of-state, husband born in Utah, husband died out-of-Utah

marry on the frontier and others had greater proportions of their children in Utah.

For the last half of the nineteenth century, the pattern is quite different. Utah-born women increase from 40 percent in 1850–59 to 80.8 percent in 1890–99. The only other group of importance are those born out-of-state who lived and had children in Utah; they decline from 54.2 percent in 1850–59 to 17.1 percent in 1890–99. The numbers of women in the residual categories are unimportant until the last two cohorts, in which they increase to a few percent. These residual cases are out-migrants from Utah, families in which the only known Utah events were the husbands' births—the wives had no Utah events and the husbands died elsewhere. Thus, the general pattern in the last half of the nineteenth century is increasingly stable. There is less change in the composition of the last three cohorts than in that of earlier cohorts. Later cohorts were dominated by life in Utah, and changes between cohorts had more to do with the changing environment of Utah as it moved into the twentieth century than with familial movement into a western frontier.

Data are provided in table 24 to identify variations in fertility behavior associated with differences in migration and settlement histories. In this table we include information on age at marriage, CEB, and age at last birth by birth cohorts. The table has summary columns for all women, as well as data for the three groups of women who constitute nearly 98 percent of the total number from table 23. There are certain statistical anomalies that need to be recognized. First, the relatively high fertility of the first cohort (1800–09) is a function of survival rather than age at marriage or social norms related to fertility behavior. Individuals (or couples) in this cohort had to survive to an older age to migrate and settle; that is, they had to survive beyond 1847—the date of the initial settlement. Of more interest is the fertility behavior of the three groups of women in the cohorts born after 1840.

These three groups are dominated by those women who were born in Utah and had their children in Utah. The second largest group consists of those women who were born out-of-state but who bore one or more of their children in Utah and generally ended their childbearing in the state. The third group is relatively small, particularly in the later cohorts, but is theoretically important.

The fertility behavior of the first two groups of women is similar in levels and trends. The women born out-of-state married later, however, perhaps responding to different marriage-market conditions in more

TABLE 24

MEAN AGE AT FIRST MARRIAGE (AM), MEAN CHILDREN EVER BORN (CEB), AND MEAN AGE AT LAST BIRTH (ALB)[a] BY TIMING OF UTAH EVENTS AND MOTHER'S BIRTH COHORT

Birth Cohort	All Women			(1)			(2)			(3)		
	AM	CEB	ALB	AM	CEB	ALB	AM	CEB	ALB	AM	CEB	ALB
1800–09	23.0	7.1	40.2	*[b]	*	*	(22.1	9.6	44.1)[c]	23.0	7.1	39.9
1810–19	23.2	6.8	40.0	*	*	*	23.1	8.1	42.1	23.5	6.5	39.2
1820–29	23.2	6.8	40.4	*	*	*	23.5	7.6	41.7	23.1	6.3	38.8
1830–39	21.9	7.5	40.3	*	*	*	21.6	8.0	40.9	22.9	6.1	38.2
1840–49	20.5	8.0	40.1	18.8	7.8	38.4	20.3	8.3	40.3	23.2	6.4	38.7
1850–59	20.2	8.0	39.8	19.3	8.3	40.0	20.7	7.9	40.1	22.0	6.4	36.9
1860–69	20.6	7.5	39.5	20.3	7.6	39.6	21.2	7.4	39.6	22.0	6.4	36.7
1870–79	21.5	6.7	38.8	21.3	6.7	38.9	22.0	6.7	39.0	22.3	5.5	35.7
1880–89	21.6	6.0	37.5	21.5	6.0	37.5	22.0	6.0	37.6	21.5	5.2	35.1
1890–99	21.7	5.0	35.6	21.7	5.0	35.5	22.0	5.2	35.8	(21.8	4.5	34.6)
TOTAL	21.4	6.6	38.4	21.1	6.3	37.7	21.4	7.3	39.5	22.9	6.3	38.3

Note: Table includes only first marriages of women who married at ages 10 through 44 and have complete fertility histories; omits women with no birthplace record and zero parity.

[a]Age at last birth is calculated only for couples who survived until the wife reached age 45.

[b]Asterisks indicate no cases.

[c]Parentheses indicate fewer than 100 cases.

(1) Mother born in Utah

(2) Mother born out-of-state, one or more children born in Utah

(3) Mother born out-of-state, children born out-of-state, mother died in Utah

settled regions. All of the women in the second group migrated to Utah at some time and generally terminated their childbearing in the state at an age somewhat later than the age at last birth of the native Utah mothers. Thus they achieved comparable fertility levels despite marrying later by persisting in childbearing to an older age. In contrast, the women who were born out-of-state and who bore all of their children out-of-state had to adapt to the socioeconomic conditions of the older, more settled regions of the United States—perhaps of Europe as well—even though their commitments ultimately led them to migrate to Utah late in life. These women also married somewhat later than the Utah-born women, completed their families with a smaller number of births, and ended their childbearing at a much earlier age.

To further explore contextual effects of childbearing, we will examine the behavior of women born outside Utah in more detail. In table 25 we distinguish between two subclasses of the women for whom data are reported in column 2 of table 23; that is, we distinguish between those whose first child was born in Utah and those whose first child was born elsewhere.

Using birth cohort groupings again causes some anomalies to appear. In the 1800–09 cohort, women who bore at least one child in Utah not only survived but remained fertile through their late 40s, and women in that cohort could have borne their first child in Utah only if they married later in life, as did the 1810–19 and 1820–29 birth cohorts.

Adult women who migrated with families, that is, who had begun childbearing elsewhere exhibited very high fertility, averaging over 8.5 children through the 1850–59 birth cohort. One might, on the one hand, speculate that these were already high-fertility families who moved to Utah knowing they would find support in terms of both values and opportunities. On the other hand, it might be that these families, although they had begun childbearing elsewhere, were not yet high-fertility but were encouraged to become so by the values and opportunities encountered in Utah. This latter explanation is supported by this group's older ages at last birth, which average over 41 until the 1860–69 birth cohort. Even among the fertility-transition cohorts, these adult migrants persisted in childbearing to older ages.[7]

The waves of migration into Utah Territory also included children, young unmarried adults, and young childless married couples; and these three subgroups are combined to form the group of married women born out of Utah who bore their first child in Utah. The age at marriage for women in this group is higher in all cohorts than for women born in

TABLE 25

MEAN AGE AT FIRST MARRIAGE (AM), MEAN CHILDREN EVER BORN (CEB), AND AGE AT LAST BIRTH (ALB), BY FIRST CHILD'S BIRTHPLACE AND MOTHER'S BIRTH COHORT, FOR MOTHERS BORN OUT OF UTAH WITH ONE OR MORE CHILDREN BORN IN UTAH

Birth Cohort	First Child Born in Utah				First Child Born Elsewhere			
	%	AM	CEB	ALB	%	AM	CEB	ALB
1800–09	2.7	*[a]	*	*	97.3	(22.1	9.6	44.2)[b]
1810–19	8.9	(33.7	3.4	42.1)	91.1	21.9	8.6	42.1
1820–29	30.2	27.5	5.6	41.2	69.8	21.7	8.5	41.8
1830–39	68.7	21.8	7.6	40.4	31.3	21.1	8.7	41.7
1840–49	82.9	20.0	8.2	40.1	17.1	21.3	8.8	41.3
1850–59	81.3	20.5	7.8	39.8	18.7	21.3	8.7	41.1
1860–69	81.0	21.2	7.3	39.4	19.0	21.0	8.1	40.3
1870–79	78.3	22.1	6.6	38.7	21.7	21.6	7.3	39.8
1880–89	77.0	22.3	5.7	37.2	23.0	21.0	7.1	38.9
1890–99	75.8	22.3	4.9	35.4	24.2	21.0	6.2	37.0
TOTAL	26.7	21.5	7.1	39.0	26.7	21.4	8.2	40.7

Note: Table includes only first marriages of women who married at ages 10 through 44 and have complete fertility histories; omits women with no birthplace record and zero parity and omits families in which the first child has no birthplace recorded.

[a]Asterisks indicate fewer than 20 cases.

[b]Parentheses indicate fewer than 100 cases.

Utah ("mother born in Utah" group, column 1, table 24). The older age at marriage for the combined three subgroups—migrated as children, migrated as young unmarried adults, and migrated as young childless married couples—probably reflects different marriage opportunities. However, their pattern of change in age at marriage parallels the change among Utah-born women, indicating that many in the first two subgroups of migrants arrived young enough to experience the same marriage market as the Utah-born women. Correspondingly, their fertility, while lower than that of the Utah-born women, follows the same pattern of decline. Beginning with the 1850–59 cohort, their age at last birth is almost identical to that of native-born Utah women. Thus, it would appear that the migration effect on fertility in this group resulted from the effect of migration on age at marriage. However, the women born outside Utah who commenced childbearing outside Utah and then continued childbearing in Utah after migrating to the state adjusted for their somewhat later age at marriage by persisting in childbearing to a much later age. Such differences among various groups distinguished by their migration experiences provide important insights.

The apparent rise in fertility across the early cohorts can now be viewed as a compositional effect due to the timing of migration. With the exception of the earliest cohort, the rise is related to the combination of the increasing proportion of mothers born out-of-state who had children in Utah and averaged approximately eight children with the decreasing proportion of women who migrated after childbearing and averaged six or fewer children. If women born before 1840 were aggregated by year of migration (instead of year of birth), one would observe individuals of varying ages and family structures migrating into Utah Territory. In other words, the analysis of data using cohorts before 1830 or 1840 does not represent changes that actually occurred in Utah but describes by age the women who migrated. These women did not migrate at the same age; they have in common only the event of migration, which occurred at different stages in their life cycles. Beginning with the 1840–49 cohort, the use of birth cohort aggregation has its traditional interpretation (Ryder 1965).

SUMMARY

Analysts of religion in America have often argued that the LDS church is the epitome of a native American religion. The church was theologically formed within the framework of nineteenth-century religious revivalism by native Americans who dominated the church's religious hierarchy. The early LDS population, however, was drawn from a crucible formed by America and the Western European nations. Through the mid-nineteenth-century birth cohorts, the married MHDP women were born predominately outside of the United States.

The midcentury date is critical for several reasons. It approximately marks the boundary between cohorts of women who were predominately foreign-born and cohorts of women who were native-born and increasingly Utah-born. It marks the boundary between the cohorts in which fertility was high and the cohorts in which fertility declined rapidly. Those two sets of phenomena—a shift in origin and a shift in fertility trends—are closely linked. Much of the earlier rise in fertility is clearly a function of compositional changes. These compositional changes are unanticipated when viewed in the context of historical studies that have compared the fertility of migrants and indigenous American groups.

Traditionally, it has been observed that the foreign-born have higher fertility than the native population of America. Such studies must now be reinterpreted to reflect the following qualifications. Since the beginning of the nineteenth century, American society has been marked by significant regional differences in fertility, with lower levels of fertility in the Northeast, particularly in urban areas within that region. Fertility in these areas began to decline early in the nineteenth century, while fertility rates in other regions, particularly on the American frontier, remained high. Comparison of the foreign-born with populations of older, more settled eastern regions thus, not surprisingly, found the fertility of the foreign-born to be higher than the fertility of the native American population. If we shift the comparison to the populations migrating to settle Utah, however, the marital fertility levels of the populations from Great Britain and northern Europe are lower than the levels of those born in the United States and the pioneer trail states. Part of the explanation stems from the high age at marriage of the migrant populations, often an important part of the European marriage patterns. Over time the foreign-born assimilated the lower age-at-marriage norms of the American-born MHDP population (Anderton 1986*a*). Such a change would suggest that the earliest cohorts arrived after marriage and the later cohorts arrived before marriage. Thus part of the rise in fertility stems from the fact that individuals born outside of the core Mormon communities (the trail states initially and Utah subsequently) experienced moderately high fertility and family size increased as a lower mean age at marriage was adopted. After midcentury the variation in the mean age at marriage among the various origin-groups was small, and the fertility differences by origin declined. Moreover, all groups, regardless of origin, shared in the decline, reflecting assimilation into a common pattern of fertility. Nevertheless, there are important differences.

Exposure to the frontier environment during the formative years of life as well as the childbearing years of life seems to be related to early marriage and high fertility, with childbearing persisting to relatively late ages (Mineau, Bean, and Anderton 1989). As the frontier began to disappear, however, it seems that the native-born group limited fertility earlier. The groups that grew up in older, more settled areas—in the United States as well as Europe—fall into distinct subgroups. Those who married and completed their childbearing before coming to Utah had lower fertility than the frontier population. The European migrants had lower fertility than the frontier population. Yet an important group of that population migrated to Utah early enough in the life cycle that all or part of the childbearing years of life were spent in Utah. The Utah-born mothers might have perceived increasingly limited opportunities for themselves and their children, relative to those expectations derived from their own childhood. The migrating population saw the territorial opportunities as good, relative to those available in the more settled areas where they spent their formative years of life.

Compositional changes in the proportions of the population born in Utah and migrating to Utah are therefore important to understanding the persistence of high fertility. The rise in fertility among the early cohorts is probably unrelated to any changes in fecundability or marital behavior. The frontier made it easier to marry and to marry early for large sectors of the population. Early missionary activity and immigrant promotion brought significant numbers of couples, who if they came early enough in the life cycle responded to the perceived opportunities by persisting in childbearing until quite late in life. As economic opportunities declined and as the proportion of the population born elsewhere plummeted, fertility declined a great deal in a short time.

CHAPTER 6

Subcultural Variations II

Residence and Religion

The dramatic fertility declines of the American nineteenth-century population were part of a larger nexus of social change encompassing social, economic, political, and denominational trends. Many of the hypotheses concerning fertility declines are thus essentially ecological in nature, referring to fertility differences among broad segments of society. Daniel Smith (1987) refers to such hypotheses as being relevant to "action groups" rather than individuals.

An example is Knodel's (1974) restatement and clarification of Louis Wirth's (1964) distinction between urbanism and urbanization. Urbanism, Knodel argues, refers to the exposure of individuals to the characteristics of urban life, and urbanization refers to the residing in such settings of an increasing proportion of the population. While urbanism may be anticipated to lower fertility among urban residents, this relationship is essentially an ecological hypothesis concerning the group of those exposed to urban values rather than an individualistic hypothesis concerning the precise amount of urbanism experienced by individuals. Easterlin's (1976) hypothesis of the marginalization of agriculture suggests a compatible process of change among those remaining in rural, agricultural areas. This hypothesis asserts that both the value of child labor in supporting household agriculture declines as increasingly marginal lands are brought under cultivation and methods of agriculture become less labor intensive. More people are displaced from agricultural life-styles into relatively urban settings and thus contribute to urbanization and swell the proportion of the population exposed to urbanism. Both the changes induced in agricultural areas and increased urbanization contribute to fertility declines. Again, however, "Easterlin does not argue that land availability has a straightforward influence on nuptiality or fertility at the individual level" (Smith 1987, p. 80).

Three successive stages of rural agriculture are found in the Utah settlements: (1) household farming, (2) wage and commercial agriculture, and (3) dry-land farming and the use of marginal lands. These stages correspond directly with Easterlin's hypothesis. Similarly, the percentage of the population residing in relatively urban areas (i.e., urbanization) and the exposure of these individuals to an increasingly commercially centered economic life within urban areas (i.e., urbanism) experienced parallel increases over time. The western settlement forms an ideal, relatively isolated setting in which to assess changes among residentially influenced social groups.

Given the unique history of the Utah settlement population, any consideration of significant social groups must also clearly include religious or denominational groups. In fact, Smith (1987) has noted the importance of such groups in understanding the general American fertility decline. For example, Charles Westoff and Norman Ryder (1977) have demonstrated the declining importance of Catholic pronatalism in American fertility patterns over the last several decades. Similarly, D. W. Hastings, C. H. Reynolds, and R. R. Canning (1972) noted a considerable lack of correspondence between contemporary pronatalist Mormon doctrine and the practice of contraceptive control by church members. Nevertheless, fertility among the Mormons continues to be higher than that of other groups in the United States. Tim Heaton and Sandra Calkins (1983) suggest a more precise direction of influence among the Mormons. They argue that contemporary Mormons are influenced by pro-family rather than anti–birth control values. Of course, the impact of pronatalist doctrines on fertility has also been questioned in the context of Muslim groups within developing countries (e.g., Chamie 1981).

The pronatalist ideology and social support provided by LDS church membership again give reason to anticipate fertility differentials among groups rather than suggesting a precise linkage between individual religious commitment and fertility. The three principle hypotheses concerning religious fertility differentials assessed within this chapter are all ecological hypotheses. These are the characteristics hypothesis, the minority-group hypothesis, and the particularistic ideology hypothesis.

It is also in this ecological sense that we must see Chamie's interaction hypothesis (1981), which, seeking a broad understanding of society-wide fertility change, attempts to relate religious fertility differentials to fertility differentials among residential groups who are in a conjoined struggle of urbanism and secularization. Rather than as a unique hypothesis Chamie's suggestion can be construed as a combination of the characteristics and particularistic ideology hypotheses.

The characteristics hypothesis generally asserts that fertility effects arise from the coincidental location of religious groups within distinctive social strata of the population (social strata as determined by, e.g., education, urban exposure, income, and occupation). However, studies have demonstrated that differences in fertility remain among religious groups after controlling for socioeconomic factors, especially for Mormons. In reaction, Goldscheider (1971) proposed an alternative, minority-group hypothesis. This hypothesis asserts that the status of some religious groups as minorities, in a particular social context, led to higher fertility as a response to both socioeconomic isolation and perceived threats connected with minority status. Both the characteristics and minority-group hypotheses neglect the possible direct effects of religious doctrine or ideology on fertility behavior. The particularistic ideology hypothesis asserts that varying identification with, or commitment to, religious pronatalist doctrine directly produces observed differentials in fertility among religious subgroups.

The three hypotheses are, of course, not mutually exclusive. A fuller understanding of the effects of religious affiliation on fertility behavior can be gained from comparative historical studies of settings in which the relative import and interaction of the three hypothesized effects can be assessed. The Utah population provides an ideal test case for such competing hypotheses. At the outset of settlement, the LDS religion embodied a distinct minority-group psychology (Ericksen 1922). This can be presumed to have been tempered over the transition as Mormonism became the heavily dominant religion within the settlement population and as Utah was assimilated into the national economic system (Heaton 1986). Such a transformation would suggest that the particularistic ideology hypothesis is most applicable to contemporary LDS church members (Heaton and Calkins 1983).

Given the presumed relationships between urbanization/urbanism and fertility as well as between religion and fertility, we initially examine the separate relationships and then the combined effects in the following sections.

RESIDENCE AND FERTILITY

Given the migration patterns of the population described in the previous chapter, we cannot simply differentiate the effects of residence on fertility behavior by using the birthplace of the mother. This strategy would omit timing of migration and length of exposure within Utah Territory while stressing the origin effects demonstrated in chapter 5. Although various residential classification procedures have been evaluated (Mineau et al. 1984; Mineau 1980), the method employed in this chapter is designed to investigate the effects of exposure to different types of communities within Utah. This classification distinguishes between two types of Utah settlements—central and agricultural. Central settlement areas are defined as the three counties within which major urban developments took place and persisted during the first decades of the nineteenth century.[1]

To focus attention on residential effects throughout the childbearing ages, two locations are used—first child's and last child's birthplace. We developed a six-category typology containing the following groups:

1. stable central-area residents: both first and last child were born in the central Utah settlement area (defined as Salt Lake, Utah, and Weber counties);

2. mobile central-area residents: the last child was born in a central Utah settlement, but the first child was not (includes couples who commenced their childbearing in Europe, the eastern United States, or an agricultural area);

3. stable agricultural-area residents: both first and last child were born in a Utah agricultural settlement area (includes couples who might have moved from one agricultural community to another but who experienced all their childbearing in largely agricultural communities);

4. mobile agricultural-area residents: the last child was born in a Utah agricultural settlement area, but the first was not (the first child could have been born in Europe, the eastern United States, or the central area);

5. residents who left Utah: one or more children were born in Utah, but the last child was born outside Utah (includes adjacent states and other Mormon settlements such as those in Mexico and California); and

6. residents with no Utah births: those who had no childbearing in Utah (one or both parents might have been born or died in Utah).

TABLE 26

DISTRIBUTION (PERCENTAGE) OF RESIDENTIAL GROUPS, BASED ON BIRTHPLACE OF FIRST AND LAST CHILD, FOR FIRST MARRIAGES OF WOMEN WITH TWO OR MORE CHILDREN

Birth Cohort	N	(1)	(2)	(3)	(4)	(5)	(6)	(7)
1800–09	939	0.0	5.5	0.0	1.1	1.0	89.7	2.7
1810–19	1,882	1.6	19.4	0.3	10.2	1.1	64.6	2.7
1820–29	3,089	7.6	19.7	4.0	23.4	2.3	40.6	2.3
1830–39	4,442	20.2	11.8	17.0	25.0	5.0	18.8	2.2
1840–49	5,423	25.3	8.4	29.6	16.1	8.1	10.1	2.4
1850–59	8,077	27.0	7.4	33.8	9.3	13.0	6.5	3.0
1860–69	10,455	26.4	6.1	35.5	6.6	15.3	8.2	1.9
1870–79	11,872	26.5	7.2	36.6	5.6	13.4	10.0	0.7
1880–89	13,363	29.2	8.5	35.3	6.0	11.7	8.8	0.6
1890–99	13,478	31.5	11.4	34.7	5.6	10.1	6.4	0.4
TOTAL%	100.0	25.7	9.3	31.0	9.0	10.9	12.7	1.4
TOTAL N	73,020	18,769	6,767	22,655	6,574	7,913	9,295	1,047

Note: Table includes only first marriages of women who married at ages 10–44 and have complete fertility histories; omits women with fewer than two children.
(1) Stable central-area residents
(2) Mobile central-area residents
(3) Stable agricultural-area residents
(4) Mobile agricultural-area residents
(5) Residents who left Utah
(6) Residents with no Utah births
(7) Missing county or state/country name

This classification requires two birthplaces, and therefore the birth of at least two children. Consequently, 3,000 families with one child were omitted from the analysis. For all cohorts combined, 41 percent of these "only" children were born in a central settlement, 32 percent in an agricultural settlement, and 27 percent outside of Utah.

The distribution of residential patterns is shown in table 26. A total of 1.4 percent of residents (column 7) were missing birthplace information and could not be used in the classification. In early cohorts, adult settlers moved to Utah after all children were born or during childbearing. For the 1820–49 cohorts, final births were slightly more likely to be in an agricultural rather than a central community. Agricultural communities maintained over 40 percent of last births for cohorts from the middle to the end of the century. The central area stabilized at about one-third of last births in the cohorts of the 1840s through the 1870s and then increased to over 40 percent at the end of the century; this pattern reflects some urbanization of the Utah population. Lastly, in cohorts born in the last half of the century, from 10 to 15 percent of families moved out of Utah.

Residential groups, as defined above, have distinctive levels of fertility during some periods. In general, families who moved into different types of communities during their childbearing years were larger than those who remained in a given type of community.

Ages at marriage and mean numbers of children ever born are presented in table 27 for residential groups by cohorts. In the 1840s cohort the two largest groups, stable central and stable agricultural residents, are very similar. The age at marriage in these groups was 20.4 and 20.1 respectively, and they both averaged about eight children. In the following cohorts, however, the individuals comprised by these two categories diverged and maintained a distinct rural-urban difference, with a higher marriage age and a smaller family size in the central areas.

The mobile residents show distinct characteristics for certain cohorts, even though their general effects are slight because these groups were small. For example, in all cohorts born in the last half of the century, families who moved into the central area were very similar to stable agricultural families with respect to average family size. This finding supports research on rural-urban fertility levels in which residents migrating into urban areas have been found to exhibit higher fertility than stable urban families (Zarate and Zarate 1975). Similarly, in the 1840–49 cohort through the 1880–89 cohort, families who moved into agricultural counties of Utah exceeded the completed family size of stable agricultural residents even though they married at about the same age. The largest families and youngest ages at marriage are found among families who moved out of Utah into the newer and more peripheral settlements. These families averaged nine or more children from the 1820–29 through the 1860–69 cohorts and may be viewed as having continued a pioneer tradition.

Beginning with the 1860s cohort, residential groups continued converging to a common age at marriage and family size, with one exception. In the last cohort the stable central residents maintained unique

TABLE 27

MEAN AGE AT FIRST MARRIAGE (AM) AND MEAN CHILDREN EVER BORN (CEB), FOR RESIDENTIAL GROUPS

Birth Cohort	Total		Stable Central		Mobile Central		Stable Agricultural	
	AM	CEB	AM	CEB	AM	CEB	AM	CEB
1800–09	22.7	7.3	*[a]	*	(22.3	9.5)[b]	*	*
1810–19	22.9	7.1	(32.3	3.7)	21.9	8.6	*	*
1820–29	23.1	7.2	26.4	5.9	21.7	8.1	28.6	5.9
1830–39	21.8	7.8	21.7	7.6	21.1	8.4	23.0	7.5
1840–49	20.5	8.2	20.4	8.0	21.3	8.7	20.1	8.1
1850–59	20.1	8.2	20.6	7.8	21.2	8.1	19.7	8.1
1860–69	20.5	7.7	21.3	7.0	21.1	7.6	20.3	7.6
1870–79	21.4	6.9	22.1	6.1	21.7	6.9	21.2	7.0
1880–89	21.5	6.2	22.2	5.4	21.5	6.5	21.2	6.4
1890–99	21.5	5.3	22.1	4.6	21.4	5.6	21.2	5.6
TOTAL	21.3	6.9	21.8	6.2	21.4	7.1	20.9	6.9

Birth Cohort	Mobile Agricultural		No Utah Births		Left Utah	
	AM	CEB	AM	CEB	AM	CEB
1800–09	*	*	22.8	7.2	*	*
1810–19	22.5	8.3	23.0	6.6	(21.2	8.8)
1820–29	22.7	8.3	22.9	6.4	(22.3	9.2)
1830–39	20.8	8.8	22.9	6.3	21.3	8.7
1840–49	20.2	8.9	22.8	6.7	19.2	9.6
1850–59	20.1	8.8	21.5	7.0	19.1	9.5
1860–69	20.6	7.9	20.8	7.4	19.6	9.0
1870–79	21.4	7.3	21.0	7.1	20.6	7.9
1880–89	21.3	6.6	21.1	6.6	20.9	7.0
1890–99	21.6	5.6	21.5	5.7	21.3	5.7
TOTAL	21.1	7.9	22.0	6.7	20.3	7.9

Note: Table includes only first marriages of women who married at ages 10 through 44 and have complete fertility histories; omits women with fewer than two children.

[a]Asterisks indicate fewer than 20 cases.

[b]Parentheses indicate fewer than 100 cases.

characteristics—an older age at marriage (22.1) and smaller families (4.6 children). Definite distinctions among the other residential groups in the last cohort are not apparent. Age at marriage was on average between 21.2 and 21.6, and couples had 5.6 to 5.7 children. In summary, the fertility of the cohorts in the first half of the century can be described by two groupings: families who migrated into a new type of community had high fertility, and those who remained in one type of community had lower fertility. Wide-scale migration effects decreased over time, those who moved out of Utah being the last group to converge to the level of the stable urban residents. For the last cohorts, the state retains only rural-urban fertility and marriage differentials. A complex pattern became increasingly simple as community differentiation produced a traditional separation of urban and rural communities.

RELIGION AND FERTILITY

In an earlier publication (Bean, Mineau, and Anderton 1983) we provided an initial descriptive analysis of fertility levels within both religious and residential subgroups of the population. Information on the occurrence and timing of religious rites (baptism and endowments) was used to decompose the population into those reaffirming religious commitment later in life and those not. (See chapter 3 for a discussion of baptism and endowment.)

We developed a religious classification that combined the wife's and husband's baptism and endowment information with the date of their marriage and of wife's death. Five categories that compare religious information are as follows:

a) lifetime commitment: baptism took place on or before the day of marriage, and endowment sometime during the wife's lifetime;

b) converts: baptism took place after marriage, and endowment during the wife's lifetime;

c) partial association: baptism took place after marriage, and no endowment occurred during the wife's lifetime;

d) nonactive: baptism took place before marriage, and no endowment occurred during the wife's lifetime; and

e) non-LDS: no baptism and no endowment were recorded for either the wife or husband.

The population's distribution among these categories is shown in table 28. The column "Non-LDS" contains both those who did not join the LDS church during their lifetime and those whose records lack

TABLE 28

DISTRIBUTION (PERCENTAGE) OF RELIGIOUS AFFILIATIONS, BASED ON BAPTISM AND ENDOWMENT INFORMATION

Birth Cohort	N	Lifetime Commit-ment	Convert	Partial Association	Nonactive	Non-LDS
1800–09	980	1.1	63.2	12.4	0.2	23.1
1810–19	1,983	8.5	61.1	10.1	1.3	19.0
1820–29	3,269	29.7	44.3	6.9	3.4	15.8
1830–39	4,644	54.5	26.2	3.9	4.0	11.4
1840–49	5,573	63.8	18.1	3.1	4.3	10.7
1850–59	8,305	68.7	13.6	2.7	4.9	10.2
1860–69	10,739	69.5	10.8	2.2	7.1	10.4
1870–79	12,267	71.5	8.3	1.9	9.8	8.5
1880–89	13,894	75.7	5.5	1.4	10.7	6.7
1890–99	14,315	79.4	3.9	1.4	11.2	4.1
TOTAL %	99.9	67.2	13.3	2.6	7.9	8.9
TOTAL N	75,969	51,063	10,132	1,984	6,024	6,766

Note: Table includes only first marriages of women who married at ages 10 through 44 and have complete fertility histories; omits women with zero parity.

information. Because the information used was for both husband and wife, the "non-LDS", including those whose records lack all four dates, account for a very small proportion.[2] Death dates are not recorded for some women; this is particularly true in the later cohorts because they may still have been alive when their family-group sheets were submitted. If a death date is missing for the wife, her death is assumed to have occurred at age 65. This assumption is required in order to determine the religious events as having occurred either during the wife's lifetime or after her death.[3]

The early cohorts represent the church's founders, their converts, and other members of their immediate of families who may not have been converted. Over 60 percent joined the LDS church as adults; about one-fifth to one-fourth never joined during their lifetime; and about 10 percent had partial association, that is, were baptized as adults but never endowed during their lifetime. Gradually the proportion of members who were raised or socialized in the church increased to almost 80 percent in the last cohort. The only other group that increased over time is the nonactive, those who were baptized as children but were not active as adults and thus never endowed as adults.

In table 29 the mean ages at marriage and mean numbers of children ever born (CEB) are presented. The mean ages at marriage are slightly higher and the mean CEBs slightly lower than those in table 27 because one-child families are included in these analyses of religious affiliation. Looking at the cohorts of 1820–89, one observes that members with lifetime commitment and converts had similar levels of fertility and that these levels were higher than the levels of the other groups. Those with partial association ranked third, nonactive fourth; and non-LDS had the lowest fertility. For example, in the 1850–59 cohort, the members with lifetime commitment and converts averaged 8.1 to 8.2 children, those with partial association had 7.6, while the nonactive and non-LDS averaged 6.9 and 6.7 children, respectively. Thus we observe a positive association between religious affiliation with the Mormon church and family size. However, there is a general convergence in family size over time, and by the last cohort there is a difference of only 0.6 between the family size of the highest (lifetime commitment and partial association) and lowest (non-LDS) fertility groups. The growing similarity in family size occurred in spite of a lack of convergence in age at marriage.

Marital age-specific fertility rates and descriptive indices of m and M (Coale and Trussell 1978) for these subcohorts are presented in table 30. Both the MTFR and M levels for subcohorts suggest that the non-LDS families in both natural-fertility and fertility-transition cohorts had substantially lower fertility. Those with lifetime religious commitment (baptized on or before marriage and endowed while living) had distinctly higher fertility levels. Among transition cohorts all m values increase, indicating the onset of age-specific (and presumably parity-dependent) fertility control. The stable central-area residents reached the greatest level of fertility control (.336), exceeding the level of control reached by the non-LDS subcohort (.330). Again, this supports the general finding that the factors encouraging fertility limitation changed; they were initially religious (i.e., being non-LDS played a role in fertility limitation), but these gave way to factors involved in residing in a central area.

TABLE 29

MEAN AGE AT FIRST MARRIAGE (AM) AND MEAN CHILDREN EVER BORN (CEB), BY RELIGIOUS AFFILIATION

Birth Cohort	Total		Lifetime Commitment		Converts		Partial Association		Nonactive		Non-LDS	
	AM	CEB	AM	CEB	AM	CEB	AM	CEB	AM	CEB	AM	CEB
1800–09	23.0	7.1	*[a]	*	22.7	7.6	22.7	6.8	*	*	23.4	5.9
1810–19	23.2	6.8	27.3	6.1	22.4	7.4	23.0	6.5	(30.7	3.8)[b]	23.5	5.5
1820–29	23.3	6.8	24.6	6.9	22.2	7.5	22.8	6.0	25.8	5.2	23.4	5.6
1830–39	21.9	7.5	21.8	7.8	21.7	7.6	22.7	6.9	23.2	5.9	22.6	6.1
1840–49	20.6	8.0	20.3	8.3	21.2	8.1	21.7	7.2	20.7	7.2	21.0	6.8
1850–59	20.2	8.0	19.9	8.2	20.7	8.1	20.8	7.6	20.9	6.9	20.9	6.7
1860–69	20.6	7.5	20.6	7.6	20.3	7.7	20.9	7.0	20.9	6.8	20.8	6.5
1870–79	21.4	6.7	21.6	6.9	20.7	6.9	20.9	6.3	21.3	6.1	20.9	5.9
1880–89	21.6	6.0	21.8	6.1	20.5	6.2	19.8	5.7	21.2	5.6	20.8	5.2
1890–99	21.7	5.0	21.9	5.1	20.8	4.8	20.0	5.1	21.1	4.7	20.8	4.5
TOTAL	21.4	6.7	21.4	6.7	21.4	7.4	21.5	6.5	21.3	5.7	21.4	5.9

Note: Table includes only first marriages of women who married from age 10 through 44 and have complete fertility histories; omits women with zero parity.

[a]Asterisks indicate fewer than 20 cases.

[b]Parentheses indicate fewer than 100 cases.

TABLE 30

MARITAL AGE-SPECIFIC FERTILITY RATES AND MEASURES OF CONTROL, BY RELIGIOUS AFFILIATION AND RESIDENTIAL GROUP, FOR BIRTH COHORTS 1830–1859 AND 1860–1889

Birth Cohorts 1830–1859

	Age at Birth of Children										
	15–19	20–24	25–29	30–34	35–39	40–44	45–49	MTFR	m	M	MSE
Religious Affiliation[a]											
(1)	459.9	466.9	428.3	390.3	333.5	185.6	26.4	11.45	−.063	.985	.0007
(2)	421.5	470.8	424.3	396.1	346.3	201.3	29.3	11.45	−.118	.974	.0016
(3)	438.0	447.6	413.5	372.1	304.0	166.1	33.2	10.87	−.008	.958	.0004
(4)	439.6	456.2	412.5	365.6	296.2	155.1	19.6	10.73	.048	.976	.0002
(5)	386.3	399.8	368.8	320.9	259.7	135.3	18.8	9.45	.056	.863	.0002
Residential Group[b]											
(1)	445.2	469.4	419.3	378.4	306.3	167.0	24.2	11.05	.017	.992	.0006
(2)	453.6	456.3	415.6	379.0	322.7	178.3	24.8	11.15	−.052	.961	.0007
(3)	444.9	460.6	426.5	390.5	346.2	191.7	28.3	11.44	−.100	.970	.0008
(4)	441.3	469.2	440.8	404.1	356.0	207.0	33.2	11.76	−.131	.987	.0012

Birth Cohorts 1860–1889

Religious Affiliation[a]											
(1)	466.9	449.4	379.3	316.6	245.2	120.1	14.3	9.96	.210	.950	.0004
(2)	452.2	440.6	382.6	321.6	259.0	141.4	14.9	10.06	.095	.918	.0018
(3)	451.5	440.4	351.2	290.4	210.2	106.4	11.8	9.31	.287	.913	.0015
(4)	472.1	435.0	356.3	280.6	211.1	98.3	14.0	9.34	.328	.919	.0005
(5)	430.8	419.6	328.6	258.4	199.5	93.1	14.8	8.72	.330	.865	.0016
Residential Group[6]											
(1)	444.0	443.7	358.6	283.8	208.4	97.6	11.1	9.19	.336	.923	.0003
(2)	469.6	449.6	379.4	319.4	249.8	124.4	15.3	10.04	.186	.946	.0006
(3)	450.9	450.2	372.8	312.6	243.2	126.9	15.3	9.86	.177	.932	.0015
(4)	481.1	454.0	393.6	340.1	279.7	139.2	17.9	10.53	.107	.959	.0005

[a]Religious Affiliation:
(1) Lifetime Commitment
(2) Converts
(3) Partial Association
(4) Nonactive
(5) Non-LDS

[b]Residential Group:
(1) Stable Central-Area Residents
(2) Stable Agricultural-Area Residents
(3) Mobile Central-Area Residents
(4) Mobile Agricultural-Area Residents

COMBINED SOCIAL HETEROGENEITIES AND INTERPRETATION

In reviewing the two indices developed from these data, one observes that each can basically be summarized by a few contrasting categories (Goodman 1981). The contrasting residential categories for the cohorts born in the first half of the nineteenth century are (1) migrants into differing types of communities and (2) stable residents of any given type of community. For the second half of the century, one can contrast (1) stable central residents and (2) all others. The contrasting religious categories from the 1820s through the 1880s are (1) families in which the wife was endowed during her lifetime (lifetime members and converts) and (2) all others. We can thus select a smaller number of highly discriminatory categories that enable these two indices to be cross-classified more easily. To emphasize community development within the new settlements, we will omit families with no Utah births and the first three cohorts, which are affected largely by the timing of their arrival in Utah, as demonstrated in chapter 5. Residential categories are then identified as (a) stable central-area residents (those families in which both the first and last children were born in the three central Utah settlement counties) and (b) mobile and noncentral area residents (those families who either experienced both first and last births in an agricultural settlement area or were residentially mobile, changing the type of community in which they resided). Religious affiliation is reclassified as follows: (a) endowed (those couples in which the wife experienced both baptism and endowment during her lifetime) and (b) nonendowed (those who lack either both rites or only the endowment rite). Thus the endowed represent those highly committed to the LDS church, and the nonendowed represent a group with little or no commitment to the LDS church.

Results of the cross-classification by both residence and religion are presented in table 31. The data are based on first marriages of women who married between ages 10 and 45, who had one or more children, and who survived with their husbands until age 45. Eliminating families broken by the early death of a spouse affects these groupings. Couples in which the wife was not endowed during her lifetime were 4 to 10 percent more likely to suffer the death of a spouse before the wife reached age 45. For example, in the 1870–79 cohort 15 to 16 percent of the endowed couples did not survive through the wife's childbearing years, as compared to 24–26 percent of those not endowed. For the

TABLE 31

FREQUENCY (PERCENTAGE), MEAN AGE AT FIRST MARRIAGE (AM), AND MEAN CHILDREN EVER BORN (CEB), BY RESIDENTIAL GROUP AND RELIGIOUS AFFILIATION

Birth Cohort	Mobile Noncentral Endowed			Stable Central Endowed			Mobile Noncentral Nonendowed			Stable Central Nonendowed		
	%	AM	CEB	%	AM	CEB	%	AM	CEB	%	AM	CEB
1830–39	64.5	21.7	8.8	22.7	22.0	8.2	10.4	22.8	8.0	2.4	25.0	6.0
Standardized[a]						8.3			8.4			6.7
1840–49	61.4	20.3	9.1	24.8	20.7	8.5	10.2	21.0	8.4	3.5	20.5	7.5
Standardized						8.6			8.6			7.6
1850–59	59.7	19.8	9.1	25.1	20.7	8.3	10.3	20.7	8.1	4.9	21.5	7.1
Standardized						8.6			8.4			7.5
1860–69	58.3	20.3	8.4	23.9	21.6	7.3	11.9	20.6	7.6	5.9	21.9	6.5
Standardized						7.7			7.7			6.9
1870–79	58.0	21.3	7.5	23.4	22.5	6.3	12.0	21.1	6.9	6.6	21.9	5.8
Standardized						6.5			6.8			6.0
1880–89	55.7	21.5	6.7	27.0	22.6	5.4	11.1	20.8	6.2	6.2	21.9	4.9
Standardized						5.7			6.1			5.0
1890–99	55.2	21.5	5.6	28.9	22.6	4.4	9.4	20.5	5.5	6.4	21.7	4.0
Standardized						4.6			5.4			4.1

Note: Table includes only first marriages of women who married at ages 10 through 44 and have complete fertility histories; omits women with fewer than two children; omits couples in which one spouse died before the wife reached age 45.

[a]The CEB for groups was standardized on age at marriage using the noncentral/mobile/endowed group as the standard. Three age-at-marriage categories were used: 10–19, 20–24, and 25–44.

cohorts of 1860–69 through 1890–99, there is no differential survival with respect to residence within the endowed group. To control for mortality effects, the following analyses eliminate couples that did not survive throughout the wife's childbearing years.

In order to emphasize the effects of social heterogeneities, a standardized CEB is presented in addition to the observed CEB. The fertility measure has been standardized on a distribution of three age-at-marriage groups using the mobile/noncentral/endowed groups as the standard; this procedure controls for age-at-marriage differences in the composition of the groups. The mobile/noncentral/endowed couples have the highest fertility in all cohorts, and the stable/central/nonendowed have the lowest in all cohorts. The other two groups are similar through the 1860s cohort, but in the last three cohorts mobile/noncentral/nonendowed couples exhibit higher fertility than stable/central/endowed couples. The pace of the fertility transition was more rapid in both of these central settlement groups (declining over 45 percent from 1850–59 to 1890–99) than in noncentral or mobile groups (35 to 38 percent). For the last three cohorts all groups maintained different levels of fertility—both of the mobile/noncentral groups had higher fertility than stable/central groups—but demonstrated some convergence. Religious affiliation still acted as a secondary factor associated with higher fertility, particularly within the stable central area. Among the last birth cohorts in the mobile/noncentral categories, religious differences diminished.

Individuals who made up the more committed religious groups and those who were mobile or had noncentral residences had the highest fertility. Even in natural-fertility cohorts, when these characteristics are combined, one finds very large family sizes, averaging about nine children, and when these characteristics are absent family size averages under eight children. These comparisons indicate the presence of heterogeneous fertility behavior even in a society that seemingly practiced no overall family limitation. All groups, however, did experience the fertility transition simultaneously. A precipitant decline began with the 1860–69 cohort across all categories. Although the groups began to change simultaneously, their rates of change differed. Those individuals with stable central locations during childbearing experienced the greatest decline, while those with other residential patterns declined at a slower rate.

Previous research (Mineau et al. 1984) on once-married couples

(ONEONE) supports these results and allows further interpretation. To capture the dynamic of changing fertility patterns across birth cohorts while avoiding over-categorizing the study population, birth cohorts were entered as a simple dichotomy: before population-wide onset of fertility limitation (birth cohorts 1830–59) and after the onset of fertility limitation (1860–89).

Tabulations presented above do not control for accompanying changes in the proximate determinants of fertility, for example, age at marriage. To overcome this limitation and to capture the interactions among children ever born, religious affiliation, residential status, age at marriage, and age at termination of childbearing, a log-linear analysis was pursued (Fienberg 1977; Goodman 1978).[4] A multidimensional frequency table resulting from classifying the population according to these five variables was used. The basic frequency distributions and categorization of all variables entered into the analysis are presented for "natural-fertility" and "fertility-transition" cohorts in table 32. The central decline in CEB (with 59 percent in 1830–59 having more than eight children, as compared to 31 percent in 1860–89) accompanied an increase in the percentage of women who married after age 20 (37 percent among the earlier cohort, as compared to 46 percent in the later cohort). Finally, those who terminated childbearing after age 39 decreased from 67 percent to 47 percent across the two birth cohorts.

Entering the proximate determinants, children ever born, and ecological subcohorts into the log-linear model, a stepwise logistic strategy was followed to identify significant interactions among the data. The model was fitted separately to natural-fertility and transition birth cohorts to facilitate interpretations. The results of the model-fitting strategy are presented in table 33 (see Mineau et al. 1984 for details and the rationale for the use of log-linear methods). For both models almost all two-way interactions between variables were significant. The absence of a relationship between residential status and age at termination of childbearing in the natural-fertility cohort provides some initial support for the argument that residential status was a less significant determinant of childbearing patterns in the natural-fertility population. Similarly, in the natural-fertility population the only significant three-way interaction was between religious, residential, and age-at-marriage variables. In contrast, the transition cohorts evidenced a complex interaction of residential, age-at-termination, and children-ever-born variables. Thus, the

TABLE 32

FREQUENCY DISTRIBUTION OF VARIABLES USED IN MODEL

Variable	Category	Natural-Fertility Cohorts 1830–59 N	Natural-Fertility Cohorts 1830–59 %	Fertility-Transition Cohorts 1860–89 N	Fertility-Transition Cohorts 1860–89 %
Children	1–4	481	8.48	4,273	22.16
Ever	5–8	1,872	33.01	8,941	46.37
Born	>=9	3,318	58.51	6,082	31.47
		5,671	100.00%	19,282	100.00%
Age at Marriage	<21	3,598	63.45	10,351	53.68
	>=21	2,073	36.55	8,931	46.32
		5,671	100.00%	19,282	100.00%
Age at Termination	<40	1,888	33.29	10,272	53.27
	>=40	3,783	66.71	9,010	46.73
		5,671	100.00%	19,282	100.00%
Religious Affiliation[a]	(1)	3,611	63.67	14,187	73.58
	(2)	995	17.55	1,307	6.78
	(3)	500	8.82	1,036	5.37
	(4)	322	5.68	2,007	10.41
	(5)	243	4.28	745	3.86
		5,671	100.00%	19,282	100.00%
Residential Group[b]	(1)	1,562	27.54	5,989	31.06
	(2)	2,226	39.25	10,156	52.67
	(3)	693	12.22	1,521	7.89
	(4)	1,190	20.98	1,616	8.38
		5,671	100.00%	19,282	100.00%

[a]Religious Affiliation:
(1) Lifetime Commitment
(2) Converts
(3) Partial Association
(4) Nonactive
(5) Non-LDS

[b]Residential Group:
(1) Stable Central Area Residents
(2) Stable Agricultural Area Residents
(3) Mobile Central Area Residents
(4) Mobile Agricultural Area Residents

TABLE 33
STEPWISE FITTING OF THE LOG-LINEAR MODELS

Model	Model Chi-Square	d.f.	Significance Probability	Marginal Chi-Square	d.f.
1830–59 Birth Cohorts					
All Two-Way Effects	213.54	183	.060	—	—
MAR[a] Added	175.98	171	.381	37.56	12
TR Deleted	184.42		.280	8.44	3
Final Model: MAR, CM, CT, CA, CR, MT, TA					
1860–89 Birth Cohorts					
All Two-Way Effects	210.10	183	.083	—	—
CTR[a] Added	188.22	177	.268	21.88	6
Final Model: CTR, CM, CA, MT, MA, MR, TA, AR					

[a]A = religious affiliation
C = children ever born
M = age at marriage
R = residential group
T = age at termination

initial examination of fitted interactions again supports the increasing importance of residential status in efforts to limit childbearing in an age-dependent fashion.

The log-linear method, of course, presents more detailed information on the nature of these interactions in the form of standardized coefficients (lambdas significant at the .05 level if greater than 1.96 or less than −1.96) measuring both the magnitude and direction of the association between particular categories of the variables analyzed. Following Mineau et al. (1984), we present only significant associations in the natural-fertility cohort and present only those which differ in the discussion of the transition cohort.

In the natural-fertility cohort, the effects of religious pronatalism can be seen in the strong associations between the lifetime-commitment groups and family sizes over eight children (lambda = 4.91) and between the non-LDS group and family sizes of less than five (4.08). Residential effects are also present: migrants to agricultural areas are associated with family sizes over eight (2.90) and stable central residents are associated with families of less than five (2.76). Indirect fertility effects of residence are also seen in the association of stable agricultural-area residents with a younger age at marriage (2.93) and in the association of migrants into the central settlement with an older age at marriage (2.36). Religious converts also evidenced their newfound pronatalism by continuing their childbearing to ages beyond 40 (1.94).

Other associations among proximate determinants and fertility levels are as one would expect in a natural-fertility population. A younger age at marriage is associated with a larger family size (11.99), and a younger age at termination of childbearing with a smaller family size (11.34). Women who married under age 21 were more likely to stop childbearing before age 40 (7.10) than those who married later. Residential stability during this early cohort also appears to have been related to religious affiliation through the effects of the proselytizing church. Stable central residents tend to be either among the lifetime-commitment group (5.64) or an enclave of those nonactive in the LDS church (2.38). Stable agricultural-area residents are associated only with the lifetime-commitment groups (6.60). Converts to the church are associated equally with migration into central (3.92) and into agricultural (3.95) settlements.

In summary, among the natural-fertility population with family sizes of five to eight children (12.07) or more (6.03), large families are associated with lifetime religious commitment, migration to an agricultural settlement, and women marrying at younger ages. Conversely, smaller family sizes are associated with the non-LDS, stable central-area residents, and younger ages at termination of childbearing. Even in the natural-fertility cohort some fertility limitation seems to have been present and associated with religious and residential subgroups.

In the fertility-transition birth cohort, lifetime-commitment LDS women are again associated with larger family sizes. However, given the fertility transition, they are associated with families of five to eight (2.59) rather than nine or more children, while converts are associated with the largest family sizes (3.06). The non-LDS group is more strongly associated with residential types. For example, they are negatively related to stable noncentral-area residents (2.99) and are weakly associated with migration to a central area (1.63). At the same time, lifetime-commitment LDS become more strongly associated with stable noncentral settlements (12.12), for there is a consistent shift in the stable agricultural area's association with large families of over eight children (1.95). These findings again support the conclusion that in the central area there emerged an enclave of women with decreased religious commitment and lower fertility in comparison with noncentral residents.

Associations with proximate fertility determinants also support this conclusion. For example, older ages at marriage and younger ages at termination of childbearing, initially associated with mobile central-area residents, came to be associated with stable central-area residents, and at the same time there was a general increase in the significance of the relationship between early termination and the smallest family sizes (23.39). Finally, the interaction of residence and age at termination was significant in the transition cohort, but it was not significant in the earlier, natural-fertility cohort.

SUMMARY

The comparison of the two cohorts—those who seemingly practiced no fertility limitation and those who adopted fertility limitation—indicates that residential status is more significant than religion in explaining variations in the proximate determinants of fertility in the second cohort. Relationships involving religious or residential subgroups with fertility patterns demonstrate an increasing division between religious pronatalism and the rise of secularism in the central-area settlements. Again, the interaction of effects of pronatalist ideologies and secularization through urbanism appears significant. The process by which pronatalist ideologies originally dominate fertility differentials and are progressively encroached upon by forces of urbanism and secularization is apparent over the course of the transition to fertility limitation.

These results support the examination of subgroup fertility differentials in assessing the relative importance of religious, socioeconomic, and minority status for fertility behavior. In a setting widely divergent from Chamie's (1981) multireligious population in the Middle East or Ron Lesthaeghe's Belgian population (1977), we find support for the particularized ideology hypothesis and the characteristics hypothesis, which are merged in Chamie's interaction hypothesis. Moreover, the longitudinal nature of the current study demonstrates a likely course of social change among ideological and social forces consistent with, and bridging the gap between, both historical European (Day 1968) and contemporary American (Ryder and Westoff 1971) studies. In the Utah population it is clear that the increasing urbanism of central settlements led to a long-term increase in the importance of socioeconomic characteristics and a corresponding decline in the significance of religious pronatalism. Yet, over the entire course of the fertility transition and settlement, both factors remained significant and in interaction. These findings are, of course, specific for the time period studied and may vary from contemporary conditions.

Equally important is the fact that, despite such effects, the fertility transition transcended these religious and residential groupings as all subgroups of the population moved to lower fertility levels with the progress of the settlement process. It is this finding that provides a basis for questioning the utility of the notion of fertility limitation as being spread through processes of innovation and diffusion. The findings are consistent with those of Carlsson, upon which he based his argument in favor of adaptation. In spite of differences in origin, time of arrival on the frontier, religious affiliation, or residential exposure, all groups initiated fertility limitation at about the same time and experienced roughly parallel precipitous declines in fertility.

While the analysis of subgroups has highlighted possible patterns of social change related to fertility declines, it does not adequately account for such dramatic declines in fertility across subgroups of the population. An attempt to isolate changes in individual fertility behaviors within the population is necessary to provide insight into the changes allowing or provoking fertility declines in nearly all segments of the population. It is to such a further decomposition at the level of individual behavior that the following chapter turns.

CHAPTER 7

Adaptive and Innovative Influences I

The Individual Life Course

George Homans, in his presidential address to the American Sociological Association, reminded us that the acts of individuals are ultimately the source or conduit of social change, no matter how socially motivated or socially constrained individual behavior may be (1964). This theme has been recently echoed in such diverse works as James Coleman's reanalysis of early capital accumulation (1986) and Tilly's call for a greater emphasis on collective action in social history (1981). Reflecting such concerns, behavioral scientists from a number of disciplines have become increasingly concerned with the linkage between macrolevel (aggregate) phenomena and microlevel (individual) phenomena. In contrast to the previous chapters' ecological focus, the analysis presented in this chapter has been undertaken to address such concerns. It is our intent in this chapter and the following one to go beyond the typical analyses of historical fertility patterns and trends in an attempt to address the actual individual-level behavioral changes associated with the fertility transition in our frontier population. The goal that we seek cannot be attained directly, and therefore it is essential to adopt a research strategy consistent with the limitations of historical data.

ANALYTICAL STRATEGY

In the absence of direct individual information on certain important variables, the analytical strategy used in this chapter involves the sequential assesssment and the successive elimination of alternative explanations. Therefore, through successive consideration of variations in behavior that produce differences in family size within and between cohorts, we propose to determine the degree to which the rapid fall in frontier fertility cannot be explained without the postulation of conscious voluntary acts to limit family size. Finally, we attempt to distinguish between those consciously directed, voluntary acts that were primarily responsive to changing social and economic conditions—that is, adaptive behavior—and those that represented solely innovative behavior.

As noted in chapter 1, Kingsley Davis and Judith Blake (1955) and John Bongaarts (1978) have created useful schemata for the organization of analyses dealing with individual behavior determining fertility. The analysis in this chapter is heavily dependent upon Bongaarts's specification of the proximate determinants of fertility. This classification is useful not simply because it systematically identifies the range of such forms of behavior but also because it provides a starting point for distinguishing between voluntary and involuntary fertility determinants.

A voluntary act that affects fertility may be consciously intended for that purpose. However, the same act in another context may be consciously selected for a different purpose, so that effects on fertility are incidental. Sterility (or infecundity), for example, may result from health and sexual practices that were not intended to limit fertility. In a number of African nations, frequent and widespread premarital sexual experimentation among a population with a high prevalence of gonorrhea has caused a high level of sterility and thus produced, unintentionally, lower-than-desired levels of childbearing; that is, the supply of children (Easterlin and Crimmins 1985) is less than the demand for children.

A typically voluntary act, postponement of marriage, reduces the number of years of potential childbearing—other things being equal—and thus reduces fertility. The decision to delay marriage may be voluntary and consciously adopted to limit final family size (Malthus 1965), but more often the decision to delay marriage is consciously made for economic or other reasons, with little concern for the ultimate effects on family size and childbearing.

These illustrations clearly indicate that any study of fertility which purports to examine individual motives must distinguish, to the extent possible, between involuntary and voluntary fertility determinants. Within the class of voluntary determinants, a distinction must also be made between those that represent conscious acts to limit family size and those to which childbearing is motivationally incidental. To make such distinctions is difficult under the best of circumstances. Historical studies are particularly limited in that the data that can be used to clarify such issues is incomplete, regardless of the amount of detailed information that might be accessible. Thus while there are enormous difficulties to be faced in determining changes in voluntary, intentional limitation of family size, several logical, methodological strategies can improve our estimation of these effects.

First, in the previous chapters we have demonstrated at the aggregate level that fertility changes are responsive to simple changes in the composition of the population, changes that may be independent of any modification of individual decision-making patterns.

Second, changes that might be associated with shifts in involuntary factors affecting fertility behavior may be estimated by means of a variety of procedures developed in recent years. Thus in the second section of this chapter, we explicate a model and related estimation procedures that provide such insights.

Third, we draw theoretical guidance from models of fertility behavior developed by economists. These models begin with the assumption that individuals (and couples) act within a framework of "bounded rationality" in assessing behavioral alternatives. That is, individuals make decisions within a limited time frame and possess incomplete or limited information. In such models the factors affecting an individual's decisions to have children (or limit family size) are either *tastes* (*norms*) or *costs*—the utility function and budget constraint of neoclassical economic theorists (Becker 1960). The problem faced by the researcher then is to develop a strategy to evaluate possible costs as plausible explanations of fertility change. For example, assume we have data for a historical population in which the involuntary determinants of fertility are randomly distributed. If, at a given time, subgroups that are assumed to have similar childbearing costs exhibit different fertility levels, then the fertility differences must be presumed to reflect normative (taste) differences among the subcohorts. Of course, further analysis might reveal some hitherto hidden differences in the structure of childbearing costs.

The elimination strategy, however, is confounded when one moves beyond a comparative static view of the fertility decision-making process into the "kaledic" realities of dynamic social change. Within this context, Nicholas Georgescu-Roegen (1971), G. L. S. Shackle (1972), and others have noted that the comparative static approach emphasizes an adaptive view of changing behavior; that is, it ascribes changes in fertility decisions to individuals who are adapting to changes in the costs of, and tastes for, childbearing. When the temporal processes of innovation occur, the comparative static model loses much of its explanatory power. Even the basic assumption of bounded rationality becomes speculative as individuals scan their futures to reach decisions that are not dependent simply on the short-run cost structure. The "infinite" costs of controlling fertility, presumed in the characterization of pretransition populations as lacking the knowledge of means to limit fertility, are radically altered through the introduction of contraceptive innovations. In such cases, the innovation and diffusion of the means to limit fertility drive the fertility decision-making process, by determining the decision-making conditions. The adaptive content of the rational decision-making model becomes a mere conduit through which social change is manifested, rather than a source of the explanation. Alternatively, if the novelty or innovation driving fertility change is one of tastes, then again the primary driving force of social change is largely exogenous to the adaptive decision-making model. In either case the historian is led to adopt adaptation as a given individual-level process and seek explanation of the innovative changes within costs of and tastes for childbearing.

In a broad sense then, both innovation and adaptation are involved in all processes of social change. However, we need not confine ourselves to such broad characterizations when dealing with the onset of fertility control in a particular population. With respect to fertility transitions, recent research has provided guidelines for distinguishing more precisely between the processes of innovation and adaptation (Carlsson 1966; Knodel 1979). Innovation explanations may be characterized as those in which the decision maker is presented with fundamentally altered possibilities for childbearing by the introduction of new variables into the decision-making context (e.g., contraceptive methods). Adaptation explanations may be simply characterized as those which attribute fertility change to changing values within existing frameworks of decision making. These characterizations are most aptly translated into behavioral expectations by Carlsson (1966); according to him, innovation explanations imply the introduction and diffusion of new factors and, hence, the likelihood of new forms of fertility behavior in a population. Adaptation explanations, in contrast, assume only compositional changes in behavior within the population arising from a changing composition of extant tastes and costs. Although it is possible that subtle innovations may arise without obvious behavioral consequences, the burden of proof lies with those who would postulate an innovation when the behavior can be explained without presuming such a discontinuity (Tilly 1986). Finally, it is likely that any social change as considerable as a fertility transition involves both adaptation and innovation. The question in all empirical settings must be one of the sequence and explanatory power of such changes.

The tasks we approach in this chapter and in the remainder of the volume are thus formidable ones. First, we seek to identify, on an individual level, the precise voluntary and involuntary factors underlying the fertility transition. To this end, we employ techniques commonplace among contemporary demographers who investigate the importance of selected proximate fertility determinants (Bongaarts 1978). Second, focusing on voluntary determinants of fertility, we investigate the differential patterns of change in these proximate fertility determinants within significant social groupings that reflect the major heterogeneities in both tastes and costs of childbearing within the population. Third, we approach the task of identifying and characterizing those specific changes in individual-level behaviors over the course of the transition that are principally responsible for the fertility decline. Finally, through an analysis of specific fertility behaviors, we provide an eliminative and demonstrative investigation addressing the potentially innovative or adaptive character of such changes. In this chapter we confine ourselves to behavioral changes within the population and its significant social groupings. In the chapter that follows we will take up similar questions, with a stronger emphasis on geographic heterogeneity and diffusion.

PROXIMATE DETERMINANTS OF FERTILITY

With historical data, the opportunity seldom arises to examine the complete set of proximate determinants (Bongaarts and Potter 1983) of fertility comprehensively. In fact, many of these determinants (e.g., risks of spontaneous abortion, contraceptive efficacy, primary sterility) are extremely difficult to measure even within contemporary populations. Nonetheless, it is possible to assess many of the most significant proximate determinants of fertility for historical populations. Perhaps the most important of these fertility effects in typical historical populations is simply the exposure to childbearing within marriage. Thus if the analysis is of marital fertility (rather than births out of wedlock), then age at marriage, risk of widowhood, divorce, and remarriage are foremost among the proximate determinants for which historical data is often available. When histories of individual events are available, many more proximate determinants, such as the duration of postpartum amenorrhea, and fecundability, can be estimated. Finally, for more problematic and less sensitive proximate determinants, such as infecundability following spontaneous abortion, approximate estimates suitable for the historical population can be drawn from secondary data sources and validated through relatively simple calculations of consistency or through simulations.

To simplify our calculation of proximate determinants in the Utah population, we continue to examine once-married couples. In addition, we restrict our attention to women who survived at least through age 49. In this study population, marital disruption occurred primarily through widowhood. (Divorce was negligible among this population of women.) The most common device for summarizing patterns of age at first marriage in populations is the marriage curve presented by Coale and D. R. McNeil (1972). The distribution of age at first marriage can be fitted to such a curve through estimates of either the mean age at first marriage and earliest age at which first marriages occur in the population or the mean age at first marriage and its standard deviation. All three parameters are presented in table 34 for five-year birth cohorts of once-married surviving women spanning the decline in fertility within the population. The data for four selected cohorts are summarized graphically in figure 15 by means of the marriage curves.

Across the cohorts examined, the mean age at marriage rose by less than one year for once-married surviving women. This delay of marriage was accompanied by a smaller variance (that is, a faster pace) in the age at marriage. This increasing homogeneity of age at marriage within the population is consistent with Anderton's (1986*a*) finding that immigrant groups within the population converged around a similar age at marriage as intermarriage among the groups became more common. The increasing mean age at marriage is also consistent with results for the population as a whole and was clearly one of the significant changing proximate determinants of fertility within the population.

The principle source of disruption in marital unions over the cohorts examined was the death of a spouse. Thus, for once-married surviving women the risks of marital disruption are easily estimated through the risk of widowhood. Table 35 presents the estimated mean yearly risks of widowhood. The data are grouped into three twenty-five-year cohorts to achieve reliable estimates of mortality. Clearly the risks of widowhood declined across all ages as mortality conditions improved in

TABLE 34

INITIAL AGE AT FIRST MARRIAGE AND MEAN AGE AT FIRST MARRIAGE, BY WIFE'S BIRTH COHORT, 1840–1899

Birth Cohort	Initial Age at First Marriage	Mean Age at First Marriage	Standard Deviation	N
1840–44	12	20.85	4.27	811
1845–49	10	20.35	3.82	1,025
1850–54	12	20.06	3.79	1,468
1855–59	11	20.14	3.45	2,125
1860–64	10	20.47	3.54	2,682
1865–69	10	20.76	3.64	2,933
1870–74	10	21.31	3.73	3,266
1875–79	10	21.76	3.63	3,496
1880–84	10	21.70	3.54	3,742
1885–89	11	21.71	3.55	3,665
1890–94	13	21.88	3.64	3,352
1895–99	10	21.57	3.56	2,931

Note: Because families in which both husband and wife were missing death dates were excluded from the analysis, the N size in the last three cohorts declines. The majority of those probably were individuals who had not died at the time that the family-group sheet was completed, and for whom the family-group sheet was not updated after their death. Some small proportion of these people are still alive.

Source: J. Dennis Willigan et. al., "A Macrosimulation Approach to the Investigation of Natural Fertility," *Demography* 19, 2 (1982): 165.

the later cohorts. However, the risks of widowhood were not extreme in any cohort and fluctuations were relatively minor. While widowhood undoubtedly influenced fertility, its effect was probably minor even in this once-married population of women. Among women who could remarry, widowhood would, of course, be even less influential, as has been argued with respect to many European populations (Coale 1986; J. Smith 1981). Given the negligible role of divorce in the Utah frontier population, these results suggest that changing patterns of marital disruption were not a major factor in the fertility decline. The increasing proportion of marriages that remained intact until the wife reached age 49 would, in fact, have tended to increase fertility slightly.

Marriage patterns, marital disruption, sterility, and birth-interval distributions combine to determine age-order-specific births in a population (Bongaarts 1978). Sterility, however, is difficult to estimate—the

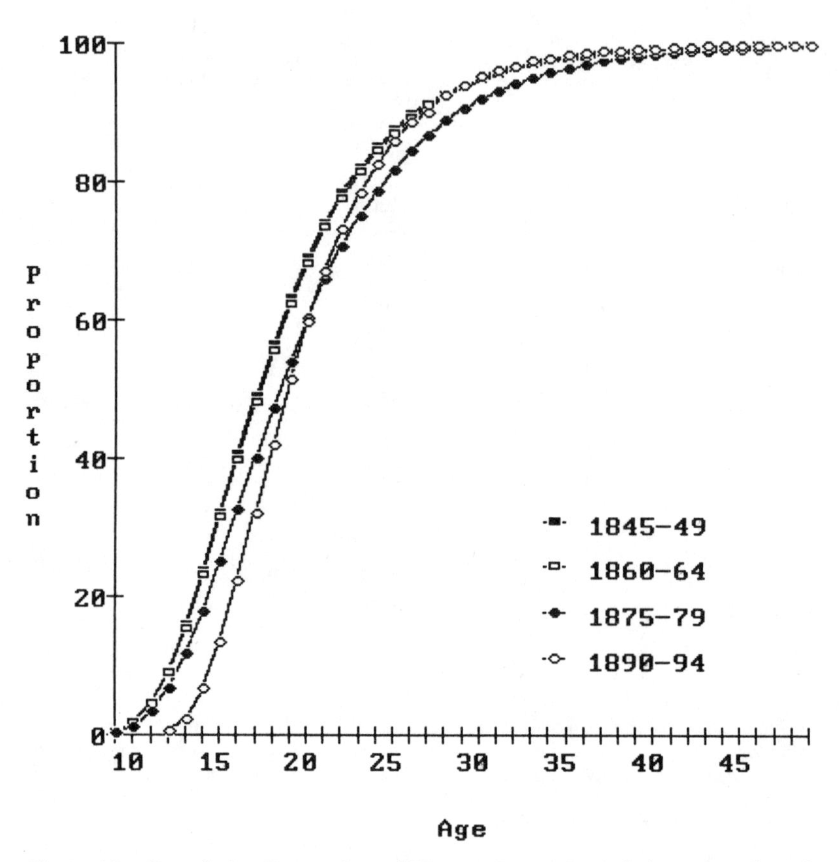

Figure 15. Cumulative Proportion of Women Ever-Married, for Selected Birth Cohorts

more so with genealogical data in which individuals with no surviving children are less likely to be recorded (Mineau and Anderton 1983). Fortunately, there is little reason to suspect abnormal levels of sterility or sterility change within the population. Given the relatively minor sensitivity of fertility levels to reasonable age-specific sterility schedules, it is not surprising that the assumption of a typical infecundability associated with sterility (Henry 1961) has proven sufficiently accurate for both the Utah population (Willigan et al. 1982) and other natural fertility populations (Bongaarts 1975).

The remaining proximate determinants are then those which contribute to the distribution of birth intervals within a population: fecundability, postpartum amenorrhea, spontaneous and induced abor-

TABLE 35

ESTIMATED MEAN YEARLY RISK OF WIDOWHOOD PER 1,000 WOMEN AND NUMBER WIDOWED, BY WIFE'S BIRTH COHORT (GROUPED), 1825–1899

Birth Cohorts	<14	15–19	20–24	25–29	30–34	35–39	40–44	45–49	50
1825–49	0.0	3.00	0.82	1.55	2.84	5.29	7.58	10.42	11.17
Number	0	7	8	22	50	85	109	162	36
1850–74	0.0	1.78	0.78	1.34	2.38	4.11	6.60	9.86	11.63
Number	0	11	34	76	133	257	397	570	131
1875–99	0.0	1.83	0.95	1.20	2.02	3.57	5.69	9.10	10.60
Number	0	11	48	96	175	309	469	645	162

Source: J. Dennis Willigan et. al., "A Macrosimulation Approach to the Investigation of Natural Fertility," *Demography* 19, 2 (1982): 167.

tion, and contraceptive use and efficacy. Bongaarts (1975) has provided methods to estimate natural fecundability within a population given there is no delay of first birth. The simplest means of estimating mean fecundability is to use Bongaarts's tabulated values for mean fecundability, which correspond to ratios of the sum of births in the ninth, tenth, and eleventh months of marriage, to all first births. The results of this extrapolation are plotted in figure 16 for five-year birth cohorts. Prior to 1885 there was a generally consistent increase in mean fecundability, compatible with generally improving health conditions. The decline in fecundability in the later cohorts is most likely an artifact of the method of estimation. It is possible that women in these later cohorts, who had most of their first births between 1905 and 1925, actually delayed first births within marriage. Changes in mean fecundability are certainly not sufficient to explain the decline in fertility among Utah women and were in fact conducive to increasingly higher fertility over much of the period of fertility decline.

Using a select group of once-married couples, those in which both spouses survived, it is possible to estimate mean postpartum infecundability in the population by subtracting the mean birth-interval following births of infants who died at less than 2 weeks old from the mean interval following births of children who survived to 2 years of age or older. The former birth intervals were not significantly affected by lactation; but the latter birth intervals presumably were, since women whose

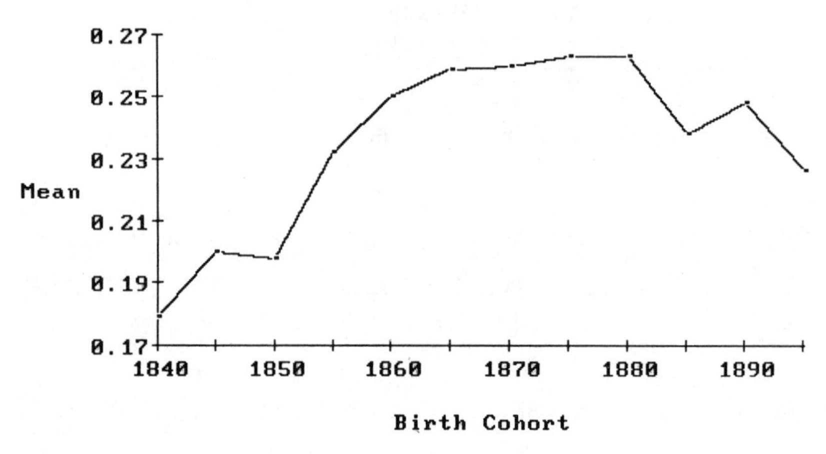

Figure 16. Estimated Mean Fecundability

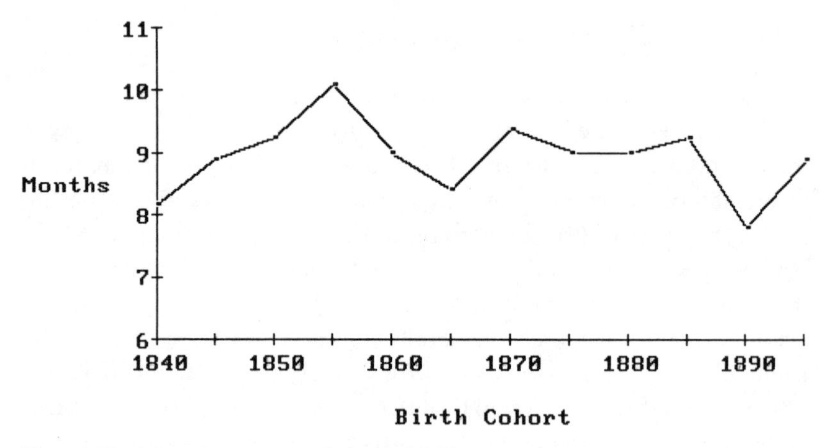

Figure 17. Mean Postpartum Infecundability

children survived at least until age 2 would likely have followed a typical pattern of breastfeeding and thereby would have experienced prolonged infecundability. The difference between these two mean intervals provides an indicative estimate of postpartum infecundability and is plotted in figure 17. During early cohorts there was a steady rise in postpartum infecundability, possibly associated with a greater reliance on breastfeeding in the settlement population. Although these estimates are not highly robust, it is fairly safe to say that from 1860 to 1899, that is, the cohorts of substantial fertility decline, postpartum infecundability fluctuated around nine months' duration, with a further decline possibly suggested by the final two cohorts. Again, the trends in postpartum amenorrhea likely did not substantially affect the fertility decline.

As in the case of sterility, it is very difficult to estimate risks of spontaneous and induced abortion among historical populations. In the contemporary population, induced abortion is becoming more widely recorded, but it is still generally underreported. Spontaneous abortion has been reliably estimated only in demanding artificial insemination experiments. Fortunately, there is sufficient circumstantial evidence to rule out any substantial role of induced abortion in the religiously pronatalist Utah population. However, we can do little more to clarify the role of spontaneous abortion than to suggest that trends were probably inversely related to natural fecundability and were at approximately the levels estimated by F. E. French and J. Bierman for the Hawaiian population (1962). The French-Bierman value has been shown sufficiently accurate for the Utah population (Willigan et al. 1982), and Bongaarts (1975) also found the value plausible for other historical populations. The sensitivity of the Utah population's general fertility levels to spontaneous abortions was likely minimal, and there is clearly no reason to suspect any changes in risks of spontaneous abortion sufficient to account for the dramatic fertility decline in the Utah population.

The remaining proximate determinants of fertility, that is, contraceptive use and efficacy, require more extensive estimation methods than the above determinants, which later cohorts held in common with the natural-fertility cohorts. Before turning to such estimates it is necessary to validate the estimates presented for other proximate determinants and evaluate their possible explanation of fertility trends within the population; that is, to assess the role that these determinants of fertility, which it is plausible to say were involuntary, played in the onset of fertility limitation.

VALIDATING ESTIMATES OF "INVOLUNTARY" PROXIMATE DETERMINANTS

Erring on the side of caution, we may assume that the proximate determinants examined thus far reflect involuntary fertility limitation; that is, while any of the above determinants can be affected by voluntary behavior (and possibly manipulated to curtail fertility; e.g., marriage can be delayed), they cannot be demonstrably connected to fertility decision-making in a historical setting without qualitative motivational data. The

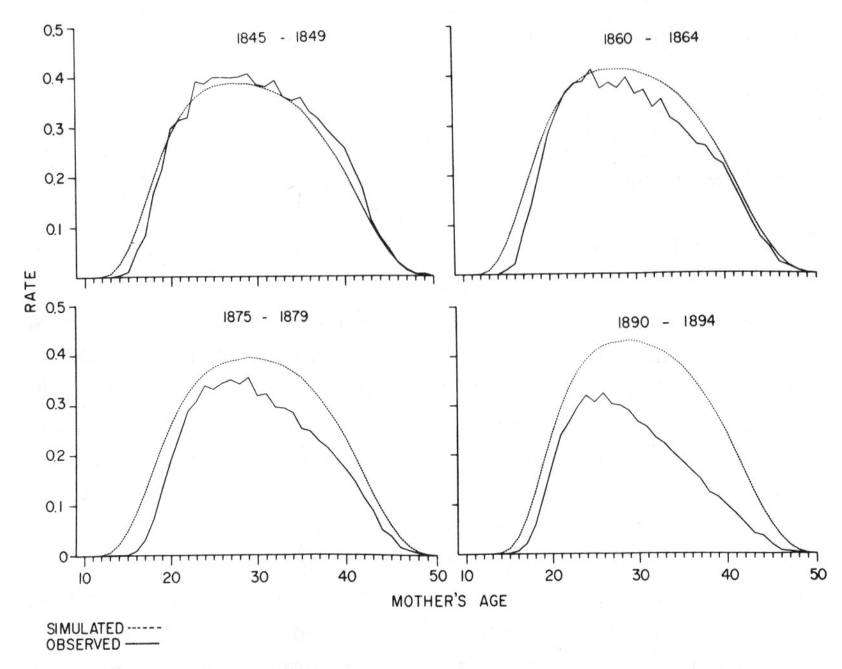

Figure 18. Observed and Simulated Age-Specific Fertility Rates by Wife's Birth Cohort, for Selected Birth Cohorts

Source: J. Dennis Willigan, et. al., "A Macrosimulation Approach to the Investigation of Natural Fertility," *Demography* 19, 2 (1982): 170.

most natural way to validate estimates for involuntary proximate determinants would be to compare the fertility behavior they imply with the observable fertility patterns of the population prior to the widespread onset of fertility limitation. Bongaarts's macrosimulation model (1976) provides such an opportunity. Making the minor additional assumption that natural-fertility cohorts did not have a limit on desired family size and using the estimated and assumed values for proximate determinants detailed in the previous section, Willigan et al. (1982) and Anderton et al. (1984) have compared simulated fertility levels to observed age-order-specific fertility patterns. Figure 18 reproduces the plot of observed and simulated age-specific fertility rates for four birth cohorts of women: 1845–49, 1860–64, 1875–79, and 1890–94. The ability of the simulation to reproduce fertility patterns so accurately for the 1845–49 "natural-fertility cohort" provides substantial confirmation of the adequacy of the estimated proximate determinants.

The use of simulation methods not only confirms the estimates of proximate determinants but, through sensitivity analysis, provides an indication of the potential causal significance of each determinant over the course of the transition. We find that results for the Utah population

(Willigan et al. 1982) are generally consistent with those of Bongaarts (1976). Excluding contraceptive parameters, fertility rates were found most sensitive to mean age at marriage, less sensitive to duration of postpartum amenorrhea, and less sensitive still to natural fecundability. Only risk of widowhood had less effect than the two determinants requiring strong assumptions (i.e., sterility and risk of spontaneous abortion).

Finally, simulation methods can also estimate the degree to which proximate determinants other than voluntary contraceptive control account for the population's fertility decline. There is no significant difference between the simulated natural-fertility rates and observed rates for birth cohorts between 1840 and 1859. The simulated rates are, however, significantly higher than those observed for all cohorts after 1860, indicating an onset of contraceptive controls. These differences are clearly evident in the panels for 1860–64, 1875–79, and 1890–94 in figure 18. The differences in simulated and observed rates also indicate that the effects of contraceptive control were far more dramatic than any accounted for by "involuntary" fertility determinants. The percentage reduction between observed rates and simulated natural-fertility rates for the 1875–79 birth cohort ranged from approximately 10 percent at ages 25–29 to nearly 30 percent at ages 40–44. By the 1890–94 birth cohort the reduction in age-specific fertility rates was nearly 30 percent for those 25–29 and over 60 percent for those 40–44. Clearly, voluntary fertility limitation was the most significant factor in the decline of fertility among Utah women.

INTRODUCING VOLUNTARY FERTILITY LIMITATION AMONG SOCIAL GROUPS

Having been used to confirm the sufficiency of the estimated proximate determinants of fertility above, simulation techniques may also be used to estimate contraceptive use and efficacy. These parameters may be examined across all plausible values to determine which estimates most accurately replicate the populations' fertility patterns after the fertility decline began.

A further attractive feature of Bongaarts's simulation model is its ability to incorporate possible population heterogeneities. We (Anderton et al. 1984) fitted the contraceptive parameters necessary to simulate controlled fertility in the population, using the four subcohorts defined in the previous chapter by the intersection of two dichotomies: endowed versus nonendowed, and stable/central settlements versus

TABLE 36

MEAN CHILDREN EVER BORN, PROPORTIONATE SIZE, ESTIMATED BIRTH ORDER AT CONTRACEPTIVE INITIATION, MAXIMUM BIRTH-ORDER, AND CONTRACEPTIVE EFFICACY FOR COHORTS, 1840–1899

Birth Cohort	Mean CEB/(Proportion)				Birth Order at Contraceptive Initiation/Maximum Birth-Order				Contraception Efficacy
	(1)	(2)	(3)	(4)	(1)	(2)	(3)	(4)	
1840–44	9.0	9.3	8.3	8.0	. . .	. . .	. . .	. . .	0.00
	(0.22)	(0.63)	(0.03)	(0.12)	22	22	22	22	
1845–49	8.7	9.2	7.1	8.8	. . .	. . .	. . .	. . .	0.00
	(0.24)	(0.58)	(0.04)	(0.14)	22	22	22	22	
1850–54	8.2	9.2	7.5	8.3	. . .	. . .	. . .	. . .	0.00
	(0.24)	(0.60)	(0.05)	(0.11)	21	22	20	21	
1855–59	8.3	9.0	7.5	8.0	5	6	4	4	0.15
	(0.26)	(0.54)	(0.07)	(0.13)	17	18	16	16	
1860–64	7.4	8.6	6.5	7.9	3	4	2	3	0.40
	(0.24)	(0.56)	(0.06)	(0.14)	15	16	14	15	
1865–69	7.1	8.2	6.3	7.2	2	3	1	2	0.55
	(0.24)	(0.57)	(0.06)	(0.13)	14	15	13	14	

1870–74	6.6	7.6	6.0	7.3	2	3	1	2	0.55
	(0.24)	(0.56)	(0.07)	(0.13)	12	13	11	12	
1875–79	5.9	7.1	5.2	6.5	2	3	1	3	0.65
	(0.23)	(0.60)	(0.06)	(0.11)	10	11	9	11	
1880–84	5.6	6.9	4.7	6.1	2	3	1	2	0.70
	(0.26)	(0.57)	(0.06)	(0.11)	9	10	8	9	
1885–89	5.3	6.2	4.7	6.0	3	3	2	3	0.75
	(0.27)	(0.57)	(0.06)	(0.10)	9	9	8	9	
1890–94	4.8	5.8	4.0	5.6	2	3	1	3	0.80
	(0.30)	(0.54)	(0.07)	(0.09)	8	9	7	9	
1895–99	4.2	5.4	3.8	5.5	2	3	2	4	0.85
	(0.32)	(0.54)	(0.06)	(0.08)	8	9	8	10	

(1) Endowed/Central Area
(2) Endowed/Noncentral Area
(3) Nonendowed/Central Area
(4) Nonendowed/Noncentral Area

Source: Douglas L. Anderton, et. al., "Adoption of Fertility Limitation in an American Frontier Population," *Social Biology* 31, 1–2 (1985): 150.

other residential groups. For an analysis of proximate determinants and individual fertility behavior, these cohorts represent the major a priori dimensions across which variations in both the tastes and costs of childbearing can be anticipated.

Three contraceptive parameters were fitted in each subcohort simulation: contraceptive efficacy, maximum birth-order, and parity at which contraceptive use was initiated. On the basis of the roughly parallel decline in family sizes across the four subcohorts documented in earlier chapters, parity at initiation of contraception and maximum birth-order were estimated across the four subcohorts as only two parameters—some number "*n*" of births less than, and some number "*m*" of births greater than, the observed mean CEB for the subcohort, retrospectively.[1] Maximum birth-orders, and hence "*m*," were fixed by empirical observation. Contraceptive efficacy and the parity at initiation of contraception (i.e., CEB $-n$) were estimated by seeking values that accurately reproduced observed fertility patterns. The results of the simulation are reprinted (from Anderton et al. 1984) in table 36.

This strategy, using the simulation model, estimates fertility behavior within prespecified subcohorts, as discussed above. Of course, different specifications of subcohorts might result in different estimates of behavior. However, two features of the Utah fertility decline suggest that the specification of subcohorts above is adequate. First, other analyses indicate that changes in both completed fertility and fertility timing during the general decline were widely distributed throughout the population and not confined to small groups of women (Anderton and Bean 1985). This eliminates the possibility that estimated contraceptive effects are the result of mixtures of women who control fertility effectively and women who do not practice fertility control. Second, the four subcohorts employed in the simulation reflect the results of our earlier log-linear analysis, which used more detailed classifications of the population. These subcohorts, then, represent the most significant contrasts in completed fertility from the prior analyses. While each of these subcohorts is clearly heterogeneous, there is no evidence of more clearly homogeneous behavioral groups with any substantively identifiable social basis.

Contraceptive efficacy increased dramatically over the onset of family limitation. Defined as the monthly probability of averting conception, efficacy went from effectively zero during natural-fertility cohorts to 85 percent by the 1895–99 cohort. This increase in efficacy, however, may be due either to innovative, or "new," behaviors or to adaptations that resulted in the increasing use or spread of existing behaviors throughout the population.

Maximum birth-orders declined from approximately twenty to around nine children over the cohorts. More surprisingly, the only reasonable fits obtained for the simulation imply that women began very early in their married lives to try to limit fertility through contraception—at parities ranging from around five for the 1855–59 cohort to under three for the 1895–99 cohort. Thus the simulation results would suggest that the initial cohorts, among whom the fertility decline is first observed, employed relatively ineffective contraceptive behaviors over a substantial range of childbearing. As the decline in fertility proceeded, contraceptive efficacy increased and the range of parities over which it was applied decreased despite an initiation of contraceptive behaviors earlier in married life.

Since parity at initiation of contraception and maximum birth-order were estimated as simple displacements from mean CEB within substantive subcohorts, it is not surprising that these parameters reflect the same trends as CEB. It is also impossible, from the simulation alone, entirely to rule out the possibility that some alternative specification of heterogeneities might reproduce observed rates without the implication of contraceptive behavior over such a wide span of the period of childbearing control. However, the simulation does clearly demonstrate that such a pattern produces an exemplary fit of simulated and observed rates. The simulated and observed values are plotted in figure 19 for specific birth cohorts. This exceptional fit, coupled with the fact that the subcohorts employed are those anticipated to reflect the major social heterogeneities in the population, lends credibility to the suggested patterns of behavior from the simulation that deserve further investigation.

The results of these simulations, however, dramatically diverge from the picture obtained through other historical fertility studies of different settings, studies that lack the benefit of longitudinal data on individual behavior. The use of ineffectual contraceptive technologies over a range of parities would, in effect, suggest a substantial lengthening of birth intervals over the course of the fertility decline. Whether these lengthened intervals were the product of deliberate motivations to "space" or "stop" childbearing is less consequential than the effective result of lengthened interbirth intervals or spacing. Most historical studies have not even investigated the possibilities of birth spacing in any thorough fashion, although it is an issue to which attention is now being turned (Knodel 1987). Instead, the common presumption has been that birth

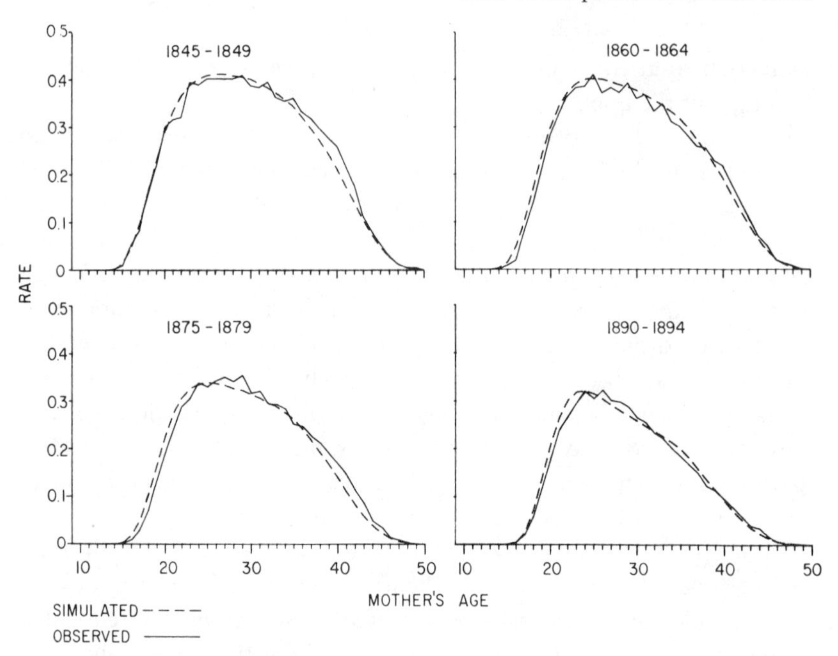

Figure 19. Observed and Simulated Age-Specific Fertility Rates by Wife's Birth Cohort and Subcohorts, for Selected Birth Cohorts

Source: Douglas L. Anderton, et. al., "Adoption of Fertility Limitation in an American Frontier Population," *Social Biology* 31, 1–2 (1985): 154.

intervals are altered only at parities close to some completed-family-size target through failed attempts to truncate childbearing once the desired family size has been achieved. Either truncation of childbearing or lengthened birth intervals may again reflect either innovation or adaptive behaviors. However, the implicit assumption of the prevailing innovation theories has been that truncation of childbearing is sufficient evidence of innovative behavior.

Because the assumption of innovative truncation has been widespread, the most common methods used to measure historical fertility limitation do not acknowledge the possibility that lengthened interbirth intervals play any role in historical fertility declines. For example, Coale and Trussell's M and m indices (used earlier in this volume) would relegate any spacing that did not affect the age at last birth to M, the estimated fertility level, rather than the index of fertility control. However, since longer interbirth intervals would also imply a longer open interval (from last birth to the end of the period of childbearing risk), the index of age-specific fertility limitation, m, would also be affected. Similarly, last closed birth-intervals (between the next-to-last and last birth) are occasionally used for indicators of failed truncation attempts but would also be influenced over time by increased interbirth intervals across parities.

Even declining age at last birth, often thought to be a clear indicator of fertility truncation, is contaminated by both truncation and spacing because increased spacing implies increased interbirth intervals, including the final, open interval. That is, if women space children widely they will have a younger age at termination, unless they abandon the practices leading to longer interbirth intervals in a late attempt to accelerate their fertility. Many other standard fertility indices—including Peter McDonald's model (1984), which was employed in the analysis of World Fertility Survey data and by Knodel (1987)—suffer from this bias (multicollinearity) and may falsely provide support for truncation in the face of lengthened interbirth intervals. Note also that this bias affecting major fertility indices would be amplified if women became more adept at avoiding births over the course of childbearing (i.e., if interbirth intervals increase across parity). Some increase in parity-specific interbirth intervals due to secondary age-related subfecundity may be expected to contribute to such biases. As a result of these implicit assumptions, there are few methodological tools available to critically assess the apparent spacing of births suggested by simulation results for the Utah population.

Fortunately, the data available are sufficient to avoid summary indices. It is therefore possible to investigate birth intervals directly over the entire course of the fertility decline. Such an empirical analysis of interbirth intervals across the fertility decline appears to be the most convincing way to clarify the simulation results, which can only suggest the possible importance of spacing rather than confirming the fact.

ASSESSING THE ROLE OF INTERBIRTH INTERVALS IN THE FERTILITY DECLINE

The clearest assessment of birth intervals and the possibility of spacing can be achieved through the graphic methods, suggested by Henry (1976) and T. H. Hollingsworth (1969), of plotting birth intervals by both parity and completed family size. Plotting birth intervals in this manner allows a simple visual inspection of the parity-specific course of birth intervals within a group of women who have achieved a given family size. Any substantial effect of failed truncation might then be identified as a disjuncture in the parity-specific course of birth intervals at the last or next-to-last interval. Since the graphic method illuminates the expected parity-specific increase in birth intervals (within family

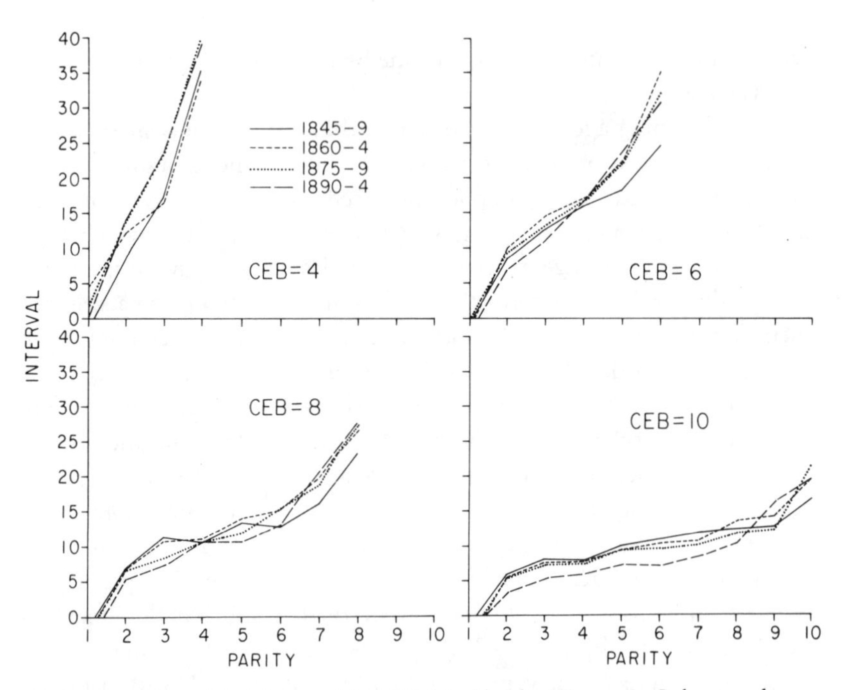

Figure 20. Mean Birth Interval (−17.5 Months) by Woman's Cohort and Parity

Source: Douglas L. Anderton and Lee L. Bean, "Birth Spacing and Fertility Limitation," *Demography* 22, 2 (1985), p.177.

size) that would occur regardless of truncation attempts, it is far superior to simplistic examples that use only ultimate birth-intervals and those that assume the equality of birth intervals at all parities when computing the anticipated effects of spacing on ultimate intervals.

Figure 20 presents such a graph for four representative cohorts (1845–49, 1860–64, 1875–79, and 1890–94) and four representative completed family sizes (four, six, eight, and ten children) (Anderton and Bean 1985). The additional advantage of examining cohorts over time is that it allows one to see how birth intervals may have been changed by innovative behaviors over the fertility decline. As is apparent from the figure, interbirth intervals within completed family sizes did not significantly change over the course of Utah women's fertility decline. There is some possible indication of lengthened last birth-intervals due to failed attempts at truncation. However, only the ultimate interval for six CEB in the 1860–64 birth cohort is longer than the preceding cohort's ultimate interval by a statistically significant amount. Anderton and Bean (1985) have also noted that variances of these ultimate intervals do not change greatly over time, although one would expect them to with increasing failed attempts at truncation.

Rather than evidencing truncation of childbearing, the empirical analysis of birth intervals suggests that the greatest portion of the fertility decline in the Utah population is attributable to a shift in composition over time among these interval schedules. For example, in the 1845–49 cohort only 2.6 percent of women had four CEB and only 7.9 had six CEB. By the 1890–94 birth cohort 17.7 percent of women had four CEB and 13.5 had six CEB. The graphic analysis makes apparent that, as women had smaller family sizes, their interbirth intervals became on the average longer at all parities (i.e., across a substantial portion of their fertility history as suggested by the simulation results). It is also clear that the interbirth-interval schedules adopted as a part of this move to smaller family sizes were indistinguishable from those of women of earlier cohorts who had the same family sizes.

Two very important interpretive results arise from confirming the suggestion of the simulation that lengthened interbirth intervals were substantial in the Utah fertility decline. First, the results suggest that the knowledge of methods for limiting fertility was present in the population even during periods that conventional indices would label as "natural fertility" periods (see chapter 1). As we have noted in our substantive review of the population's characteristics, this knowledge was, in fact, available even to the initial immigrant population, many of whom came from areas in which fertility decline had already been initiated. Most previous studies of historical fertility decline have not examined interbirth intervals with an equivalent precision. These studies have relied upon indicators of fertility control which we have argued are not robust in the face of significant birth spacing. If upheld in other populations, the results of this behavioral investigation would then challenge both the methods for assessing natural fertility and the theoretical conceptualization of populations that have been characterized as natural-fertility populations, populations ignorant of the means of fertility limitation. If studies supporting a significant role for the spacing of births across fertility declines are confined to similar American settings, these results clearly demonstrate the inadequacy of many of the standard indicators employed by historical demographers which a priori assume only truncation effects and neglect the multicollinearity between age at last birth and lengthened interbirth intervals.

Second, in turn, the patterns of fertility control in our study population do not reveal any significant population-wide innovation, defined as fundamentally altered possibilities of fertility limitation. It is, of course, possible that only enclaves of the population were initially aware of these fertility-limiting behaviors and that the revelation of these means of fertility control to others was a very rapid diffusion of behavioral innovation. However, the fact that all of the analyses by significant social subcohorts suggest simultaneous fertility decline (chaps. 5 and 7) argues somewhat against such a diffusion argument. In fact, Anderton (1983) has demonstrated that the birth-interval schedules in figure 20 are similarly stable over the fertility decline both within and across the four religious and residential subcohorts used in the simulation analyses. Social diffusion seems an unlikely possibility within the population. On the large geographic scale represented by the core-noncore dichotomy there is also no evidence of geographic diffusion. However, the possibility of geographic diffusion among specific communities or immigrant groups is reserved for more detailed analysis in the following chapter. The present behavioral analyses do not reveal significant behavioral innovation and are more compatible with recent theories, such as John Caldwell's (1982), which emphasize fundamental changes in the costs of and tastes for childbearing rather than for the production possibilities of children; that is, they are consistent with an adaptive perspective.

ANALYSIS OF SHORT-RUN ADAPTATIONS IN INTERBIRTH INTERVALS

The analysis of interbirth intervals over the fertility decline provides suggestive evidence of adaptation by the apparent absence of innovation. The fact that interbirth intervals increased across all significant social groups suggests that fertility adaptation in the population occurred largely in response to long-run changes in costs of and tastes for children which cut across the entire population. There is certainly substantive evidence to support such a possibility, evidence bearing on the fact that as the religious settlement developed, it came into contact with the secular, mainstream U.S. economy. Unlike the European populations that have provided our principle historical view of the fertility transition, the Utah population was not an isolated and indigenously developing capitalist economy. Instead, the frontier settlement, facing the pressures of modernization brought by the hegemonic progression of the United States across the continent, was similar to contemporary, less developed economies. The simultaneous progress of the economic,

TABLE 37

CORRELATION OF TREND-CONTROLLED, PARITY-SPECIFIC MEAN BIRTH-INTERVALS WITH PRECEDING THREE BIRTH-INTERVALS

	Parity								
With Parity	2	3	4	5	6	7	8	9	10
−1	.536	.444	.902	.873	.791	.905	.717	.829	.594
−2	n/a	.897	.609	.885	.496	.809	.751	.876	.397
−3	n/a	n/a	.916	.403	.743	.531	.630	.873	.512

social, political, and ideological penetration of the population, however, render any specific demonstration of the forces creating adaptive pressures difficult.

Continuing to focus on behavioral analyses, it is possible to address the question of whether interbirth intervals were adaptive to short-run situations. Any major disruptions in conditions relevant to fertility decision-making might be expected to affect fertility decisions across women at different stages of childbearing. It is, of course, possible that birth intervals at different stages of the childbearing career were differentially adaptive or sensitive to immediate conditions. However, if birth intervals were adjusted to immediate circumstances, some degree of association across different parities should be discernible.

Table 37 presents the yearly correlation among mean birth intervals at different parities; the birth intervals are controlled for long-term trends (i.e., the correlation of the residuals from a polynomial regression against year). The correlation of the mean birth-interval, controlled for trends, is presented for each parity from two through ten, with the immediately preceding birth interval, the birth interval two births prior, and the birth interval three births prior.

The correlation (or coherence at frequency zero) between the residual mean birth-intervals is remarkably high, indicating that yearly deviations in birth intervals at any parity were significantly similar to those of women at the immediately preceding three parities. These correlated short-run fluctuations in birth intervals thus suggest common responses across a range of parities to similar yearly conditions. The magnitude of the correlations suggests both that birth intervals were adaptive in the

TABLE 38

CHANGES IN BIRTH INTERVALS OF UTAH WOMEN AT PARITIES FOUR, FIVE, AND SIX, ASSOCIATED WITH THE ECONOMIC DEPRESSIONS OF 1867–68, 1893–94, AND 1929–30[a]

	Mean Birth-Intervals by Parity			Percentage Change in Mean Birth-Intervals by Parity		
Year	4	5	6	4	5	6
1867	2.027	2.068	2.041			
1868	2.176	2.353	2.077	7.37	13.78	1.78
1869	2.185	2.273	1.998	.41	−3.41	−3.81
1894	2.376	2.472	2.469			
1895	2.443	2.569	2.520	2.80	3.92	2.07
1896	2.539	2.552	2.599	3.94	−.65	3.13
1928	4.059	5.150	4.299			
1929	6.591	5.294	4.625	62.38	2.80	7.56
1930	5.473	5.190	5.176	−16.97	−1.97	11.93

[a]Specific years were selected for the largest increase in birth intervals across parities (1868, 1895, and 1929) in the ten year interval surrounding the depressions.

short-run and that these adaptive responses were distributed over a reasonable range of parities.

Fortunately, the long period of observation covered by the Mormon data also encompasses dramatic social events that lend further evidence of adaptation through birth spacing. In table 38, the changes in mean yearly birth intervals associated with the U.S. economic depressions of 1867–68, 1893–94, and 1929–30 are presented for women who bore their fourth, fifth, and sixth children during these events. The tabulations are restricted to these middle-range birth orders, since they are apparently sensitive to economic conditions among Utah births. Associated with each of the three depressions is at least one year in which birth intervals experienced substantial increases. In each case, the increase was greater than that in the previous trend in birth intervals.

The increase in birth intervals in 1868 was apparent only after the decline in economic conditions and seemed to be short-lived. By 1869 birth intervals either declined toward their previous levels or, at a minimum, stabilized. Some of the birth intervals affected by this economic decline would have occurred before the mothers arrived in Utah, and hence while they were in less isolated settings than the frontier.

The increase in intervals in 1895 came somewhat later than the economic decline, and consequently birth intervals had less of a tendency to decline immediately after the increase. It was only several years after 1895 that a return to prior trends of increase was reached. The less severe impact of this depression might well have been due to the fact that many of the births in this period, whether the mothers were migrants or Utah natives, occurred in Utah, which was still isolated and agrarian—a setting that may have diminished the impact of the economic decline. Nonetheless, there was at this time an identifiable period of substantial increase in birth spacing, reflecting the growing dependence of Utah on the national economy.

Finally, compatible with the fact that the depression of 1929 actually followed the erosion of consumer confidence, the impact of the crash in 1929 appears to have been nearly simultaneous with (or even prior to) the economic decline. The increase in birth intervals appears to have been both stronger and more immediate among those with smaller family sizes. At higher birth-orders the impact is somewhat delayed, perhaps reflecting a greater confidence among those with larger families. While somewhat of a leveling off is observed in birth intervals, they remained substantially longer than before. The dramatic effects of this relatively late depression clearly indicate the severity of the depression and the nearly complete economic integration of Utah into the U.S. economy.

Another major event with identifiable impact upon birth spacing in the population was the outbreak of World War I and the subsequent armistice. Figure 21 presents the percentage change in mean first and second birth-intervals from the year after the Belgian incursion (1914) to one year following the armistice (1919). Early birth-intervals are examined because families established by young men were most likely to have been disrupted by the events surrounding the war. The rush to establish families at the time the United States entered the war (1917) is clear in the dramatic decline in first birth-intervals. The correspondingly dramatic increase in first birth-intervals (marriage to first birth) during the war years is also evident. Second birth intervals display a much more subdued response until 1918–19, when there was a substantial increase. However, there was clearly a dramatic decline in both first and second birth-intervals, creating a small "boom," following the armistice. These effects were short-lived and affected far fewer women than the eco-

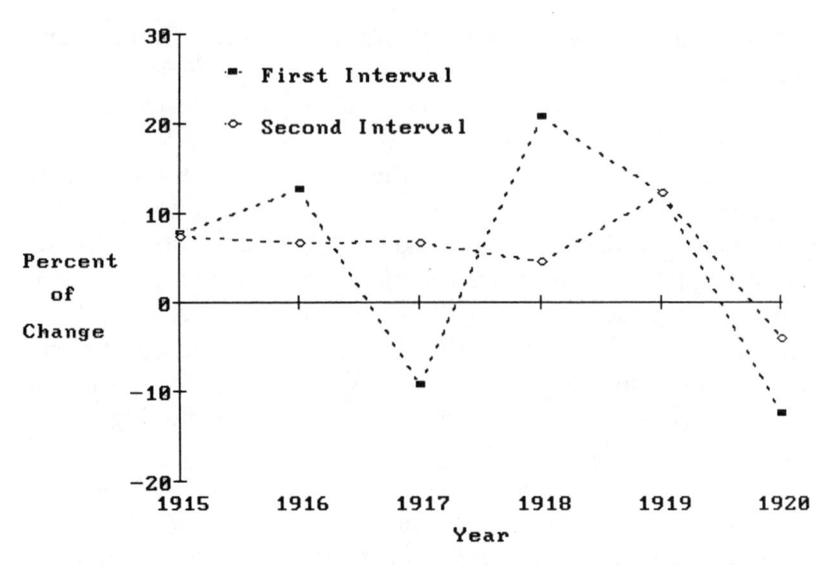

Figure 21. Birth Intervals from the Year of the Belgian Incursion to One Year After the Armistice

nomic fluctuations noted above. Nevertheless, they again provide clear support for the observation that the timing of births was adjusted in response to short-run socioeconomic conditions.

The apparent relevance of the adaptation perspective for short-run phenomena also points to a further weakness in an innovation paradigm. That is, the adaptation paradigm is applicable to both short-run and long-run fertility changes, while the innovation perspective provides little help in explaining short-run fertility behavior. The apparent short-run adaptive behavior in interbirth intervals does suggest the possibility of motivations to space children in response to prevailing conditions. In this sense short-run behaviors are compatible with the preceding analyses, which suggest that control of interbirth intervals was substantial during the Utah fertility decline.

SUMMARY

The longitudinal and individual-level data available from the genealogical records for this population clearly provide an atypical opportunity to suggest causal mechanisms and relations among the proximate determinants of fertility during a substantial onset of family limitation. Much of the fertility limitation within the Utah population can be clearly attributed to voluntary behavioral factors. Our analysis of proximate determinants suggests that the changes in some of these determinants would have tended to increase fertility during the course of the fertility decline. Fertility simulations confirm that involuntary proximate determinants that would have tended to lower fertility could not account for the patterns of fertility decline within the population.

The analysis of the present chapter has also raised a question about the accuracy of prior studies in presuming that fertility limitation is primarily accounted for by the onset of fertility truncation, or stopping behavior, alone. In particular, it is difficult to dismiss the hypothesis that contraceptive behavior was increasingly employed over a long period of marital life to achieve the levels of fertility limitation described earlier in this volume. Significantly, from a methodological perspective, these changes were not made obvious by the indices that have been employed in most prior historical studies. Only by examining interbirth intervals across both parity and completed family size was it possible to demonstrate that an onset of fertility control within the population did not necessitate radical changes in the behaviors used to achieve smaller families prior to the fertility transition. Rather, a substantial portion of the fertility limitation in the population can be accounted for through an alternative explanation stressing a compositional shift of the population to the birth-spacing schedules found in enclaves prior to the transition.

Also important to an understanding of the fertility transition in this population is the fact that the changes in proximate determinants and fertility behavior cut across the major social heterogeneities that presumably reflected differences in costs of and tastes for childbearing in the population. While relatively consistent behavior differentials are substantiated cross-sectionally, trends across cohorts indicate only a minor urbanization-secularization interaction; there was a far greater consistency of decline in all groups.

If birth spacing was in fact a significant adaptive behavior within the population, then one might assume that short-run variations in birth spacing would also reflect adaptation to circumstances in specific time periods. Our analysis of period fluctuations confirms short-run adaptations of interbirth intervals across a reasonably similar range of parities. However, it does not necessarily follow from a demonstration of short-run adaptations that long-term trends were similarly adaptive. To demonstrate this we must rely on both the eliminative argument, that no pattern indicative of a behavioral innovation or its diffusion can be identified, and a demonstrative argument, that a plausible source of pressure to adapt through fertility limitation can be identified. The analysis of interbirth intervals contributes importantly to the eliminative argument in failing to reveal any behavioral innovation not already present within subgroups of the population. To the contrary, the analysis confirms not only that the means of adaptation were available within the population but also that they were actively employed to facilitate short-run adaptations or fertility adjustments.

In combination, the findings of this behavioral analysis make a substantial case for believing that adaptive birth spacing was a major component of the Utah fertility transition. In response to the four areas of inquiry outlined at the beginning of this chapter, the analyses demonstrate (1) that the fertility decline was a result of voluntary behavior rather than nonvoluntary proximate determinants; (2) that the fertility decline was apparently consistent across major social groups within the population; (3) that one important, specific behavioral change in part responsible for the fertility decline was the adoption of lengthened interbirth intervals; and (4) that the adoption of lengthened interbirth intervals reflects both short-run and long-run adaptation by means of behaviors present within the population prior to the fertility decline.

Our analysis of geographic patterns has thus far been confined to a broad comparison of the central core settlement to other areas: that is, the analysis has not exhausted the possibility of the geographic diffusion suggested by some innovation theories or demonstrated possible geographically specific patterns of adaptation. In a more refined geographic analysis we might hope to clarify whether fertility limitation was, on an individual level, an innovation diffused throughout the population from enclaves in specific geographical areas or whether the fertility limitation reflected adaptive pressures in specific geographical areas. Thus the next step in our analysis is to explore the eliminative argument further by assessing geographic diffusion. These geographic patterns of fertility limitation are the subject of the following chapter.

CHAPTER 8

Adaptive and Innovative Influences II

The Geography of Fertility Change

This chapter focuses on geographic units—communities and counties—to provide a spatial characterization of the patterns of fertility change in Utah. This geographic level of analysis is comparable to European studies that rely on aggregated data to trace patterns of fertility change among subnational administrative units—provinces or districts. The purpose of such an analysis is to assess the relative importance of regional patterns of fertility limitation. Regional patterns serve as a direct test of assumptions underlying the innovation argument, which suggests that a pattern of geographic diffusion throughout the population follows the initial innovation of fertility limitation within the population centers. Regional fertility patterns are also useful in assessing the effects of unique local settings upon fertility behavior. Thus, our goal is to identify both regional fertility patterns and the changes in these regional patterns over the course of the fertility decline.

To achieve this goal, three analytical strategies are employed. First, the initial analysis examines differences in levels of fertility among communities and counties for three successive time intervals. Second, the analysis is expanded beyond the study of fertility levels to the investigation of changes in forms of fertility-limiting behaviors (e.g., delaying marriage and adoption of spacing as well as truncation). Third, cluster analysis is used to identify regional or community similarities in the patterns of fertility change over time and the underlying forms of fertility-limiting behavior.

Aggregate-level European studies have tried to assess the importance of regionally specific demographic adaptation in comparison to behavioral or technological innovation as an explanation of differences in the timing and extent of fertility limitation. Although the basic outlines of the adaptation/innovation issue were presented in chapter 1, the issue warrants further elaboration at this point.

Previous studies have drawn conflicting conclusions about the merits of these two influences, adaptation and innovation. Carlsson (1966) noted the theoretical and substantive importance of the diffusion of technology when distinguishing between long-term adaptive and innovative demographic change. He argued that the adoption and diffusion of innovations such as contraceptive knowledge or technology among a population would evidence fertility patterns separable from those created by pressures to adapt to local circumstances. Carlsson proceeded to make a substantial case for the prevalence of adaptive behavior in the fertility transition, but there have been few significant attempts to extend his analysis of diffusion to comparable historical settings. Those which are available have been conducted with European data.

Lutz Berkner (1973) summarized a number of European historical studies and critically evaluated hypotheses of both cultural and regional diffusion. From these earlier studies Berkner concluded that regional differences in social, economic, legal, and political structures were the primary determinants of demographic variablity. On a larger scale, Coale and Watkins (1986) summarized the Princeton European Fertility Project studies conducted with aggregated European data. Their findings generally support Coale's earlier demonstration of geographic fertility variations (1969) and his argument that the geographic distribution of socioeconomic pressures toward fertility adaptation do not explain pre- or post-transition regional fertility differences in Europe (1973). A number of the individual Princeton studies (e.g., Knodel 1974; Lesthaeghe 1977) provide similar conclusions. Andorka (1986), using Hungarian data, illustrated the difficulties in assessing the diffusion hypothesis. He noted that the regional characteristics that affect fertility through adaptive mechanisms are also spread by a process of diffusion, paralleling the spread of fertility limitation. As a result, it is difficult to distinguish the diffusion of new means of limitation from that of new environments or contexts that stimulate modifications in fertility decision-making processes.

The body of accumulated fertility-transition research suggests that neither the geographically variable distribution of socioeconomic fertility settings nor autonomous diffusion processes are likely to provide a simple account of regional distributions of fertility limitation. However, rather than suggesting that neither influence is at work, prior studies suggest that both influences may be important; but the results of such studies still provide only partial explanations of geographic fertility patterns. Furthermore, previous research suggests that broadening the definition of the object of diffusion to include behavioral and cultural innovation (e.g., changes in family-size norms) as well as technological innovation makes it even more difficult to separate the influence of diffusion from that of adaptation. Examining both paradigms with greater specificity, however, might allow the effects of one to be distinguished from the effects of the other.

One possible way to increase specificity would be to assume that geographic differences may create differences in the relative import of the two influences, as suggested by Lesthaeghe's (1977) examination of two relatively homogeneous cultural areas within an ethnically heterogeneous country. A second way to gain specificity would be to refine the definitions of socioeconomic environments, as suggested by Knodel's (1974) attempt to narrow the definitions of terms such as "urbanization." In light of recent studies suggesting that the introduction of fertility limitation might be more complex than the simple introduction of fertility truncation, a third way to specify the discussion would be to expand upon Coale's (1969) separation of marriage and fertility behaviors within marriages, and to examine the geographic distribution of a series of life course events. Most prior studies have only considered fertility levels and age-specific patterns of marital fertility. Finally, it may be useful to consider patterns of behavioral change. Heterogeneous pre-transition populations might retain some of their initial heterogeneity and thus confound specific behavioral trajectories over time.

The analyses presented in this chapter make modest gains in each of the four areas, listed above, that have the potential for increased specificity. First, the population analyzed was for the most part a culturally homogeneous one, in spite of the differences in origin, migration history, religious commitment, and residential history detailed in chapters 5 and 6. For example, E. E. Ericksen (1922) characterizes the Mormon population as one having a "highly unified minority group consciousness" welded from common religious beliefs and experiences. Second, while specific socioeconomic indicators are not employed, the regional characteristics of the population are reasonably well defined in comparison with other settings. The frontier settlement was characterized by one clearly identified central settlement, several emergent satellite towns, and largely rural surrounding counties. Some less-hospitable desert counties and outlying mining communities were exceptions, which are clearly identifiable in the analysis. Third, the family-group sheets (genealogies) make it possible to analyze specific life course behaviors underlying fertility levels: behaviors affecting age at marriage, interval to first birth, average birth-interval, length of final birth-interval, and age at last birth. Fourth, because of the considerable period of time covered by the data set and the availability of individual-level data, both absolute levels of fertility behavior and patterns of change in fertility behavior over time can be distinguished and analyzed separately.

In the next section of this chapter we outline additional details involved in the community and county analyses and the types of data examined. In the third section we study variations in levels of CEB and various behavioral determinants of fertility. Section four details patterns of change among the various counties and communities. The final section of the chapter lays out the theoretical implications of the analysis.

COMMUNITIES AND COUNTIES

In previous chapters geographic units were explicitly included in our analysis. In chapter 5 our analysis distinguished between Utah and other states as well as European nations. In chapters 6 and 7 we focused our attention primarily on events in Utah but introduced greater geographic specificity. We have demonstrated the importance of distinguishing between residence in central and noncentral (agricultural) areas. To investigate the geographic spread of fertility management over the course of the transition, the present analysis uses community or city data as well as county data.

A diverse selection of communities that captures both ecological and distal variation is used for the analysis of diffusion patterns of fertility behavior. The analysis of ecological diffusion patterns serves to evaluate adaptation pressures. To ensure that the ecological variation of the sample communites is sufficient, we have made our selection from communities with known agricultural and industrial variations. In turn, the analysis of distal diffusion patterns serves to evaluate the potentially innovative character and contagion, or dissemination, of fertility-control behaviors. An examination of the changing geographic clusters or constellations of similar fertility behavior over the course of the fertility transition will allow us to make an inferential case about the regionally adaptive or innovation-diffusion character of the transition. As with all regional studies these ecological findings provide suggestive guidance to more detailed individual-level analyses rather than definitive conclusions.

The communities used in the analysis include the thirteen principle settlements in the frontier population and twenty-nine counties. For reference these are identified in figure 22. Ten of the thirteen communities form a nearly linear path from the northcentral to the southwestern boundaries of present-day Utah, following the western slope of mountain ranges through the state. There are three communities that fall outside the linear north-south path of colonization, transportation, and communications networks: Moab (Grand County); Price (Carbon County); and Vernal (Uintah County). These three communities should represent ones in which family limitation would appear relatively late, if family limitation largely involves a process of geographic diffusion.

Each of these three communities, which are somewhat isolated from the other ten settlements by intervening mountain ranges, was settled later. Although the initial settlement in Moab took place in 1855, the community was abandoned and was not resettled until 1880. Price was not settled until 1897, although a number of smaller Utah communities had been established in the late 1870s to mine coal. This has remained the dominant industrial activity in the county to the present. Vernal was settled in 1878. Among those communities that fall along the north-south line of development only Logan was not settled in the first decade of colonization, but it was settled shortly thereafter, in 1859.

The penetration of communities by improved transportation networks, for example, roads and rail trunk-lines, brought them into contact with the outside world over the periods covered in this study. All but two of the communities on the north-south axis were linked into rail transportation by 1890. A spur was completed to Manti after World War I, and although St. George was bypassed, both were linked to the central communities by other means of transportation. During the 1860s Brigham Young maintained separate households in St. George for some of his wives and spent part of each year in residence. Of the three communities east of the central settlement line, Price was reached by rail transportation in 1890. The line continued to Denver, but ran north of Moab, which remained isolated until the uranium-mining boom of the 1950s. Vernal remains to this day without rail transportation.

The largest settlement by far was Salt Lake City. Next in size were Ogden and Provo. These three communities are still the three largest

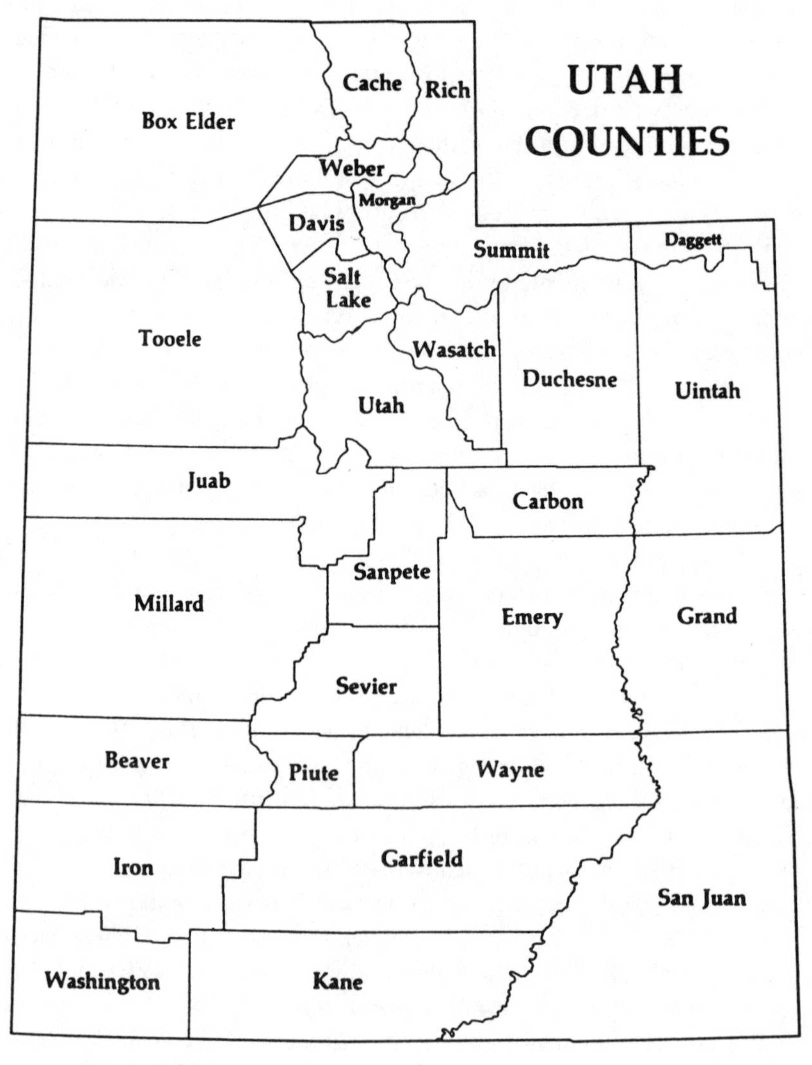

Figure 22*a b*, Utah Counties and Cities

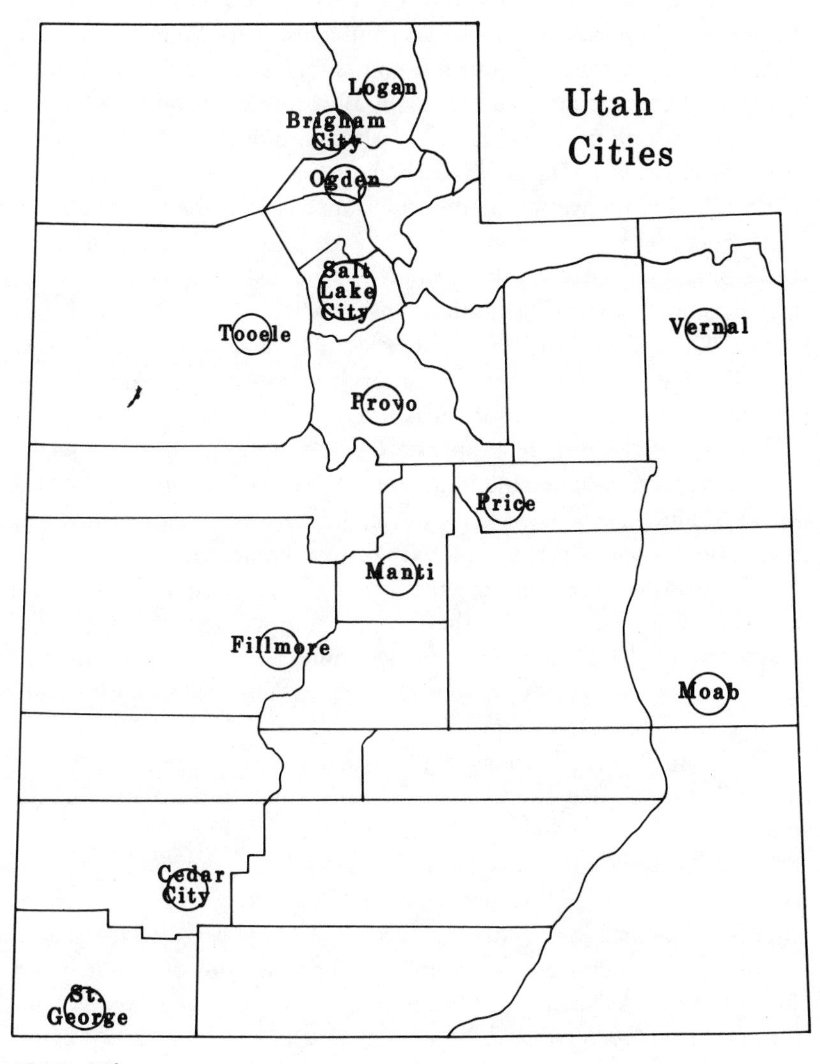
Utah
Cities
Logan
Brigham
City
Ogden
Salt
Lake
City
Tooele
Vernal
Provo
Price
Manti
Fillmore
Moab
Cedar
City
St.
George

Figure 22*b*

cities in Utah. The central or core area of settlement also roughly corresponded to these three settlements and contained approximately 70 percent of the state's population during the periods under study (Wahlquist 1977). This core settlement area was the center of emerging urbanism and contact (through the transcontinental railroad in 1869) with the larger U.S. economy. The remaining ten communities are of varying size and distance from the central settlements.

All demographic events that did not occur in the thirteen major communities but did occur within Utah are associated with one of the twenty-nine counties that exist today. Exclusive of the thirteen major communities, there were no sizable communities during the time period studied. Therefore, the counties essentially represent rural populations.

Utah's current twenty-nine counties received their final form in 1917 with the creation of Daggett and Duchesne counties. For the most part the counties in the western half of the state have retained stable boundaries since the separation of Nevada and Arizona. Like Daggett and Duchesne, several of the other counties in the east were formed later by the division of existing counties. These include Garfield (1882), San Juan (1880), Grand (1890), Carbon (1894), and Uintah (1880). As mentioned above, in the analysis of fertility patterns by county we use the county configuration as it exists today. In allocating to the counties demographic events that happened outside the thirteen major settlements, we were usually able to accept county designations as recorded on the family-group sheets. However, because our analysis involves comparing counties across time, yet county boundaries changed over time, it was necessary to reassign events whose county locations were affected by such changes. In these cases the town designations on the family-group sheets allowed us to determine the appropriate present-day counties to which to assign the events. Such reallocations were necessary only in a few cases.

In the analysis, it becomes evident that the number of events that occur in the various counties is often too small to calculate reliable indices. For example, the population of Daggett County since 1920 has remained around 400. After the initial settlements, the commercialization of agriculture, and the decline of selected mining industries, several counties remained stable after 1900 or 1910, and several experienced major population losses. For example, the populations of Wasatch and Juab counties declined after 1910; Sanpete, Beaver, and Emery went through a period of decline beginning in 1920. Piute County has remained relatively stable, with a population of less than 2,000. In addition, several counties have large, if not majority, populations of native Americans: Duchesne, Uintah, and San Juan counties in particular. (See table 1 for a summary of the county patterns of population change.)

Longitudinal analysis of genealogical data requires certain decisions to be made when dealing simultaneously with locations across various time periods. In the MHDP data set, the location of individuals is recorded only at the time of a demographic event such as marriage, birth, or death. However, many common fertility measures are life course measures (e.g., CEB, average birth-intervals) not necessarily tied to specific locations. For classification purposes measures that span the life course are assigned to place of first birth as a convenience and to avoid some subtle biases that otherwise arise. We use the specific location for measures that do not span the life course, for example, age at marriage, first birth-interval, and last birth-interval. Similarly, a time period must also be specified for measures that do and those that do not span the life course. Measures that do not span the life course are tied to a specific time. All measures that span the life course (including age at last birth) are tabulated by time of first birth. This is necessary because reporting life course results by time of last birth leads to a bias. For example, reporting age at last birth by time of last birth biases the report with respect to individuals with later ages at last birth in the later periods.[1]

Given these measurement assumptions, mean children ever born (CEB), mean age of wife at marriage (AM), mean first birth-interval (FBI), average closed birth-interval (ABI), mean last birth-interval (LBI), and mean age at last birth (ALB) were tabulated for each of the geographic regions. Average closed intervals, which are the mean of women's average intervals, avoid bias toward higher family sizes (Wolfers 1968).

All measures were computed for three twenty-year time periods for the sake of including a sufficient numbers of cases. Wife's age at marriage is reported by date of marriage for three periods: 1871–90, 1891–1910, and 1911–30. Mean Children ever born, average closed birth-interval, mean first birth-interval, and age at last birth are tabulated by date of first birth in the same three intervals. Last birth-interval is tabulated by date of the last birth falling in the intervals 1891–1910, 1911–30, and 1931–50.

An additional problem associated with our geographic analysis is that there is no precise means of ascertaining whether unit differences in levels and patterns of change exactly conform to a predicted pattern of diffusion. In a general way, however, certain patterns should be obvious. Typically, from the assumptions of innovation and diffusion, we would predict, first, that increased levels of fertility limitation would appear earlier in the communities than in the counties; second, that fertility limitation would occur initially in the largest communities and the core counties; and third, that fertility limitation would spread among those communities and counties on the north-south axis. This type of pattern is, in point of fact, represented in our initial analysis of "levels."

ANALYSIS PHASE I. LEVELS OF CHILDBEARING AND FERTILITY LIMITATION

Simple cartographic presentations of fertility measures are given in figures 23 through 28, with each of the three time periods in a separate panel. The thirteen cities are represented as circles within their respective counties; the large circle represents the principle settlement of Salt Lake City. Figure 23 presents the data for mean children ever born. Even within the very first time period considered, 1871–90, the mean number of children ever born was slightly lower in the central regions of the state than in outlying areas, where the women of ten communities and counties average more than 8.5 children. This pattern is consistent with earlier studies that date the fertility transition to birth cohorts of women born from approximately 1860 onward (Willigan, Anderton, et al. 1982; Mineau et al. 1984), and with studies suggesting that some amount of fertility limitation preceded the general fertility transition (Anderton and Bean 1985). By the second time period a moderate decline in CEB had spread throughout the state, with a definitively lower fertility leading the decline in the central settlement and surrounding satellite cities. Women commencing their childbearing in the second period complete their families with between 5 and 6.4 children, in eight areas. Again, by the third time period this smaller family size (5–6.4 children) had spread throughout most of the state; central settlements declined to even lower family sizes (fewer than 5 children).

Wife's age at marriage, in figure 24, is initially more heterogeneous than children ever born. It is also somewhat less effective in explaining fertility differentials than in Coale's European analysis (1969). By the later time periods, especially the last period of 1911–30, the substantially older ages at marriage in the central cities are apparent. In eight areas the average age at marriage for females is age 22 and higher.

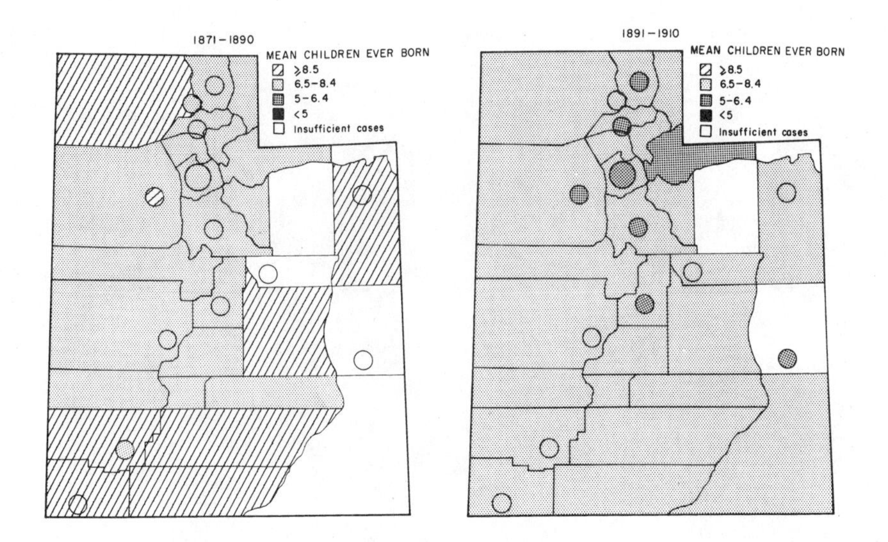

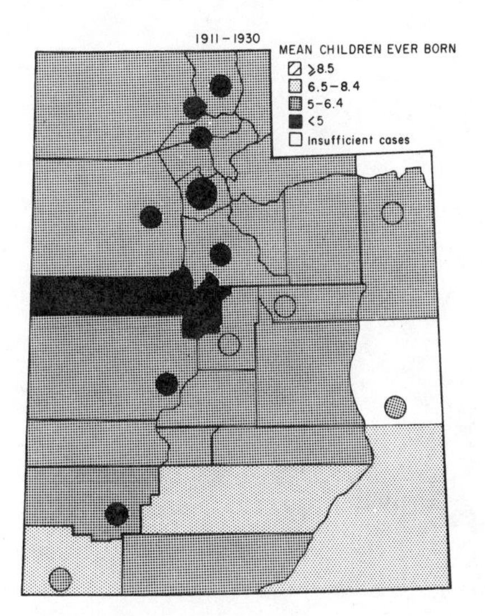

Figure 23. Mean Children Ever Born, by County and City, 1871–1890, 1891–1910, and 1911–1930

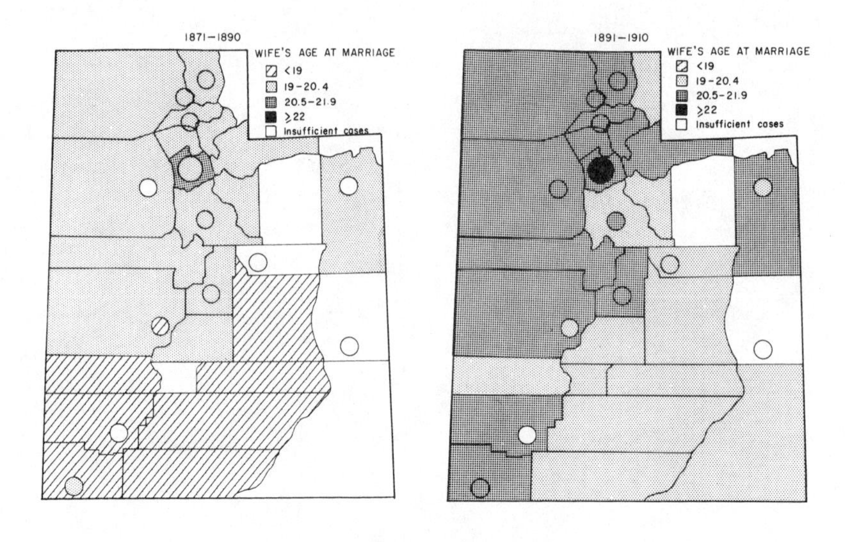

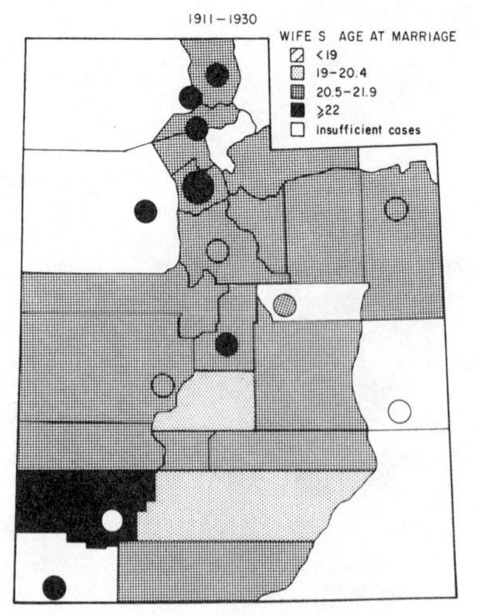

Figure 24. Wife's Age at Marriage, by County and City, 1871–1890, 1891–1910, and 1911–1930

However, the pattern is not sufficiently consistent to suggest a strong diffusion argument. Again, this is consistent with earlier studies demonstrating geographic variations in marital fertility not accounted for by age at marriage (Bean, Mineau, and Anderton 1983; Mineau et al. 1984; Anderton 1986*a*).

The maps of mean first birth-interval presented in figure 25 show a similar initial heterogeneity, which coalesces in the central cities by the final period, 1911–30. Longer first birth-intervals persisted in both Salt Lake City and the city of Logan throughout the first two time periods as well. The substantial lengthening of first birth-intervals over the course of the transition is supportive of earlier research suggesting that fertility behavior early in the life course was altered over the course of the transition. For example, in the first period the average first birth-interval is less than sixteen months in all communities for which sufficient data are available. In the second time period four widely separate areas evidence average first birth-intervals in excess of sixteen months; and in the last time period thirteen areas fall into this category, with the average first birth-interval exceeding eighteen months in eleven areas.

Average closed birth-intervals, shown in figure 26, are initially more heterogeneous than first birth-intervals. In the first period, 1871–90, this may simply reflect the greater variability of average intervals in periods of less fertility limitation. By the second period, 1891–1910, central cities are uniformly among those with longer intervals. By the final period, women of the two major cities, Salt Lake City and Ogden, are among the few groups with very long average intervals (over 3.5 years). The modal average birth-intervals are less than 2.75 years in the first period (thirty-two areas), 2.75 to 2.9 years in the second period (twenty-three areas), and 3.0 to 3.4 years by the last time period (twenty-seven areas).

An increase in the length of the last, closed birth-interval is a commonly used indicator of fertility truncation, for the increase is presumed to indicate failed truncation attempts. (See fig. 27.) However, last birth-intervals would also be lengthened disproportionately by attempts to delay or avert births throughout the life course. There is a consistent pattern, again, of longer last intervals in central cities throughout the three time periods. Of interest, however, is the fact that longer terminal intervals are also found in a few more remote counties during the last period. These counties are found among the more harsh environments of the state, and they are the less solidly aligned with the prevalent pronatalist religion of the state. Across the three time periods there is a

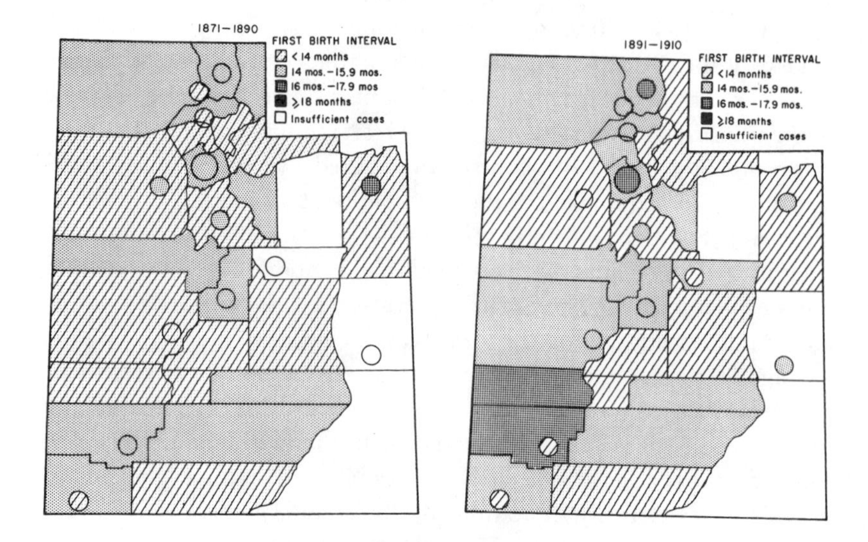

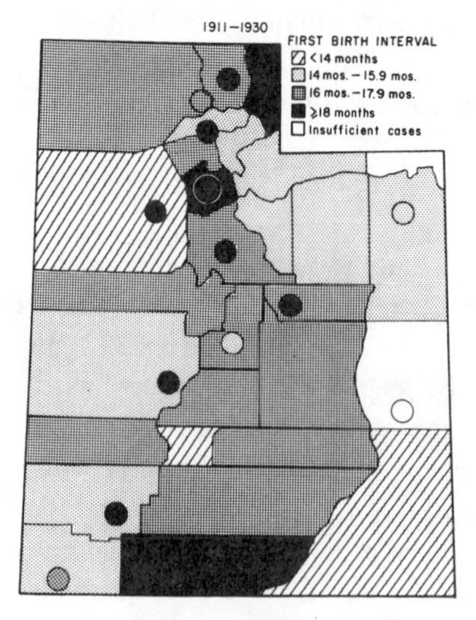

Figure 25. First Birth Interval, by County and City, 1871–1890, 1891–1910, and 1911–1930

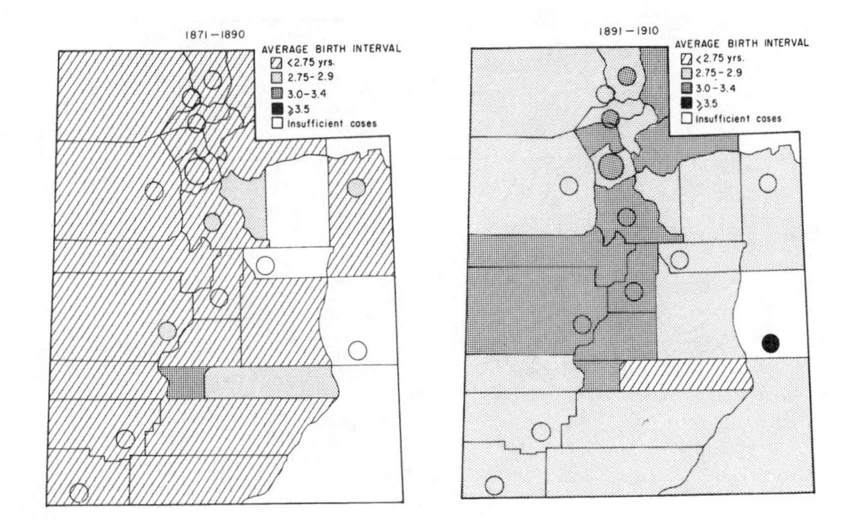

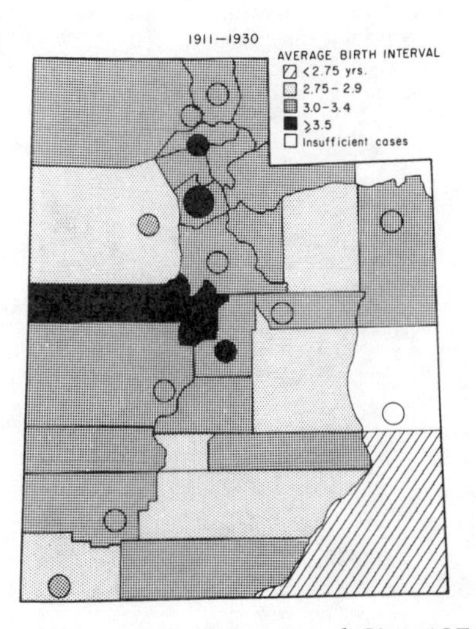

Figure 26. Average Birth Interval, by County and City, 1871–1890, 1891–1910, and 1911–1930

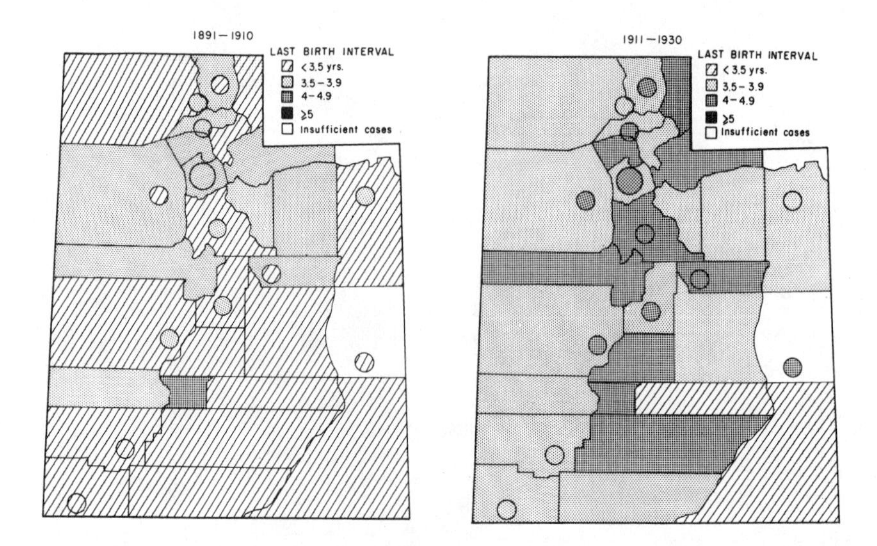

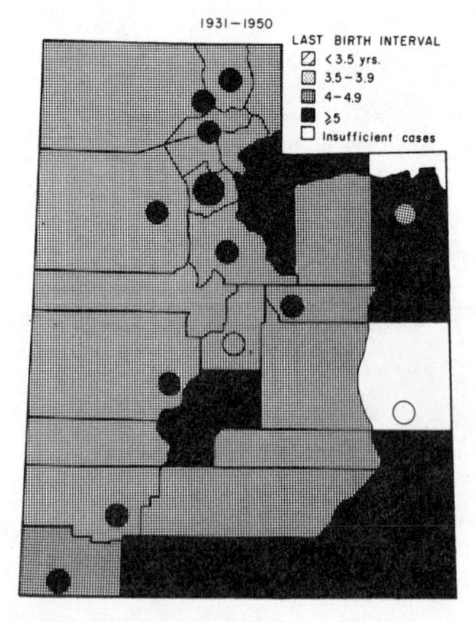

Figure 27. Last Birth Interval, by County and City, 1891–1910, 1911–1930, and 1931–1950

consistent increase in the modal values of the last birth-intervals: for 1891–1910 there are twenty-one areas in the category of less than 3.5 years. For 1911–30 there are twenty-two in the category of 3.5 to 3.9 years. In the last period, twenty-two areas are in the category of 4.0 to 4.9 years.

Finally, age at last birth (figure 28), not surprisingly, follows a pattern similar to that of last birth-intervals over time, being initially lower but diffuse in the central reaches of the state, more clearly associated with the central settlement in the second period, and common in both the central settlements and dispersed outlying counties in the last period. By the last time period the average age at last birth is less than 35.5 years in thirteen areas.

The maps of fertility measures confirm much of what has been suggested in prior studies. The entire range of life course events was altered by the transition to lower fertility; those behaviors most conducive to lower fertility were consistently strongest in the central cities of the state; and there was, nonetheless, substantial variation in fertility across other areas.

ANALYSIS PHASE II. CLUSTER PATTERNS OF CHANGE

It is difficult to interpret the vast amount of information contained in geographic presentations such as those of figures 23 through 28. In addition, initial conclusions drawn from such an analysis may prove to be misleading given the initially heterogeneous fertility levels of the population.

Consider two areas that each evidence a decline in CEB of three children from their initial levels. We might tend to regard such areas as similarly declining. However, if one of these areas began at a high level, for example, ten CEB, and the other at a lower level, for example, seven CEB, the higher-level area might appear similar to an area experiencing an increase from three to six CEB rather than to the area with similar declines. Thus the initial differences in fertility levels obscure the patterns of fertility change over time which are central to a longitudinal analysis of fertility change.

The cartographic analysis presented above, as well as similar analyses of European data, also tends to distort longitudinal patterns of change. If central cities (or other regions) begin the fertility transition at lower levels of fertility, cross-sectional mappings of fertility levels such

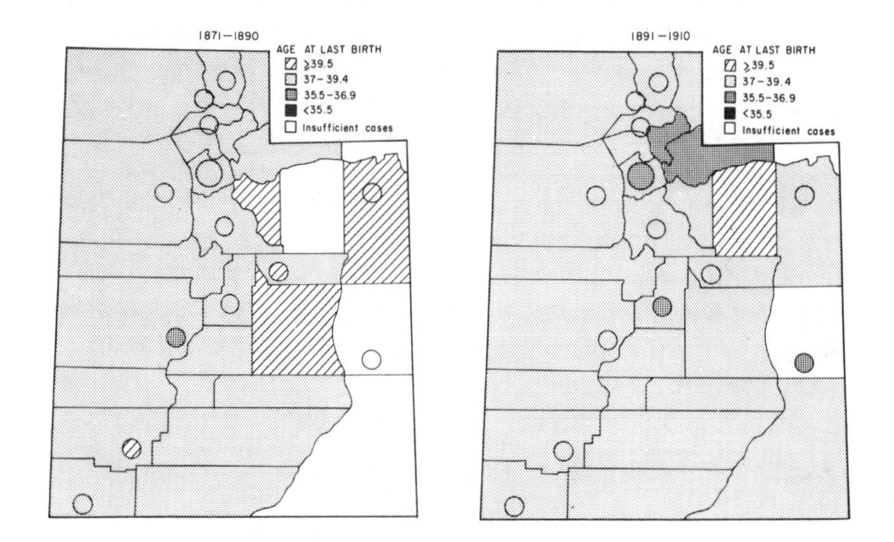

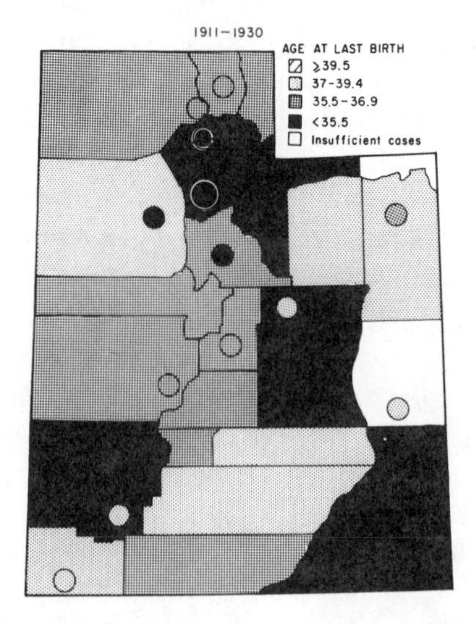

Figure 28. Age at Last Birth, by County and City, 1871–1890, 1891–1910, and 1911–1930

as those presented above will generally show lower levels of fertility in such areas throughout the transition as fertility declines in all areas. Over time these cross-sectional mappings look as if the central areas are consistently the leaders in fertility control, which diffuses outward to other areas. However, if initial heterogeneities are substantial, such results might equally well reflect a geographically uniform adoption of fertility control (or even a higher level of adoption in areas with initially higher fertility levels) superimposed upon initial heterogeneities. The only solution to such confusion is to isolate the analysis of patterns of fertility change from heterogeneities in initial fertility levels.

The analytical approach employed in the following section is that of cluster analysis, that is, the search for groups of geographic areas with similar fertility characteristics over the fertility decline. Each of the fertility indices used in the cartographic analysis, including specific life course behaviors, are successively employed to identify common geographic clusters with respect to that fertility measure. However, control for the initial level of the measurement in each area is introduced to isolate patterns of fertility change over time. Thus, in the analysis that follows we seek to identify groups or clusters of geographic areas that displayed similar patterns of change in a fertility behavior across the three time periods.

There are a variety of means to transform the measurements presented above into "pattern" variables which control for initial levels. Anderton and Bean (1987) have clustered complex-pattern variables for this population. In the present case, it is sufficient simply to examine the change (first differences) in fertility measurements across the three periods mapped above. That is, rather than analyze CEB measured at all three periods (1871–90, 1891–1910, and 1911–30), we analyze the change in CEB from the first to second period, and from the second to third period.

Several types of clustering (e.g., Smallest-Space, Centroid, and K-Means; see Spath 1980) were also investigated and produced generally consistent results. In the present analysis K-Means clustering was used to cluster the two variables indicating change between periods across the geographic regions of the state. By means of cluster analysis, then, we identify groups of regions that had similar patterns of fertility change across both these intervals.

Before relying upon such analysis to identify patterns of geographic change possibly indicative of diffusion, it is important to note the cluster patterns we should expect to find in the case of a simple geographic

TABLE 39

CLUSTER DEFINITIONS DERIVED FROM K-MEANS CLUSTERING OF THE CHANGES IN SIX FERTILITY MEASURES BETWEEN 1871–90 TO 1891–1910 (INTERVAL 1) AND 1891–1910 TO 1911–30 (INTERVAL 2)

	Cluster One		Cluster Two		Cluster Three	
Measure	Interval 1	Interval 2	Interval 1	Interval 2	Interval 1	Interval 2
CEB	−0.76	−1.46	−1.51	−1.07	−1.63	−1.61
AM	1.12	0.63	1.31	1.47	2.80	0.21
FBI	0.70	−0.74	0.70	2.07	−0.22	6.10
ABI	2.61	1.02	2.59	5.71	4.65	3.81
LBI	3.00	15.56	5.71	5.43	8.44	12.81
ALB	0.00	−1.24	−1.66	−1.43	−1.59	−2.86

Note: Changes in first birth-interval (FBI), average birth-interval (ABI), and last birth-interval (LBI) are measured in months. Changes in age at marriage (AM) and age at last birth (ALB) are measured in years. Changes in children ever born (CEB) are measured by the number of children.

diffusion of fertility limitation. First, we should expect some region(s) to be clearly associated with an earlier initial adoption of the fertility-limiting behavior analyzed (i.e., the change in the first period should be relatively more conducive to smaller family sizes here than in other areas). Second, we should expect to find surrounding regions in a cluster evidencing a relatively later adoption of the fertility-limiting behaviors. Finally, we might expect some "hinterland" areas in which no, or little, onset of the limitation behavior is found. To identify a simple pattern of diffusion clearly, these clusters should be arranged in a geographic pattern plausibly indicating paths of communication and transportation in the state but relatively independent of alternative pressures for adaptive fertility limitation. In the section below we first discuss the clusters of similar regions identified by the analysis and subsequently turn to the geographic distribution of those clusters that might reveal consistent patterns of diffusion or adaptation.

The clustering of fertility measures indicates that for each measure approximately three unique clusters or regional groupings can be identified which adequately account for variations within the state. In table 39 interval one represents the difference in variables between 1871–90 and 1891–1910, and interval two is the difference between 1891–1910 and 1911–30. In each case, the strongest and earliest fertility-limiting behavior is identified by the cluster labeled number three and the weakest or latest fertility limitation by the cluster labeled number one.

For children ever born (CEB), the weakest pattern of change (cluster one) still represents a decline in mean fertility of three-quarters of a child (−.76) during the first interval and of nearly a child and a half (−1.46) in the second interval. However, while all clusters display a decline in CEB, the change in the first interval is more substantial for both clusters two and three. In cluster three, CEB declined by over one and a half children in both intervals (−1.63, −1.61). Thus, all regions declined in CEB, but areas in clusters two and three declined more strongly in the initial stages of statewide fertility decline. The decline continued most strongly in cluster three, while areas in cluster two declined at a slower pace than other areas after their initial decline.

Clusters for wife's age at marriage (AM) are somewhat more ambiguous. All clusters display an initial increase in age at marriage. Again, cluster three comprises regions with the greatest increase in age at marriage (2.8 years). However, cluster two has a more gradual and continual increase of nearly equal magnitude distributed across both periods (1.31 + 1.47 = 2.78 years). Only cluster one contains regions with appreciably less increase in age at marriage. The delaying of marriage appears to have been initiated by all areas in the first interval and carried to the same extent within all but one area by the final interval.

Changes in the first birth-interval (FBI) seem more heavily concentrated in the later stage of the fertility transition, as one might suspect. Other than minor fluctuations, the most significant adoption of longer first birth-intervals is by cluster three in the second interval (6.1 months) followed by cluster two in the second interval (2.07 months). Combined with results for age at marriage, this suggests that early regulation of initial birth relied upon age at marriage, whereas first birth-intervals came under individual control during the later stages of the transition.

In contrast to the initial birth, spacing between other births is affected earlier in the transition. All three clusters of average closed birth-intervals (ABI) show increased birth-intervals during the first period of change from about two and one-half months to over four and one-half months. Cluster three represents a geographic region with the earliest strong, and continuing, increase in spacing. Cluster two appears to contain areas that began spacing somewhat later but then increased dramatically, while cluster one has a fairly modest adoption of birth spacing.

Last birth-intervals (LBI), which might reflect either spacing or failed truncation, increase across both intervals of observation and most dramatically within the second interval of change. In the first interval, cluster three clearly has the greatest incidence of longer terminal birth-intervals. However, the pattern becomes confused in the second observation. One plausible explanation for both the confounded patterns of change and the greater uniformity of increase in last birth-intervals might be that increases during the early stages of the transition arose from longer birth-intervals in general (i.e., spacing), while increases in the later stages reflect a greater influence of attempts to truncate childbearing. If this is the case, then cluster one may reflect a more substantial later reliance upon truncation among areas that did not adopt spacing in earlier stages of the transition.

Such an argument might also be consistent with clusters derived for age at last birth (ALB). Some areas (cluster one) appear not to have terminated births earlier in the initial stages of the transition. All groups terminated at earlier ages during the second stage of the transition. Age at last birth, like last birth-interval, is affected by both spacing and truncation (see Anderton 1989). Some areas thus appear to have avoided both means of limitation in the early stages of the transition. The bulk of the evidence thus far indicates that both forms of limitation were practiced by the later stages of the decline.

A summary of the clusters helps to identify the behavioral heterogeneities across geographic regions over the course of the transition. Not only do individuals in the Utah population appear to have practiced different paths to fertility control but regions also appear to have varied substantially in the means of fertility limitation employed at different stages of the transition. The decline in fertility (CEB) is most nearly uniform across the state. Wife's age at marriage (AM) increased early in all regions and proceeded to a similar level of increase in most reaches of the state. Later-life-course increases in average birth-intervals (ABI) and last birth-intervals (LBI) persisted across the transition, with a greater increase in last birth intervals during the later stages of decline. While one might expect truncation to explain this, these intervals were also affected by spacing; and first birth-intervals also increased most dramatically during the later stages of the decline. At least some groups of the population did not achieve younger ages at last birth in the early stages of the transition, although all regions did so in the later stages.

Again, it would seem that the early stages of the transition may have involved the multiphasic adoption of different methods of fertility limitation and planning throughout the life course. As contraceptive control became more certain and manageable in the later stages of the transition, birth spacing, initially ineffective, became more effective and more widely practiced, even to the extent of delaying first births. At the same time it appears that some regions relied less heavily upon spacing and perhaps more heavily upon truncation. Thus the explanatory options we applied earlier to individual behavioral change appear to be applicable on a regional level, with substantial heterogeneities in the paths of an otherwise nearly uniform fertility decline.

To address more adequately the possible geographic patterns of diffusion or adaptation in the population, we must examine the geographic composition of the clusters identified. Table 40 identifies the cluster to which each geographic region belonged for each of the six measures clustered. For an indication of population density, cities and counties are presented in decreasing rank order of the total number of births that occurred in them during the period 1891–1910.

The patterns that emerge provide a further indication of the heterogeneous paths to fertility limitation within regions. Nearly all of the major cities and towns were in the cluster with the greatest decline in children ever born. However, these communities were in clusters with less dramatic increases in age at marriage than other areas of the state. Major cities did experience increases in first birth-intervals during the later stages of the transition. These increases were most dramatic in the two central cities of the state, Salt Lake City and Ogden, and several other areas. Average birth-intervals also increased most substantially within major cities. However, the patterns of increase in last birth-intervals appear very heterogeneous within cities and towns. Age at last birth is somewhat more consistently younger in cities and towns, although again heterogeneity is greater than for birth-spacing measures.

The first eleven counties, ranked by total number of births, appear largely similar to communities. Decline in fertility (CEB) was somewhat less uniform in the lowest-fertility cluster. These counties generally experienced the least increase in age at marriage and were in the second cluster of increasing first birth-intervals. Again, average birth-intervals generally increased throughout the transition in these areas, and the first six counties are all in the cluster with the greatest increase in average birth-intervals. Patterns for changes in last birth-interval and age at last birth are again somewhat heterogeneous. However, major counties

TABLE 40

CLUSTER MEMBERSHIP OF UTAH CITIES AND COUNTIES FOR CHANGES IN SIX FERTILITY MEASUREMENTS

Cities:	CEB	AM	FBI	ABI	LBI	ALB
Salt Lake City	3	2	3	3	1	2
Ogden	3	1	3	3	3	2
Provo	3	1	2	3	1	3
Logan	3	2	2	3	3	1
Brigham City	3	2	2	2	1	3
Manti	2	1	2	2	2	2
St. George	3	2	3	3	3	1
Tooele	3	1	3	2	1	3
Fillmore	1	2	2	1	1	1
Cedar City	3	3	3	2	3	2
Vernal	2	3	1	1	1	2
Price	n[a]	n	n	n	3	2
Moab	n	n	n	n	n	n
Counties:						
Utah	2	1	2	3	3	2
Cache	2	1	2	3	3	2
Sanpete	3	1	2	3	3	3
Salt Lake	3	1	3	3	1	2
Weber	2	1	2	3	2	3
Davis	3	1	2	3	2	3
Summit	2	1	2	1	2	2
Sevier	3	1	2	2	3	2
Box Elder	3	1	2	3	1	2
Juab	3	1	2	2	1	2
Wasatch	3	1	2	2	1	3
Beaver	1	2	2	1	1	1
Washington	1	3	1	1	2	1
Millard	2	1	2	1	2	1
Tooele	2	n	1	1	1	1
Iron	3	3	1	3	1	3
Garfield	1	1	2	1	2	2
Morgan	3	2	2	2	3	2
Kane	3	2	3	3	1	1

TABLE 40 (continued)

Counties:	CEB	AM	FBI	ABI	LBI	ALB
Emery	1	2	2	1	2	3
Rich	3	n	3	3	2	1
Uintah	2	1	1	1	2	2
Wayne	1	3	2	2	1	1
Piute	2	2	1	1	2	2
Carbon	1	n	1	3	2	3
Duchesne	n	n	n	n	n	3
San Juan	n	n	n	n	2	3
Daggett	n	n	n	n	n	n
Grand	n	n	n	n	n	n

Note: For illustrative purposes cities and counties are listed in decreasing order of the total number of children born in them during the period 1891–1910.
[a]n = Insufficient cases

appear to have had more uniformly lower ages at last birth than did the major cities.

If a pattern of diffusion is plausible within these data, it would seem to be that of increasing length in average birth-intervals and, ultimately, first birth-intervals. This contrasts with what might be expected from an "innovation of truncation" premise. No consistent pattern of diffusion in last birth-interval or age at last birth seems apparent. Wife's age at marriage seems, at best, inversely related across regions of fertility decline and spacing of births. Although spacing may have diffused throughout the population, the early increases in average birth-intervals across all three clusters and the lack of a distinctive discrimination of spacers early in the transition and of adopters of spacing late in the transition seems to suggest that the onset of spacing was not clearly diffused over time.

The picture that emerges from the cluster analysis is that of a largely uniform adaptation to the features of life in the central regions by the lengthening of duration between births. As the transition proceeded this spacing of births extended to the delay of first births within the regions most familiar with spacing. Fertility truncation certainly increased throughout the state, but in a more heterogeneous fashion than birth spacing. Later ages at marriage were nearly uniform across the state in the early stages of the transition. No single pattern of diffusion emerges. Instead, we see a largely uniform decline in fertility achieved by varying means in different regions of the state. The greatest evidence of interpretable regional variations appears to be the greatest regulation of fertility by means of birth spacing over the entire life course in more densely settled areas. Given the lack of temporal diffusion patterns for this birth spacing, it seems plausible to suggest that this greater reliance on birth spacing reflects the greater life-long opportunity costs and alternative consumer goods available in the more densely settled areas.

It is readily apparent that a very different picture emerges if one clusters patterns of change over time than if one examines levels of fertility measures and behaviors. While the profiles that emerge from the two analyses are not entirely inconsistent, the delineation of specific patterns of behavior supporting the greater fertility declines in the cities are distinctly clarified if one controls for heterogeneities in fertility levels and examines patterns of change over time. The analysis of fertility levels translates a somewhat uniform decline in fertility levels into a misleading picture of diffusion of fertility behaviors.

The more detailed analysis of geographic patterns of change in proximate fertility determinants, or fertility behaviors, reveals far more complex patterns of change and cannot be subsumed under a simple geographic diffusion hypothesis. None of the clusterings resulted in a clearly identifiable dichotomy of characteristic areas, those that experienced an earlier fertility decline and others that followed at a later time after some diffusion of behaviors.

Even a summary of patterns found is difficult. Generally speaking, fertility levels (CEB) were found to decline most substantially in central regions of the state but were geographically heterogeneous outside the central cities, evidencing no simple direct transmission to nearly rural communities. Patterns of change in wife's age at marriage varied greatly by region, suggesting that marital behavior itself was similarly not simply a geographically diffused phenomenon. Birth spacing, as reflected in increasing first, average, and last birth-intervals, became more common in central cities and was more narrowly confined to these geographic regions. The relative regional confinement of birth spacing, and especially delay of first births to central areas, suggests a possible role of the commercial environments within these areas, environments with greater alternative consumption possibilities or householding requirements early in the life course. These patterns of change may suggest a case of diffusion outward from central cities, perhaps paralleling the outward spread of commercial alternatives. Finally, the patterns of change in age at last birth are not centered within these core cities, although these areas did have progressively earlier ages at last birth. Significant, but scant, evidence of spacing and truncation as alternatives comes from the fact that the greatest declines in age at last birth occurred among some areas with less consistent patterns of increase in birth spacing.

Again, neither the analysis of fertility levels nor the analysis of patterns of change is sufficient to address the debate of adaptation and innovation in full. However, the particular adoption of fertility limitation across the life course within cities seems to support inferential adaptive arguments. The more narrowly defined is the specific behavior or technology under question, the more tractable and realistic the questions of adaptation and innovation become.

SUMMARY AND DISCUSSION

The process of transforming a population characterized by high fertility to a population characterized by low fertility can be described in several ways. Often researchers focus simply on completed family size, examining the average family size among specific categories at sequential intervals. This type of analysis for the MHDP population was the beginning point for the geographic analysis of fertility change presented in this chapter. The result of the analysis (see fig. 23) suggests, in a general way, that one might be observing a process of innovative behavior adopted by the populations of the major central settlement areas, replicated in (or diffused to) surrounding regions in later time periods. As one would anticipate for women initiating childbearing during the period 1911–30, the lowest levels of completed family size are found in the major communities, which lie along the northcentral-southwestern axis of the state.

Small families had not yet become the pattern for the three communities to the east of the central mountain chain—Price, Vernal, and Moab. There are only a few additional exceptions to the anticipated pattern. St. George and its county, Washington, in the southwest corner of the state, are represented with somewhat higher than expected levels of completed fertility, but each was separated somewhat from the major transportation and communication links in the last period, 1931–50. With the death of Brigham Young and the termination of polygyny, these areas lost their function as second homes for certain leaders of the community who were resident for most of the year in the central cities. Additionally, the rail network ran south to Iron County and then west toward Los Angeles, leaving Washington County somewhat isolated. Juab County was also an anomaly, having achieved a low level of fertility comparable to that of the central cities; yet Juab was an area of declining economic opportunities, as reflected by a significant decline in population size. The last exception to the predicted pattern, Manti, in Sanpete County, more than other communities, continued as an agricultural center.

Before one can accept the seeming validity of the diffusion notion, however, one must, we have argued, extend the analysis in two ways. First it is necessary to ascertain whether the pattern of change in mechanisms associated with declining fertility are consistent with changes in levels, and second it is essential to supplement the visual inspection of changes with a more comprehensive statistical analysis to identify common clusters of communities with respect to patterns of fertility change.

The analysis presented above indicates that there is no one common pattern of behavioral changes associated with the shift from high to low fertility. In each measure examined—age at marriage, various spacing indices, as well as truncation measures—there is considerable heterogeneity in the patterns observed. Yet one might anticipate some heterogeneity if one distinguishes between spacing and stopping. We previously argued that early fertility control was dependent upon the use of ineffective technologies, which would encourage early "testing" if couples were to achieve a smaller family size. With improvements in technologies, couples might be able to delay testing and implementation. Thus one would predict that early adoption in the central communities would be reflected in a more common pattern of spacing, while more isolated communities, adopting the idea of the small-family norm later, would be more likely to truncate. The first set of communities would be marked by delays of marriage, increased first birth-intervals, and increased average birth-intervals. The second set of communities would be marked by rapidly declining age at last birth and increasing last birth-intervals.[2] Consequently, in the last step of our analysis, clustering was performed on patterns of change in fertility behaviors.

There are several important conclusions that must be drawn from this analysis. First, the pattern of change in children ever born is less complex and more uniform than patterns of change in the behaviors used to achieve these lower fertility levels. All clustered regions displayed declines in fertility, which differed primarily in magnitude. Only one cluster represented areas that experienced a slight delay in their fertility decline. Central cities and counties were among those areas that experienced the greatest decline in fertility. Second, there are relatively uniform differentials in the geographic distribution of birth spacing over the entire life course. Those areas that achieved the greatest decline in fertility also appear to have made the greatest use of interbirth delay of childbearing. However, the lack of any temporal pattern of diffusion seems to suggest that the spacing of births was an adaptive feature of the more "urban" life in these areas rather than a process of innovation and diffusion. Third, the spacing of births appears to have occurred alongside an early onset of delayed marriage. There is some slight evidence that delaying of marriage and spacing were inversely related and represented alternative means of early-life-course fertility reduction. Finally, there is no evidence of geographically bounded or diffused reliance upon fertility truncation. While truncation was doubtless a feature of the fertility transition, its appearance and spread during the fertility transition was extremely heterogeneous, without clear patterns of either innovation-diffusion or adaptation.

The evidence would seem to suggest a uniform statewide fertility decline, with regions employing multiphasic means to limit fertility. A somewhat greater decline occurred in central parts of the state, where opportunities, costs, and alternative consumption possibilities perhaps led to greater efforts to avert or delay childbearing across the entire life course.

Throughout recent research the innovation-diffusion hypothesis has been progressively broadened in scope. In Carlsson's (1966) discussion the hypothesis has a narrow focus, referring explicitly to dissemination of a contraceptive technological innovation. Subsequent research on the hypothesis has included analysis of behavioral innovations. Ultimately, as Rudolf Andorka (1978) notes, broadening the definition of the object being diffused leads to an intractable and inseparable concept. While a diffusion hypothesis is potentially meaningful and testable for a clearly identifiable innovation, it becomes progressively less so as the object of diffusion is less separable from other diffusion processes.

In the Utah transition, there is clear evidence of "multiphasic" (Davis 1963) fertility limitation patterns. Ages at marriage tended to be heterogeneous but clearly on the rise. It is not unreasonable to suppose that early-life-course opportunity costs were responsible for much of the marital delay within the population. Similarly, increases in spacing of early births were strongest in central cities but were apparent throughout the state and likely reflect similar early opportunity costs and some intentional fertility avoidance or delay based upon ultimate desired family sizes and current conditions. Fertility truncation, or termination, is also evidenced in the later life course, when desired family sizes were approached or exceeded. There is no question that fertility levels were lower within cities and their surrounding reaches, but it is clear that no one behavioral innovation of a clearly identifiable nature was responsible for changing fertility levels.

The diffusion hypothesis, however, goes further than this, by suggesting a causal ecological relation between the city declines and those of the surrounding areas. But the relatively heterogeneous patterns of change in specific fertility-limiting behaviors within the frontier population do not support such a simple diffusion thesis. We might expect such heterogeneous patterns to have emerged in that the differences in the pace of adopting such behaviors in the different regions were negligible, that is, in that the adoption of fertility-limiting strategies across regions of the state occured simultaneously; for this timing suggests that interregional influence was not the cause of the adoption but was instead largely random. In the MHDP population, it is arguable that the major influence on fertility behavior came from the rapid incorporation of the Utah population into the mainstream U.S. economy over the period under consideration. Both initial heterogeneities in behavior and the persistence of these initial differences throughout the transition support the suggestion that regional fertility declines were part of a population-wide response to changing socio-economic environments across the state. This is consistent with the fact that the spread of public education, dry farming and marginal agriculture, commercial enterprise, and so forth have all been associated with lower fertility and were not confined to urban areas.

CHAPTER 9

Fertility Change on the Frontier

Fertility change on the American frontier is a distinctive phenomenon, and although the change was transitory within specific regions of the frontier, it was present among some sectors of the population for as much as three centuries. The analysis presented in this volume covers more than one hundred years of fertility behavior and confirms certain demographic consequences of frontier settlement. Our analysis documents an initial frontier effect when fertility increased, reaching high levels similar to those of populations selected to represent maximum, uncontrolled fertility. Consistent with the proposition that frontier effects are transitory, within a few decades fertility declined. The decline on the American frontier appeared at approximately the same time as the secular decline among many populations of Western Europe (Coale and Treadway 1986), identified as "the fertility transition." Consequently, it is possible to investigate the question of whether theoretical descriptions of Western European fertility transitions are consistent with the frontier fertility decline in the latter decades of the period covered by our analysis (Lee 1987).

At the beginning of this volume, we noted that the study dealt with the phenomena of fertility changes rather than fertility transitions per se. The concept of "fertility change" was adopted to describe two periods, one marked by a "frontier effect," or increase in fertility, and the second marked by a fertility decline, or transition from high to moderate fertility. As a convenience, we have employed the term "fertility transition" frequently to refer to both processes. In this concluding chapter we summarize the results of our analysis to clarify both the distinction between the frontier effect and fertility transitions and the relationship between the two.

In the first major section of this concluding chapter, we examine the notion of the frontier effect and its implications for fertility analysis. In the next section we focus on the period of fertility decline, the fertility transition among the population as it became more urbanized, more commerical, and more closely integrated into the national economy. This section provides a summary of the adaptation-innovation argument and an assessment of the degree to which an initial frontier effect may predispose populations in such environments to adopt behavioral patterns different from those of European populations that have been selected to model the classic fertility transition.

These two sections emphasize general theoretical issues. However, it is important not to lose sight of the fact that this study deals with a population whose motivations for settlement were related to a particular religious movement. Thus the population involved in the settlement of the region was perhaps different from other populations. The population has been identified as a high-fertility population, and the traditional explanation for this is that the population was and still is largely composed of members of the LDS church. The church is noted for its pro-family and pronatalist values, and these have traditionally pointed to a normative explanation of fertility. In the last section of this chapter we examine specific contextual effects that suggest that a simple normative explanation of fertility behavior in this population is inadequate.

THE FRONTIER EFFECT

Frontier settlement should be viewed, from the perspective of social science methodology, as a classic social experiment. It is a distinctive phenomenon that can be isolated in time and space. It is a process that dominated some part of the American scene from initial colonization until the late nineteenth century, and in a few areas until the early twentieth century. It is not, however, exclusively a New World phenomenon, but includes vast reaches of the world, historically and contemporarily. Within the last several years new frontier settlements have been identified even in Africa. For example, the Kofyar, an ethnic group of Plateau State Nigeria, has colonized the Benue valley savana within the last thirty-five years (Stone, Netting, and Stone 1987). Other examples are found in Indonesia, which through its transmigration policies aggressively pursues frontier settlement on sparsely settled islands; the Soviet Union, which continues to encourage Siberian settlements; and Brazil, whose government encourages settlement and development of the Amazon basin.

The value of treating the frontier as a social experiment in part derives from the fact that the demography of frontier populations is different from that of other populations. Ronald Lee, in his presidential address to the Population Association of America in 1987, argued that "there are many kinds of evidence for homeostasis in human populations, including the rapid expansion of some frontier populations" (1987, p. 445). Robert Johnson attributes the rapid population growth on the island of Mindanao to high fertility, declining mortality, early age at marriage, and "a large 'frontier stream' of migration to Mindanao from the more settled islands of Luzon, Bicol, and the Visaya" (1985, p. 243). Migration is an important factor in the rapid growth among frontier populations, but an important frontier effect seems to be the encouragement of early family formation and high fertility. Coale's explanation of high fertility in America summarizes the argument succinctly:

> When there is a large change in the availability of resources, traditional restraints on fertility are generally modified. An example is the settlement of North America by West Europeans. The settlers brought with them the technology of Europe, which was applied, with adaptation to new conditions, to extensive and very fertile land, until then sparsely settled by a population still dependent at least partly on hunting and fishing. The native population was progressively displaced; the supply of agricultural land the colonists could occupy was, by European standards, enormous. In Europe, the colonists had been accustomed to marrying late because only at an age in the late twenties or higher had men come into possession of land or qualified for the steady positions that customs dictated marriage required; custom also sanctioned only a slight difference in age between bride and groom, so that women as well as men married late. In America, the young European immigrant or his descendants could always settle at the frontier; also the plentiful supply of land meant a relatively high demand for labor, if individuals chose to work for wages. Indeed, the high fertility in the United States (TFR over 7 in 1800) was highest near the frontier, and much lower in the long-settled seaboard areas. (1986, pp. 19–20)

High fertility on the American frontier has been widely recognized among scholars of American historical demography. Following from such research, the concept of "land availability" has been suggested as a major explanation of regional differences in fertility (Yasuba 1962;

Forster and Tucker 1972; Easterlin, Alter, and Condron 1978; Stern 1987). Vinovskis (1976,1978) has criticized the land-availability thesis, but his study of Massachusetts in 1860 is an inappropriate test because it deals with a region with well-established property rights, relatively small land parcels, and a population in which family limitation had become widespread. Nevertheless the simple notion of land availability may be much too restrictive.

Economic opportunities arise on the frontier not simply because available land provides new opportunities. The institutional structures that govern access to and distribution of land must be considered. As David Kertzer and Caroline Brettell argue in their reanalysis of studies of Iberian and Italian family history, "no family system can be understood apart from the political economic context in which it is found" (1987, p. 88). The linkage of resource availability and political economic systems is evident, as well, in Malthus's *An Essay on the Principle of Population.* We argue that a more satisfactory concept linking land availability to political economic systems is the notion of the frontier. The concept of the frontier essentially presents a region—geographic, temporal, or economic—within which perceived economic opportunities are substantially greater than in other, more populated regions and within which the political-economic system supports relatively open access to resource exploitation. The demographic response to the frontier involves, of course, mass migration, as well as high fertility.

Increases in fertility occur in a wide range of situations, however. They are noted among many populations during the initial stages of industrialization and modernization. Such increases are attributed in some cases to changes in reproductive capacity (Trovato 1987). In other cases increases are attributed to reductions in length of birth intervals associated with relaxation of postpartum taboos (Bongaarts 1979) as well as to reductions in the practice or intensity of breastfeeding (Romaniuk 1974). However, initial stages of modernization and industrialization may be conceived as simply a special case of the frontier effect. Virginia Abernethy, for example, has suggested that the delayed fertility-decline in many developing countries may reflect a "rising-tide-of-expectations" (1979). Thus there may be a theoretical similarity between the initial rise in fertility on the American frontier and the initial rise in fertility in Russia (Coale 1986, p. 20), Kenya, and other countries. The concept of frontiers may have more general applicability than is implied by its common use in reference to the settlement of sparsely occupied regions during particular periods.

The frontier effect generates a rise in fertility, but data presented in this volume provides greater specification of the underlying mechanisms associated with the increase. Two changes were important in the study population: a change in age at marriage and a change in fertility behavior within marriages. Data presented in chapter 4 indicates that during the period of increasing fertility the mean age at marriage declined. Among the oldest cohorts (1800-04) only 30 percent of the women married before age 20. These women married in settled regions of the United States and Western Europe. Among the cohorts born at midcentury, who achieved the highest fertility levels, 58 percent married before age 20. Most of these women married on the frontier.

Changes in age at marriage do not account fully for the rise in overall fertility levels. Within each age-at-marriage category—less than 20, 20–24, and 25 plus—the number of children ever born (CEB) increased as well. These later changes suggest modifications of behavior within marriages. We find that the migrant women who accounted for much of the relative rise in fertility among earlier cohorts persisted in childbearing to older ages. For example, in a further analysis of migrant fertility behavior (Mineau, Bean, and Anderton 1989), we found that, among the 1830–59 cohorts of women born in Great Britain, those women who initiated childbearing in Great Britain and completed childbearing on the frontier had their last birth at the average age of 41 years and 6 months. Women who completed childbearing in Great Britain and then migrated to the frontier had their last child over three years earlier, at the average age of 38 years and 5 months. The difference among migrants from Scandinavia was 41 years and 10 months versus 39 years and 6 months. Bean and Mineau (1988) also show that women who migrated to the frontier during the childbearing years of life after initiating childbearing in Europe experienced an increased birth interval during the migration process, which was then followed by a shorter birth interval.

One should not, however, romanticize the American frontier as an area of unlimited equal opportunities. Political-economic systems on the frontier provided greater opportunities for some but not all of the settlers. In Utah the early settlers were more likely to have access to land as well as economic and community support if they were strict adherents to the LDS faith and responsive to the dictates of the ecclesiastical leaders who initially dominated the political system. The rise in fertility was greater among the "committed" LDS and the converts than it was among the non-LDS, the nonactive, and those with partial association;

yet within each of these groups fertility increased. This parallel increase in fertility among each of these groups further documents the ubiquity of the frontier effect.

In contrast to other studies of rising fertility, our analysis suggests, on the basis of various tests of proximate determinants affecting fertility within marriages, that the changes are the result of shifts in voluntary determinants of fertility. The data suggest a rational adaptation of marriage and childbearing to opportunities on the frontier. Thus the migrants to the frontier not only adapted technologies imported from Europe and the settled eastern regions of the United States to the frontier but adapted patterns of marriage and fertility to the frontier. How this adaptation strategy was subsequently modified as the territory, and later the state, became more urban and more industrialized is an issue that is addressed through an examination of the period marked by a fall in fertility levels.

FERTILITY DECLINE ON THE FRONTIER: ADAPTATION OR INNOVATON?

The Utah frontier and its frontier effect lasted for less than half a century. By the 1880s the beginning of the end of the frontier was in sight, and fertility had started to decline. Period fertility rates decrease by 19 percent from 1885–89 to 1905–09. However, the pace of decline is more evident in fertility rates for birth cohorts. The rates fell by 31 percent from the 1845–49 cohort to the 1895–99 cohort, with 20 percent of the decline occurring among the 1875–79 to 1895–99 cohorts of women.

The Utah economy had been linked to the national system by 1869, when the transcontinental rail link was completed in Utah. Mining, primarily a "gentile" (non-LDS) activity, began to reach its potential when ores could be economically transported to eastern smelters and markets. The federal government exercised increased control over the territory. During the 1880s federal agents forced leaders of the church into an underground existence as the marshals sought to prosecute church leaders for polygyny. The Perpetual Emigration Fund, which supported migration of converts from Europe, was declared illegal. Accessible land had been successfully exploited, and few new communities would be established in the next decade. Did these changes result in a simple adaptation to modified economic and political systems, or did the changes create a new climate in which the value of smaller families and the acceptance of technology to achieve those smaller families represented an innovation that rapidly diffused through the population?

Three closely linked assumptions or propositions can be derived from a review of the literature supporting the argument that the European fertility transition is best described in terms of a process of innovation and diffusion. These are:

1. Before the transition, European populations were marked by natural-fertility schedules; fertility behavior was not parity dependent.

2. The initial adoption of parity-dependent control is marked by increasing truncation of the childbearing experience.

3. Parity-dependent control appears first among a select subset of the population, and then appears later among other groups. That is, there is a lag between the initial adoption among specific groups and adoption among other groups.

Several forms of analyses presented in chapters 5 through 8 lead us to reject various propositions associated with the characterization of the documented fertility decline among the MHDP population as a form of innovation and diffusion. The conclusions drawn from these analyses are summarized as follows:

1. Fertility limitation was not completely absent during periods when the MHDP population appeared to follow natural-fertility regimes. Our research went beyond the traditional modes of analysis and eliminated possible confounding effects of involuntary determinants of fertility, determinants presumed to account for variations in levels of fertility among diverse natural-fertility populations. We examined childbearing across the entire life course of mothers and specifically examined birth intervals within completed-family-size groups. Small clusters of seemingly highly motivated couples achieved limited numbers of children through the use of ineffective technologies early in marriage, and became increasingly adept in their use over the childbearing years of life.

As a consequence of this finding, we do not suggest that some pockets of fertility controllers will be found in every presumed natural-fertility population, although other researchers suggest that the phenomenon is more common than previously thought (David and Sanderson 1987; David and Mroz 1986). However, determination of the presence or absence of couples who limit family size through spacing cannot be accurately determined in many cases. Aggregate-level data obscure such differences. Bongaarts's macrosimulation model, used in this study, and other traditional methods designed to index the presence of natural-fertility schedules and increasing shifts toward control are not sensitive to spacing as a fertility-limitation strategy.

2. Widespread adoption of increasingly effective family limitation does not depend upon a single strategy, as suggested by previous studies emphasizing innovation and diffusion. These studies conclude that increasing fertility limitation is parity-dependent and involves primarily truncation after a given family-size target has been achieved. Analytical methods employed in these earlier studies are able, however, to identify only this type of change. For example, shifts in the curve of marital age-specific fertility rates from convex to concave and increasing values of Coale and Trussell's *m* are seemingly sensitive only to truncation and the decline of fertility at older ages.

The simulation studies presented in chapter 7 indicate that the observed marital age-specific fertility curves across those cohorts of women with progressively smaller family sizes can only be replicated if one changes parameters to reflect (1) increasing adoption of conception early rather than late in the childbearing experience and (2) increasingly effective use of contraception across the range of cohorts.

In addition, our tabular analysis of birth intervals—within parity groups across the range of cohorts representing minimum to maximum fertility limitation (within the MHDP population)—indicates that birth-interval distributions within final-parity groups is largely invariant across the transition. Falling fertility indicates what might be described as an important compositional change: the growth of subcohorts with small numbers of children achieved by birth spacing and the decline of subcohorts with moderate and large numbers of children born at short intervals.

The increasing adoption of birth-spacing strategies is, of course, coupled with increasing truncation. Both are important and suggest the adoption of multiple strategies. The adoption of alternative and perhaps multiple strategies to achieve more limited family-size targets is further documented in the analysis of geographic patterns of change presented in chapter 8. The pace of the decline in CEB varied among different communities and counties, and there was little consistency in the changes in age at marriage, truncation, and birth spacing.

3. Increasing family-size limitation occurred simultaneously among

a wide range of subcohorts rather than sequentially. This conclusion directly addresses the assumption of initial adoption of family-size limitation among specific groups and subsequent diffusion across other groups. The evidence supporting our conclusion is consistent across a wide range of subcohorts defined by marriage type, age at marriage, origin, time of arrival on the frontier, religion, and residence history.

Chapter 8 provided an extensive geographic test of the diffusion argument. Analyzing changes in fertility levels across three time periods, for populations initiating childbearing in thirteen communities and twenty-nine counties, we find some support for the notion of diffusion from urban to rural communities at the most general level of analysis. Further analysis of cluster patterns of change indicates that the preliminary conclusion is incomplete. The initial conclusion reflects the same type of erroneous judgment that one might make after looking at subcohort fertility differences cross-sectionally. At any specific time, the variations in levels of fertility would suggest initial adoption among groups traditionally assumed to adopt fertility limitation earlier than other groups. For example, women resident in Utah's central areas evidenced lower fertility than women resident in other, largely agricultural areas of the state. However, as noted above, those differences are consistent at the beginning of the observed period of the fertility decline, across the period, and at the end of the period.

In the geographic analysis presented in chapter 8, clustering of patterns of change clarified the process. The patterns of change in age at marriage, age at last birth, and birth intervals did not reflect a simple pattern of diffusion across the geographic regions. The conditions leading to changes in tastes for and costs of children emerged simultaneously across a wide range of communities linked together through the spread of effective means of communication and transportation, but the methods employed to reduce family size varied among the various communities and counties.

In summary, the process of fertility change documented for the MHDP population appears to have been somewhat different from that found among Western European populations. There were two phases. First, there was a period of rising fertility, reflecting a frontier effect. Fertility during the frontier period indicates a strategy of adaptation to a distinctive setting in which settlements expanded rapidly, matured quickly, and were soon integrated into larger (national) socioeconomic environments. Second, there was a systematic decline in fertility across a wide range of subcohorts. Rapid change and evolution was virtually imposed on the population by a social process of settlement over which initial settlers soon lost all control.

These findings, however, pose a further, important theoretical question: What is the relevance of normative explanations of fertility levels and change? This question stems from the observation that, among a population dominated by a pro-family, pronatalist religion, fertility declined in an amount and at a pace similar to that observed among many Western European populations. However, like that in the populations of many developing societies, the level of fertility in the MHDP population at the outset of the transition was considerably higher than the level of fertility in the settled, eastern regions of the United States or in Western Europe, where many of the migrants were born, were married, and commenced childbearing. Perhaps by exploring possible reasons for a decline of such a magnitude within a normative system favoring high fertility, it will be possible to suggest lines of investigation to clarify the importance of normative explanations of high fertility.

THE FRAMEWORK FOR FERTILITY CHANGE

Our study of fertility change has demonstrated the validity of the conclusion of Kingsley Davis and its restatement by Charles Hirschman that when "something" motivates successive cohorts of women to limit family size, multiple strategies are employed. Strategies used by the MHDP population were the delaying of marriage, truncation, and spacing. Our data suggest that the rise in fertility also reflects more than one mechanism, and that the rise in fertility may not be attributable simply to unintended acts or circumstances such as increased fecundability, shortened birth-intervals due to decreased breastfeeding, or simply marrying at younger ages to take advantage of actual or perceived lower costs of establishing new families. While we can clearly document the mechanisms of and paths to changing family size, we can only speculate on the most important question: What specifically motivated ever-larger proportions of sequential cohorts of women to adopt multiple strategies for achieving family sizes different from those achieved by women in earlier birth cohorts?

Therefore it becomes more interesting to ask: What happened to shift the costs of and tastes for children almost simultaneously among a variety of different groups, generating first a rise and then a decline in fertility? In the first section of this chapter we discussed the relevance of the frontier environment to this question. In this concluding section we suggest several reasons for the decline in fertility. Issues related to the means of controlling fertility were discussed at the end of chapter 1 and will not be repeated here. Particular attention will be given to the changes that contribute to an explanation of a shift in the desire for a large family to a desire for a small family. We focus on (1) institutional discontinuity and (2) economic integration.

INSTITUTIONAL DISCONTINUITY

We use the concept of institutional discontinuity to refer to the rupture of economic, political, educational, and religious institutions. The notion of institutional discontinuity is not, of course, a new idea, for it has similarities to Caldwell's discussion of the reversal of wealth transfers and the development of educational systems. In China the concept applies to the revolution and the implementation of a comprehensive political system that displaced traditional authority structures and institutions. In certain Middle Eastern Islamic countries, failure to control fertility stems not from lack of commitment but rather from continuity of institutional structures, not only Islam but also the tribe and ethnic groups.

On the American frontier, fairly soon after the initial successful settlement and colonization, the institutional structure of the community was threatened. During the first quarter-century of colonization, the authorities of the LDS church were generally successful in maintaining social, political, and economic control over the region. Settlement was directed by the central church authorities, and land allocated to the "faithful" by the church. A church-controlled commercial and industrial program was developed, and an education system organized and operated by the church. Even with the replacement of Brigham Young as governor of the territory by an outsider who was not a member of the church, mobilization of the population was sufficient to control the nonfederal political system at the city and county levels.

Two decades after the initial settlement, the completion of the railroad and broadened federal control increased the flow of non-LDS into the region. The development of the mining industry began to concentrate wealth in the hands of the non-LDS. Federal laws designed to eliminate polygyny undermined religious authority; stripped women of the right to vote; eliminated the Perpetual Emigration Fund, thus cutting off resources for converts in Europe to join the settlement; and drove the polygynous leadership of the church underground as they were hounded during the 1880s (the period of the "raid"). By 1890 the church had capitulated to national pressure, eliminating plural marriage as a right—in some cases a virtual responsibility—of the righteous men who were the leaders of the church. Before the beginning of World War I religious educational institutions (academies) had generally been replaced by a secular education system. No longer could one plan on an economic future dictated by the church. Land control and distribution passed to federal authorities; easily irrigated land was fully occupied; dry land farming was more expensive; and fragile agricultural communities had become ghost towns.

Whatever the dictates of the church regarding the value of having a large family, the economic reality mitigated such behavior. Zion had become a symbol rather than a fully integrated, developed economic system controlled by religious authorities who could guarantee a future, a place, a position, and employment for the children of the faithful. LDS children had to compete educationally and economically with children from gentile families. At least by the end of World War I the growth of the economy was no longer sufficient to absorb the growing numbers of young people seeking employment opportunities. Utah became a population-exporting state. Some young people would find a place and future in Utah, but others joined the exodus from Utah. Utah could produce children, but it could not keep them. (See, for example, Frost 1949.)

These economic, political, educational, and religious changes, however, did not simply affect the populations within the central cities and then become evident to populations in other communities. Persecution of polygynous leaders occurred throughout the state, and mining communities controlled by the gentile community emerged in a variety of settings across Utah. The formal, hierarchal structure of the church, with its apex in Salt Lake City, allowed issues of concern to the Saints in the major urban community to be rapidly communicated down the structure, throughout the state. Leaders from across the state assembled twice a year in Salt Lake City, for guidance and direction. Communication was therefore both indirect and direct.

Thus the high period of natural fertility was temporary, stimulated by the settlement of the frontier but quickly undermined by the inability of the community to maintain a separate economic system with its own comprehensive institutional system. The institutional system of the early economic empire of the LDS population was weakened, but certainly not shattered. The LDS church and its population remain central to the state of Utah to the present. They did, however, undergo a series of dramatic changes, which we summarize by the concept of institutional discontinuity.

ECONOMIC INTEGRATION

Easterlin has suggested that one of the major factors accounting for the decline in fertility on the American frontier was the increased availability of consumer goods that changed the preference maps of individuals. Given limited financial resources, consumers of the new goods had to forgo other valued goods—large families, for example. Although there has been much criticism of classifying children as "consumer durables," it remains clear that when budgets are constrained, shifts in preference maps, including preferences for certain numbers of children, do occur. Perhaps the most forceful argument for the emergence of the American consumer society, dating from the nineteenth century, is made by Daniel J. Boorstin in his *The American: The Democratic Experience*:

> And there were created many communities of consumers. Men who never saw or knew one another were held together by their common use of objects so similar that they could not be distinguished even by their owners. These consumption communities were quick; they were nonideological; they were democratic; they were public and vague, and rapidly shifting. Consumption communities produced more consumption communities. They were factitious, malleable, and as easily made as they were evanescent. Never before had so many men been united by so many things. (1974, p. 90)

As we showed in chapter 2, the Utah community was not isolated from, or immune to, the consumer communities springing up elsewhere in the United States and intruding into Utah with the gentile mercantile establishment. Rather than reject such intrusions, Brigham Young joined and aided the movement, creating the cooperative stores that spread quickly throughout the region. Women in the rural communities did not have to wait for Montgomery Ward's first, single-sheet price list (published in 1872) because they already had access to a "co-op." These were linked to major stores in the central urban core, stocked by products from the manufacturing enterprises of the Saints, and supplemented with goods made available by the newly completed railroads. Rural Mormon women were probably linked into consumer markets earlier than women in other rural communities because of their unique settlement pattern, which differed from that typical midwestern pattern described by Boorstin as the American norm.

When economic integration came to Utah, it perhaps affected a greater area more quickly than it did when it came to other frontier regions. From the outset the church had fostered an integrated, internally controlled economic system. Intrusion into and integration of one sector of the system changed other components of the integrated system simultaneously. The process was perhaps furthered by the Saints' "buying into" the national system. For example, Brigham Young purchased stock in the Union Pacific Railroad for the church and contracted with the railroad to complete certain sections of the system (Arrington and Bitton 1979). The integration of the Utah economy into a national system thus created new consumer opportunities and new cost structures, which seemingly stimulated a decline in family size.

CONCLUSION

The notion of the fertility transition among Western European societies assumes the existence of natural-fertility schedules prior to the onset of the adoption of fertility limitation. The argument that in natural-fertility populations individuals uniformly fail to limit fertility within marriages, however, presupposes a wide range of additional behavioral tenets. These include, first, the view that the capacity to control family size is absent. It is assumed that the value structures of traditional Western European societies define the notion of fertility limitation as "unthinkable." Crude technological means to prevent conception may be known but are limited to illicit sexual "connections." There is no carryover from one sphere of sexual behavior to another, from the illegitimate to the legitimate—the hallowed family unit formed with the blessing of religious authority.

A second tenet flows from the first. It is the idea that rational decision making applies only when control is adopted. This tenet denies the fact that under existing family and economic systems large families may represent rational adaptations (Caldwell and Caldwell, 1987). The recognition that large families may represent rational choices rather than unintended denials and absent technologies has perhaps not been investigated as systematically as it should. We have suggested that the rise in fertility among the MHDP population not only reflects significant compositional shifts but also appears to represent decisions to continue to bear children later in life. During the early period on the frontier children were a good source of labor requiring minimal investment. This conclusion stands out as an aberration, however, because most studies attribute the rise in fertility during initial stages of modernization and industrialization to changing age at marriage, reduced levels of infecundity, or serendipitous reduction in the length of birth intervals. These studies, however, being based upon aggregate data, at best identify interesting correlations and suggests plausible conclusions. It has yet to be demonstrated for European populations, through individual-level, longitudinal data sets, that there have not been important modifications in behavior within marital unions across sequential cohorts.

In the behavioral sciences rational-choice theory has been studied primarily within a political-economic framework, but it may be fruitfully extended to research on variations in family size. The theory should not, however, be limited to accounting for the decline from periods of peak natural fertility to periods of low fertility that represent rational control within marriages. High fertility, too, may be a rational adaptation to new or expanding economic opportunities, whether actual or perceived. Research in this area is essential, for it is more theoretically useful to assume that fertility behavior is always rational than to assume that it is only sometimes rational; the former assumption in the long run simplifies our investigation of the causes of rapid fertility declines.

Without such an assumption we must explain three conditions: what factors move decisions related to family size from some null category into a range of rational decisions; what factors account for the change in family-size goals; and what factors account for increasingly effective attainment of limited fertility. Explanations of fertility change are more likely to be fruitful if we deal only with the last two rather than all three questions.

A third tenet presupposed by the natural-fertility argument, a tenet in part encapsulated in the first, is that fertility limitation in any society depends upon contraceptive technology that is highly effective, inexpensive, available, and aesthetically acceptable—in short, the sort of contraception that only became available a quarter of a century ago. Yet anthropologists, albeit without attempting to detail mechanisms as precisely as one might like, have argued repeatedly that family limitation occurs in a wide range of primitive societies, and that remarkably low levels of fertility had already been achieved among many populations by the time modern contraceptives began to appear.

In the study of fertility transitions, beyond the basic notion of the shift from natural fertility to family limitation—a notion having various questionable assumptions—is the incomplete effort to capture the range of conditions that alter both tastes for and costs of children. Preferences for particular family sizes, large or small, are formed not simply within economic frameworks but within social-cultural systems. Easterlin, in his attempt to marry social and economic theory by incorporating the concept of "norms" into the concept of "tastes," clearly recognizes this fact (1978). The expanding interest in "contextual" effects suggests a methodological strategy that might be pursued in clarifying the issue. It is incorrect, we would argue, to assume that preference maps, tastes for children, are dictated by competing options for and costs of consumer goods, no matter how precise the calculus of rational economic planning within the family. Tastes are formed within particular social-cultural conditions, and the attempt by Western nations to introduce family-limitation programs into less-developed countries may well be unsuccessful unless there is a systematic internal restructuring of the societal system within which family values are formed. Fertility began to fall among MHDP women for a variety of reasons, but certainly critical was the disruption of the political-religious system and the integration of the Utah economy into the national economy. Even as the population responded to these pressures, which increased the cost of children and provided alternate consumption schedules, the religious system continued to maintain a preference for more children than one would find among comparable socioeconomic groups.

The high fertility that continues to the present in Utah is not simply a reflection of a particular set of normative standards. While these pro-family, pronatalist norms influence consumer preferences, they are only effective within a particular social system. In chapter 2 we suggested an explanation for high fertility among the Mormons according to which family-size preferences do not simply arise from a positive, pro-family set of values. Pro-family values, relative to other values, are shaped within the normative context of the religion and are reinforced and rewarded within the structure of the church. There are rewards, psychological but real, which accrue to the families of moderate rather than small size. Indeed, family size represents a rational decision-making process in a wide range of societies and cultures across a wide range of time periods.

Appendix

Period, Birth Cohort, and Marriage Cohort Data

The materials presented in this appendix provide further justification for limiting the analysis presented in this volume to the fertility of birth cohorts of women. Table A.1 contains the age-specific fertility rates and a summary measure, the MTFR, for synthetic cohorts, that is, period rates. In addition the MTFR for actual birth cohorts is presented. We compare the data for two synthetic cohorts (1870–74 and 1915–19) and two birth cohorts (1835–44 and 1880–89). For reference purposes the synthetic cohorts are read across the rows and the birth cohorts are read along the diagonals and are identified by underlining. The MTFR peaked in 1870–74, at 11.40 and fell to 9.23 in 1915–19, a decline of 19 percent. Comparing the age-specific fertility rates for the two synthetic cohorts, it would appear that the decline in fertility is general for all age groups; the decline is surprisingly high for the young women age 20–24, 11.5 percent (.4662 to .4126).

In the case of two birth cohorts, the decline from the peak MTFR of 11.14 for women born in 1835–44 to the MTFR of 9.12 for women born in 1881–89 is similar to the decline between the two time periods that reflects the experience of synthetic cohorts—18.1 percent. While MTFR declines at about the same rate over the same number of years, the reduction among birth cohorts is greater among older women and less among young women relative to the change observed between the two synthetic cohorts. For the women age 20–24 the reduction is 4.6 percent, less than half the rate of decline identified by comparing two

TABLE A.1

MARITAL AGE-SPECIFIC AND MARITAL TOTAL-FERTILITY RATES, 1815–19 TO 1940–44

Period	Age at Birth of Children							Period	Birth Cohort[a]
	15–19	20–24	25–29	30–34	35–39	40–44	45–49	MTFR	MTFR
1815–19	(.3556)[b]								
1820–24	.3717	.4512							
1825–29	.4027	.4393	.4023						
1830–34	.4199	.4656	.4154	.3728					
1835–39	.4257	.4355	.4138	.3632	.3351				
1840–44	.4055	.4454	.4172	.3602	.3207	.2181			
1845–49	.3719	.4143	.3988	.3611	.2905	.1734	.0461	10.28	10.91
1850–54	.4088	.4521	.4093	.3659	.3171	.1785	.0342	10.83	10.59
1855–59	.4217	.4448	.4160	.3765	.3178	.1820	.0212	10.90	10.66
1860–64	.4367	.4605	.4279	.3872	.3254	.1858	.0255	11.25	10.79
1865–69	.4379	.4548	.4274	.3927	.3299	.1814	.0238	11.24	10.82
1870–74	.4531	.4662	.4282	.3879	.3270	.1906	.0275	11.40	10.70
1875–79	.4506	.4620	.4176	.3862	.3279	.1894	.0294	11.32	10.89

1880–84	.4621	.4650	.4210	.3803	.3228	.1781	.0256	11.27	11.08
1885–89	.4650	.4562	.4143	.3729	.3179	.1787	.0249	11.15	11.14
1890–94	.4523	.4507	.4024	.3554	.3057	.1713	.0214	10.80	11.14
1895–99	.4703	.4438	.3876	.3435	.2864	.1716	.0236	10.63	11.07
1900–04	.4523	.4470	.3839	.3361	.2719	.1587	.0241	10.37	11.05
1905–09	.4662	.4391	.3784	.3244	.2767	.1472	.0197	10.26	10.75
1910–14	.4667	.4190	.3475	.3010	.2437	.1376	.0174	9.66	10.50
1915–19	.4518	.4126	.3352	.2786	.2317	.1217	.0145	9.23	10.34
1920–24		.4004	.3197	.2646	.2082	.1116	.0153		9.93
1925–29			.2789	.2242	.1729	.0901	.0121		9.76
1930–34				.1847	.1383	.0708	.0088		9.12
1935–39					.1107	.0537	.0077		8.68
1940–45						.0326	.0047		8.10

[a]These cohort rates are computed along the diagonals. They are not totally consistent with other birth-cohort rates because these aggregate and overlap different years; e.g., those ages 15–19 in 1820–24 were born 1801–09 and those ages 15–19 in 1825–29 were born 1806–14.

[b]Parentheses indicate fewer than 20 births.

synthetic cohorts, as noted above. Thus the use of period rates is less precise in identifying the time and age during which changes occur.

A further example is provided in figure A.1 in which age-specific fertility rates of women in age groups 15–19 through 40–44 are plotted on the basis of the data presented in table A.1. Note in figure A.1 that after approximately 1875–79, the age-specific fertility rates begin to decline for the age groups 25–29 through 40–44, with the amount of the decline increasing with age. To illustrate the period and cohort differences, we have drawn three lines marked A, B, and C through the age-specific-fertility line segments. Line A connects the points that would be included in the calculation of the period MTFR for 1870–74. Line B begins with the apex of line A, and then traces the fertility rates of women age 15–19 as they age. Their actual fertility rates as they age may be compared with the rates of the synthetic cohort of women (women married and exposed to the risk of childbearing in 1870–74) that is anchored by the same group that was age 15–19 in 1870–74 (line A). During this initial period of fertility decline, the cohort of women age 15–19 in 1870–74 did not behave a great deal differently from women in similar age groups in 1890–94, although by the time these women (age 15–19 in 1870–74) were age 40–44 they had a slightly lower probability (9 percent) of having a child than women age 40–44 in 1870–74. Line C traces the age-specific fertility rates of women age 15–19 in 1890–94. By the time these women were 40–44, in 1915–19, their probability of having a child relative to women age 40–44 in 1895–99 had been reduced by 30 percent. These illustrations indicate, again, that a comparison of synthetic cohorts underestimates the decline in fertility in older ages and overestimates the decline in fertility in younger ages.

Regardless of the particular numerical values that result from various types of fertility calculations, it remains evident that the patterns are consistent. To validate that conclusion further, we present one final measure: parity progression ratios for birth cohorts of women. Parity progression ratios indicate the probability that a woman, once having achieved a given parity, n, would continue to have at least one additional birth, $n + 1$. Whether women purposefully exerted control over fertility or not, one anticipates that parity progression ratios will fall within increasingly higher parities. Because parity is related to age and age in turn is related to fecundability, the predicted decline is in part physiologically determined. Data summarized graphically in figure A.2 confirm the obvious and indicate the consistency of the decline in the

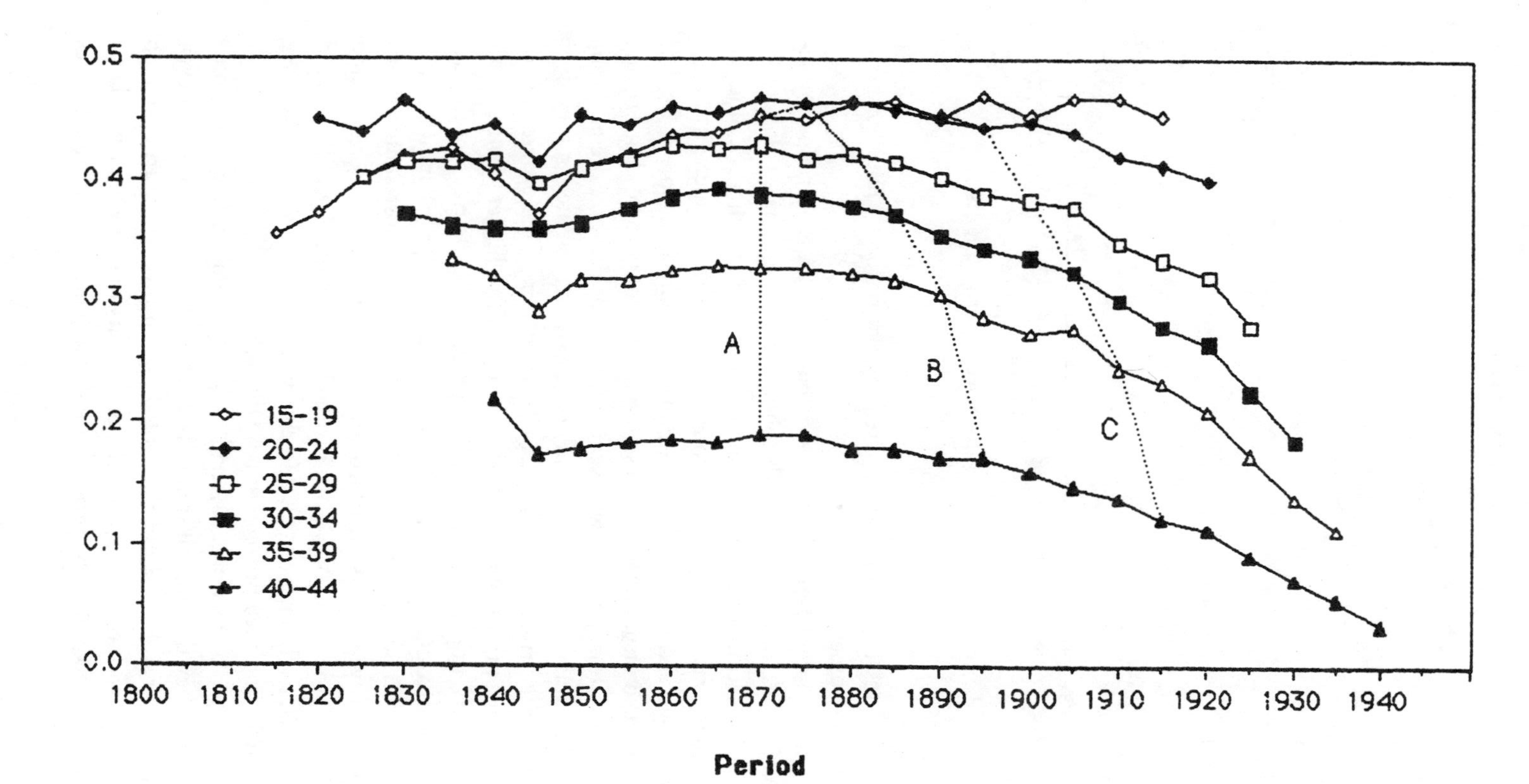

Figure A.1. Marital Fertility Rates by Age and Period of Observation

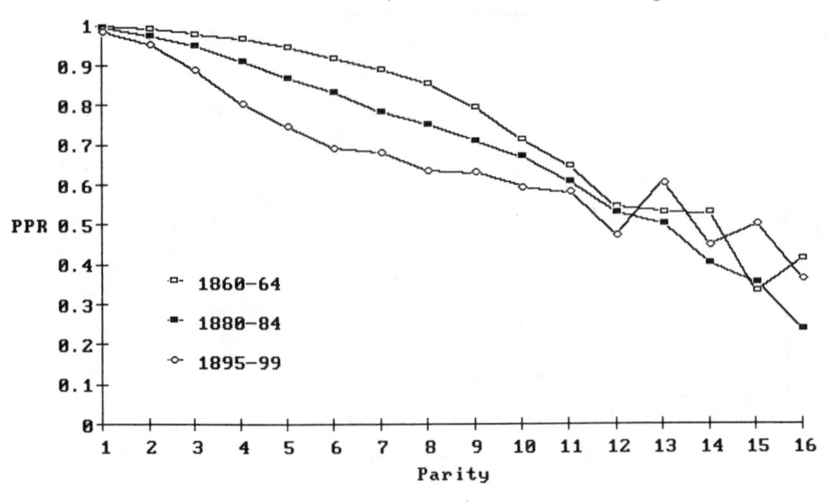

Figure A.2. Parity Progression Ratios for Selected Birth Cohorts

parity progression ratios, with increasing parity for a sample of birth cohorts of women.[1]

Of more interest are the values of parity progression ratios for selected parities for successive birth cohorts of women. These values more precisely indicate the degree to which the decline in fertility is a function of changing final-parity distributions. Probabilities of achieving parities of two, four, six, eight, and ten are plotted in figure A.3. Note again that these data confirm our earlier description of fertility trends but provide additional information. If we exclude from consideration the first four cohorts because of the smaller number of cases represented, it is evident that the initial rise in fertility is largely a function of the progression of an increasing proportion of women on to relatively higher parities. Thus the rise in average completed fertility reflects to a certain extent the fact that an increasing proportion of women had quite large families. However, the decline in marital fertility indicates an almost simultaneous drop in parity progression ratios for women at parities four, six, and eight. The proportion of women proceeding from the first to the second birth is relatively unchanged, and the proportion of women who have nine births and then proceed to ten falls only modestly.

Thus once women already had very large families (e.g., over nine children), they did not substantially alter their progression on to even larger family sizes, nor did the probability of proceeding from first to second births change. However, the probability of ever achieving a large family in the first place by progression through intermediate family sizes

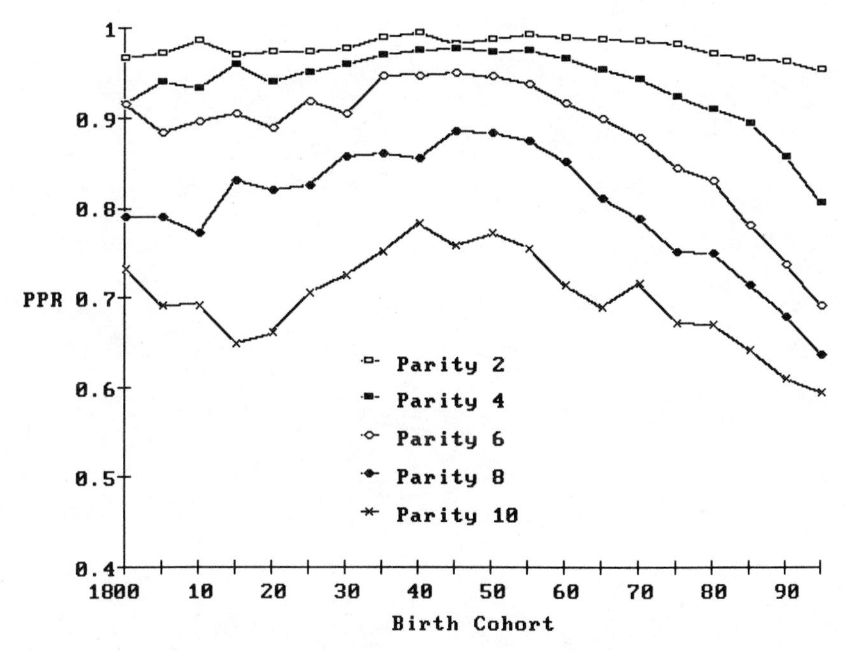

Figure A.3. Parity Progression Ratios by Parity, by Birth Cohorts

(e.g., four, six, and eight) dropped significantly, a fact that accounts for most of the decline in overall average family size.

These results suggest the importance of examining in detail, as we did in chapter 7, the relationship between changing fertility behavior—spacing—within completed-family-size groups.

Notes

ACKNOWLEDGMENTS

1. Investigators associated with the development of the Utah Population Database gratefully acknowledge support provided under the following grants: NIH/NCI/CA 16573 and 28854 (Skolnick); NIH/NICHHD/HD 10267 and 15455 (Bean); NIH/NICHHD/HD 16109 (Jorde); NIH/NHLBI/HL 21088 and 20455 (Williams); NSF BHS-8700864 (Anderton-CASBS).

1. FERTILITY CHANGE ON THE AMERICAN FRONTIER

1. One must assume, however, that prior to the beginning of the secular, modern decline in fertility in Sweden (circa 1880), Sweden possessed a relatively tightly integrated national economic system. One must also assume that the population was homogeneous in language, culture, and religion, so that no "barriers" impeded the nearly immediate effect of socioeconomic changes in one region on other regions.

2. For an application of M and m to these genealogical data see table 19 in chapter 6. For a recent critique of these indices, see Blake 1985 and Wilson, Oeppen, and Pardoe 1988.

3. By "imperfect technology" we imply two characteristics: first, a technology that is less than 100 percent effective in preventing conception, and second, a technology that poses certain aesthetically undesirable features, such as being action-specific or limiting spontaneity. Adoption of imperfect technologies early in the family life cycle may be followed by other forms of behavior after the desired family size is achieved. One should note that in the case of imperfect technology, multiple methods may be employed simultaneously where commit-

ment to preventing conception is very high. See, for example, Freedman, Whelpton, and Campbell 1959, p. 174.

4. For example, the extensive bibliography in Rodman Paul and Richard Etulain's *The Frontier and the American West,* comprising 2,973 citations, basically excludes the issue (1977). The bibliography's thirty-six sections include several dealing with population composition. One section is devoted to the Mormons, but the extensive literature on the Mormon family and fertility is not noted. In the section on "Women, the Family, and Women's Rights in the West," one paper is cited with reference to demography.

5. Readers of Yasuba's study should note that the early fertility ratios cited for Utah on pp. 52 and 53 are incorrect, owing either to a typographical error or to a calculation error. The figures published are too low.

6. Coale, for example, includes among the three conditions he identified as essential to stimulate a major reduction in marital fertility the fact that effective techniques of fertility reduction must be available (1973). Ron Lesthaeghe and Chris Wilson, however, question the explanatory power of this condition (1986).

2. THE CONTEXT OF CHANGING FERTILITY

1. See chapter 3 for an example and description of a family-group sheet.

2. Conflict over the issue of who would succeed Joseph Smith resulted in some splintering of the church, but the majority elected to accept Brigham Young as the church's legitimate, divinely ordained leader.

3. Leonard Arrington and Davis Bitton describe the settlement process in Utah, its organization and pattern, as a direct continuation of a form used by the church members during the preceding quarter of a century in their frequent relocations. A preliminary church-sponsored exploration would be followed by a selected company equipped to pioneer a settlement. New colonists would follow, arriving before spring planting to provide time to construct shelters, develop irrigation works, and prepare land for planting (1979, p. 20).

4. By moving from the Midwest to Salt Lake Valley, the LDS jumped ahead of the recognized frontier line of the United States, and it was three decades before the traditional frontier line caught up with the Utah settlement (Arrington and Bitton 1979).

5. Adult single women may be called on missions, although this is a relatively recent phenomenon. Retired couples may also be asked to serve on missions. In addition to the proselytizing missions, individuals may be called on to direct agricultural, medical, educational, or construction programs in missions located in the developing nations of the world. Proselytizing missionaries compose the bulk of the program and are typically single males between the ages of 19 and 22. Early missionaries were generally adult males, often married and with young children, whom they left in the care of their wives and the church while they worked in the field. On these missions they worked without financial support from the church, depending instead on the good will of sympathizers and converts. Today the missionaries are supported by their families, which arrangement makes it possible for the church to maintain over 30,000 voluntary

workers in many regions of the world—North America, South America, selected Asian countries, Western Europe, and a few locations in Africa.

6. There is some confusion in the literature regarding this name. Arrington notes that the legal title was "Perpetual Emigrating Company, commonly known as the Perpetual Emigration Fund, or PEF" (Arrington and Bitton 1979, p. 130). Thomas O'Dea uses the name "Perpetual *Emigrating* Fund" but continues to link it to the term "Company" (O'Dea 1957, pp. 94–95). We adopt the common identification, mentioned by Arrington, Perpetual Emigration Fund.

7. Charles Dickens, in *The Uncommerical Traveler,* describes a group of Mormon converts shipping out of England: "They had not been a couple of hours on board when they established their own police, made their own regulations, and set their own watches on all the hatchways. Before nine o'clock the ship was as orderly as a man-of-war . . . there was no disorder, hurry, or difficulty" (n.d., p. 635).

8. By 1880 a significant number of non-Mormons had settled in Utah: "According to the 1880 United States census, Utah's population included 120,283 Mormons, 14,136 Gentiles (non-Mormons of *any* other religious persuasion), and 6,988 apostates" (Larson 1947, p. 100).

9. In the LDS church one may be "called" to various positions of authority, to be a missionary, a colonist, or perhaps even a faculty member in one of the church's educational institutions. Today consultation takes place in advance of the formal "call" issued by the appropriate authorities of the church, although during the early days of settlement such consultation may not have occurred, and accepting the call was anticipated. It has been said, for example, that when Brigham Young said to jump through a brick wall, one jumped first and asked why upon recovery.

10. The directed-settlement pattern of the church established an ecological structure not typically associated with agricultural settlement in the United States. The isolated farm household surrounded by its agricultural land, common to most of the rest of the country, did not become the dominant pattern in Utah. Rather, the pattern of agricultural settlement in Utah was more common to what is even today found in the Middle East: a community of farmers resident in villages from which they travel out to their agricultural lands in the surrounding area. This pattern of concentrated agricultural settlement also provided the basis for the establishment of small-scale industries necessary to sustain the agricultural community and in some cases to produce commodities using local resources for shipment to the major settlement communities.

11. A handcart was a box mounted on two wheels, which could hold minimal household goods, and be pushed not only across the plains but also through the mountain passes.

12. A significant number of polygynous families left Utah and established a colony in Mexico. This was but one of several new colonies established outside the core during the period 1877–96, when intense persecution of polygynous males, and other pressures, initiated a new wave of colonization (Wahlquist 1981, p. 93).

13. Unpublished data made available by Dr. T. Lynn Lyon, Department of Family and Community Medicine, University of Utah.

14. Federal action also resulted in the disenfranchisement of Utah women, who had been granted the right to vote by state law in 1870. Women's right to vote was eliminated in the 1887 Edmunds-Tucker Act, which also declared the Perpetual Emigration Fund illegal.

15. The last decade of the nineteenth century also witnessed a new prophetic revelation in the LDS church eliminating the practice of polygyny. The relationship between polygyny and fertility is, however, discussed in chapter 4.

16. For a lucid description of the theological foundations for the belief, see O'Dea 1957.

17. See also Heaton 1986; Heaton and Goodman 1985; and Thomas 1983.

18. In recent years the Davis-Blake categories have been replaced with Bongaarts's "proximate determinants," which are generally consistent with the Davis-Blake listing. We retain the original set because of its integration into the Freedman scheme.

19. A stake president is a second-level official. At the base of the church's organizational structure are wards, each of which is presided over by a bishop and his two counselors. A stake is a unit containing between six and twelve wards that is presided over by a stake president and his two counselors.

20. Ordination as deacon normally takes place at age 12, as teacher at age 14, as priest at age 16, and as elder at the time of undertaking a mission, prior to marriage in the temple, or later.

21. An additional important feature of the LDS church stems from its organizational structure. The co-worshiping group of members, the congregation, is a ward. The ward consists of a bounded geographic area limited in size to between 400 and 600 persons. When the population in the ward increases beyond this level, the ward is divided. Thus the co-worshipers consist of a moderately small number of people residing within the same area; they are co-worshipers and neighbors. Whether members are active in the church or not, they are routinely visited monthly by representatives of the church. Members of the priesthood (males) attempt to meet with the entire family, and in addition members of the Relief Society (females) meet monthly with the adult women of the family. During such visits attention is often given to the welfare of the family, economic and social; among the topics of concern are marriage plans for single adults in the household and problems of couples who might remain childless. As a consequence of the perceived pressures on unmarried people, special arrangements have been made to allow such individuals to form "singles wards," but these remain rare. Special arrangements—alternatives to the geographic ward—are also made for non–English speaking convert-migrant groups. Again these are exceptions to the rule. As a result of this unique ecological structure in the LDS church, young couples are constantly exposed to contact with neighbors and co-worshipers who might express informal concern (pressure) if the couple delays childbearing too long.

22. Economically the members of the LDS church have recourse to perhaps one of the most dynamic, effectively organized support systems to be found in any organization. Through the ward leader—the bishop—the Welfare program provides food, clothing, rent or housing assistance, and medical care. The Wel-

fare program is supported through voluntary work programs. Wards or stakes maintain farms, ranches, orchards, food-processing and storage plants, clothing factories, and distribution facilities. In the major areas of LDS settlement in the West the LDS church also operates an extensive hospital system, and in mission areas particular attention is given to agricultural, health, and education programs. Thus in time of crisis—say unemployment—the active LDS family with several children can find assistance, in the private sector.

23. Tim Heaton, in a more recent study of Mormon fertility, finds no significant regional differences but confirms the importance of reference groups in maintaining pronatalist values. He argues that acceptance of a pronatalist theory requires, in part, "maintenance of a Mormon reference group through weekly church attendance" (1986, p. 256).

3. A GENEALOGICAL APPROACH TO HISTORICAL DEMOGRAPHY

1. For a more extensive summary of the Genealogical Society of Utah's holdings and data-collection procedures, see Bean et al. 1980. This paper, which was designed to describe the significance of the collection for historical demographic research, is of course out-of-date with respect to the size and coverage of the records because of the rate of expansion of the collection, but the description of the structure and significance of the holdings remains accurate.

2. At the time of the selection of the records, the family-group sheets were filed in two collections, the "Main" and the "Patron" sections. The Main collection contained approximately seven million family-group sheets. The Patron section was developed beginning in 1968 when members of the LDS church were "instructed" to complete records for four generations. The Patron section was sampled initially.

3. To enter data from a family-group sheet, an operator brought to the screen four formats in succession. The format listed items to be entered. This list was accompanied by a highlighted section to be filled with data typed exactly as it appeared on the family-group sheet. Each section had to be filled or a specific command entered indicating that the information was missing before the operator could continue to the next block or the next screen. Failure to complete the information or issue the skip command locked the keyboard and keyed a buzzer to inform the operator that information had not been entered.

4. If there were variations in name spelling or birth date, an individual who entered the database as a child from his or her parents' family-group sheet might not be identified by the computer as the identical person when he or she was entered a second time as a married person with spouse and children. Thus another entry would be created with the appropriate relationships, but the pedigree would be fragmented. This required a lengthy verification project to identify duplicate individuals and to combine their information to form more complete pedigrees.

5. For a discussion of strengths and weaknesses of different forms of records used in historical genealogical studies, see Willigan and Lynch 1982.

6. Of married women who were born in the period 1800–99 and have complete fertility histories, 1.14 percent had no children. The distribution is U-shaped across the birth cohorts. Early cohorts have over 1.5 percent nulliparous women; this declines to 0.5 percent at midcentury and increases to 2 percent in the youngest cohort. For comparison, Sheps's study (1965, p. 73) of Hutterite fertility indicates that 2.3 percent of the marriages were estimated to be childless.

7. As indicated in chapter 2, the LDS church members constituted approximately 60 percent of the population in 1906, the last date when the Census Bureau provided information on religious affiliation in the United States. Given the relationship between religion and fertility, one would anticipate that the LDS population would contribute a higher proportion of births. Thus the data set implies that the genealogy is a relatively complete reflection of LDS births in 1910.

8. The founders and their wives "enter" the population as adults drawn from a wide range of birth cohorts, but members of later cohorts appear in the file beginning at birth.

9. Throughout the remainder of this book, those individuals who entered the data set only as children in sibships will not be included in tables or analyses that discuss marriage patterns because we have only partial marriage information for them (the dates of marriage and the names of their spouses); they will only be studied as offspring of their parents' marriages. All individuals included hereafter were married, and for each of these marriages a family-group sheet was created.

10. The mean length of the interval from marriage to the birth of the first child for cases with complete information was 1.35 years. The mean value varied over time in a U-shaped manner from 1.43 years for the 1800–09 cohort to 1.27 for the 1850–59 cohort, to 1.42 for the 1890–99 cohort. Thus when the marriage dates were missing an imputed value was calculated for each case as the first child's birth date minus 1.3 years. Further analysis of families with missing marriage dates indicates that they had fewer children. For example, women in the 1820–29 cohort had on average 6.97 children; those with marriage dates had 7.21 while those without had 6.11 children. In this period, having fewer children is associated with an older age at marriage; and the imputed data are consistent with this pattern. Again for the 1820–29 cohort, mean age at marriage was 23.25; those with known marriage dates were age 23.03, and those with imputed dates were age 24.04.

11. An indication of the role of the professional genealogist is that in many cases they check birth intervals to determine unusual patterns. If unusually long birth intervals are observed, genealogists check alternate records for information that might indicate events during the interval: a stillbirth, a child who died very young, or the birth of a child unrecorded for some unspecified reason. If no such information is recorded, the later child's name is underlined to indicate no evidence of missing events in the preceding long interval.

12. Each event, baptism and endowment, reflects a certain level of commitment to the LDS church. In addition, endowment, which occurs in adulthood,

implies not only individual commitment to participate in the event but certification of conformity to church doctrine by religious authorities, as ascertained during an intensive personal interview.

13. The assumption that European fertility was stable prior to the modern fertility transition has been proved incorrect on the basis of a number of studies that have documented significant shifts in birth rates often reflecting changes in nuptiality. The assumption of stability has been replaced by the assumption of uncontrolled marital fertility, or natural fertility.

14. For a summary report on the Princeton European Fertility Project see Coale and Watkins 1986; Watkins 1986; and the reviews of the Coale and Watkins volume by Tilly (1986), Andorka (1986), and Levine (1986).

15. Genealogies have in some cases, however, been constructed from censuses and vital statistics, and so approximate family reconstitutions. Among the significant examples of these types of records is C. Tanquay's construction of eighteenth-century Canadian genealogies, which have been used by Bongaarts in his analysis of natural fertility (1976).

16. While not central to the analysis presented in this book, the fact that in the MHDP database family records may be linked into sequential generations provides the opportunity to examine the transmission of fertility behavior across generations (Anderson, Tsuya, et al. 1987).

4. FERTILITY AND NUPTIALITY

1. Only women whose marital histories are complete are represented in table 14. Women with more than one marriage are assigned to marriage cohorts by age at first marriage.

2. Two categories (TWOINM and TWOINP) have incomplete marital or fertility histories and are omitted from all previous and subsequent analyses. These two groups account, respectively, for 7.2 and 0.7 percent of the cases. Two other categories (ONELAP and TWOCFP) are very small (1.1 and 0.7 percent). These two groups are not shown in the separate analyses involving extensive cross-tabulations but are retained in the summary tables for ever-married women. The category reflecting incomplete dates, ONEAMB, is retained in the analyses and needs further explanation. We are certain that each ONEAMB woman married only once and that her husband married two or more times, but we are not certain whether the subject wife is the first or a higher-order wife. The group is moderately large, 5.9 percent of the total, and during the early decades includes approximately one in every ten ever-married women. Our analysis suggests that the group is made up predominately of first wives because their behavior (age at marriage, CEB, etc.) corresponds to the values of the group represented as ONEFRS.

3. That is, the statistical relationship itself between age at marriage and fertility is likely to change across cohorts with changing fertility behavior. Thus, controlling for age at marriage within cohorts (rather than for the effect of age at marriage as determined across cohorts) removes all variation in fertility attributable to the interaction of age at marriage and cohorts. It is possible that

the interaction of fertility and cohorts works through the relationship between fertility and age at marriage across cohorts and that this accounts for some of the variation in fertility removed by controlling for age at marriage. Therefore changing fertility may partially explain the variance this tabular presentation attributes to age at marriage over cohorts.

4. We calculate the partial marital total-fertility rates beginning with age 30 to reduce the effect of short intervals between marriage and first birth which would occur among the women married between the ages of 25 and 29. For similar computations and analysis among historical German populations, see Knodel 1979.

5. SUBCULTURAL VARIATIONS I

1. J. R. Kearl and Clayne Pope (1987) note that as early as 1870 there was substantial economic inequality among the Utah population, LDS as well as non-LDS.

2. Selected ethnic groups are underrepresented in the file. Conversion of Catholics (Irish initially and later Italians) and the Greek Orthodox was minimal; thus few descendants are available who might be interested in submitting family-group sheets or other genealogical information to the GSU.

3. Because table cells multiply with the introduction of these new variables, in the remaining analyses we will combine cohorts into ten-year or larger groups in order to maintain within cells numbers of sufficient size to meet the requirements of various analytical techniques.

4. European aggregate levels of fertility might have been lower than U.S. rates, overall, owing to the European marriage pattern, the effects of which are controlled in our study through the restriction of the analysis to marital fertility and the control of age at marriage.

5. Easterlin (1961) showed how marriage markets among the foreign-born affected their aggregate fertility after World War I, but we are examining marital fertility only.

6. Since approximately 1900, marriages for devoted members of the LDS church have been solemnized in temples. Up to 1900, temple ceremonies (or "sealings") also took place in homes, tithing offices, ward chapels, the president's office, and "Endowment Homes." After 1900 the restriction of sites for "sealings" meant that marriages often took place in a few communities where temples had been built. Thus couples traveled to communities with temples for the official marriage ceremony. Consequently the record of place of marriage may indicate the temple's location rather than the couple's usual residence.

7. Because age at last birth is calculated only for women who remain in an intact marriage until age 45, groups can exhibit differential survival rates and therefore different family sizes. For those who migrated as adults and were born from 1840–99, 83.3 percent of couples were intact when the wife reached age 45. This compares with 81.7 percent for Utah-born women and 77.2 percent for women born outside Utah who had their first child in Utah.

6. SUBCULTURAL VARIATIONS II

1. During initial stages of development these three counties also included a substantial agricultural population, yet the three counties were anchored by important cities—Salt Lake City, Provo, and Ogden.

2. Also included in this category are those who were rebaptized or reendowed after death. Among these are rare cases in which information on baptism and endowment was lost. In these cases, it is possible that family members who failed to find religious information for deceased relative had these rites performed again, by proxy.

3. Although the analyses are based on this assumption, we also calculated the results using the age 50 as the age at death for women with unrecorded death dates. Comparing the two sets of results, one observes a total shift out of endowed and into nonendowed and non-LDS categories of 1.3 percent. The major change was a 1 percent loss of members with lifetime committment and a 1 percent gain of nonactive members. Because 63.3 percent of the affected cases were concentrated in the 1890–99 cohort, this cohort was studied separately; a 4.3 percent shift out of endowed categories and into nonendowed and non-LDS categories was observed. Thus lowering the age at death decreases the percentage of those with stronger religious affiliation, and raising the age at death increases the percentage.

4. Log-linear analysis was selected over regression analysis because some of the relationships were non-linear.

7. ADAPTIVE AND INNOVATIVE INFLUENCES I

1. Bongaarts's original formulation of the model fixed $n = m-3$. However, applications to the Utah data proved incapable of simulating observed fertility without allowing n to vary. This is clearly a result of the lengthening of interbirth intervals over the course of the transition, as discussed below.

8. ADAPTIVE AND INNOVATIVE INFLUENCES II

1. The analytical procedures employed assume that the effect of mothers' moving from one area to another, during any phase of the life course, introduces no systematic bias. It is correct that we have noted that women who move from one type of area to another tend to have somewhat higher fertility than women in stable populations. In the time periods studied in this chapter, however, the population tends to be more stable than the population in earlier periods, as discussed in chapter 6. Data presented in that chapter also indicate that the proportion of women mobile across the life course was relatively small in comparison to those who were stable in the core and non-core areas. Of that small proportion of movers, a majority migrated from rural areas to towns, or from rural areas and towns to the major core settlements. Migration from the core settlements to towns or rural areas was less common. Given the levels of fertility associated with those who stayed and those who moved in combination with the

patterns of migration, the procedures adopted are likely to introduce minimal biases.

2. These types of changes may be conceptualized in terms of the Coale and Trussell indices, M and m. Reductions in M, often seen as changes in level, would occur with a reduction in fertility across the entire range of childbearing, while changes in m would reflect truncation.

APPENDIX

1. Because of space limitations, tabular presentations of parity progression ratios are not given. Such tables are available on request from the authors.

References

Abernethy, Virginia. 1979. *Population Pressure and Cultural Adjustment.* New York: Human Sciences Press.

Anderton, Douglas L. 1983. A quantitative analysis of behavioral change in the Utah frontier fertility transition: Women's birth cohorts, 1840–1899. Ph.D. dissertation, University of Utah.

———. 1986*a*. Intermarriage of frontier immigrant, religious and residential groups: An examination of a macrostructural assimilation hypothesis. *Sociological Inquiry* 56:341–353.

———. 1986*b*. Urbanization, secularization, and birth spacing: A case study of an historical fertility transition. *The Sociological Quarterly* 27:43–62.

———. 1989. Comment on John Knodel's "Starting, stopping, and spacing during the early stages of fertility transition: The experience of German village populations in the 18th and 19th centuries." *Demography* 56, no. 3.

Anderton, Douglas L., and Lee L. Bean. 1985. Birth spacing and fertility limitation: A behavioral analysis of a nineteenth-century frontier population. *Demography* 22:169–183.

———. 1987. Regional adaptation or geographic diffusion: Community differentiation during the onset of fertility control on the frontier. Paper presented at the Population Association of American meetings, Chicago, Illinois, 1987.

Anderton, Douglas L; Lee L. Bean; J. Dennis Willigan; and Geraldine P. Mineau. 1984. Adoption of fertility limitation in an American frontier population: An analysis and simulation of socio-religious subgroups. *Social Biology* 31:140–159.

Anderton, Douglas L.; Tsuya O. Noriko; Lee L. Bean; and Geraldine P. Mineau. 1987. Intergenerational transmission of relative fertility and life course events. *Demography* 24:467–480.

Andorka, Rudolf. 1978. *Determinants of Fertility in Advanced Societies.* New York: The Free Press.

———. 1986. Review Symposium: *The Decline of Fertility in Europe.* Edited by Ansley J. Coale and Susan Cotts Watkins. *Population and Development Review* 12:329–334.

Arrington, Leonard J. 1963. *The Changing Economic Structure of the Mountain West, 1850–1950.* Monograph Series, vol. 10, no. 3. Logan, Utah: Utah State University Press.

Arrington, Leonard J., and Thomas G. Alexander. 1974. *A Dependent Commonwealth: Utah's Economy from Statehood to the Great Depression.* Provo, Utah: Brigham Young University Press.

Arrington, Leonard J., and Davis Bitton. 1979. *The Mormon Experience.* New York: Alfred A. Knopf.

Arrington, Leonard J.; Feramorz Y. Fox; and Dean L. May. 1976. *Building of the City of God: Community and Cooperation among the Mormons.* Salt Lake City: Deseret Book.

Bailyn, Bernard. 1986. *Voyagers to the West: A Passage in the Peoplying on the Eve of the Revolution.* New York: Vintage Books.

Barclay, George W. 1958. *Techniques of Population Analysis.* New York: John Wiley and Sons.

Bardet, J. P.; K. A. Lynch; G. P. Mineau; M. Hainsworth; and M. Skolnick. 1981. La mortalité maternelle autrefois: Une étude comparée. *Annales de Demographie Historique,* pp. 31–49.

Bean, Lee L.; Dean L. May; and Mark Skolnick. 1978. The Mormon historical demography project. *Historical Methods* 11:45–53.

Bean, Lee L., and Geraldine P. Mineau. 1984. Linking the 1880 manuscript census to family genealogies: Methodological techniques and problems. Paper presented at the Social Science History Association in Toronto, Ontario, October.

———. 1986. The polygyny-fertility hypothesis: A re-evaluation. *Population Studies* 40:67–81.

———. 1988. Theoretical and methodological limitations of the concept of natural fertility. Paper presented at the Population Association of America meetings, New Orleans, La.

Bean, Lee L.; Geraldine P. Mineau; and Douglas L. Anderton. 1983. Residence and religious effects on declining family size: An historical analysis of the Utah population. *Review of Religious Research* 25:91–101.

Bean, Lee L.; Geraldine P. Mineau; Katherine A. Lynch; and J. Dennis Willigan. 1980. The Genealogical Society of Utah as a data resource for historical demography. *Population Index* 46:6–19.

Bean, Lee L.; Geraldine P. Mineau; Yung-chang Hsueh; and Douglas L. Anderton. 1987. The fertility effects of marriage patterns in a frontier American population. *Historical Methods* 20:161–172.

Becker, Gary. 1960. An economic analysis of fertility. In *Demographic and Economic Change in Developed Countries.* Princeton, N.J.: Princeton University Press, for the National Bureau of Economic Research.

Berkner, Lutz K. 1973. Recent research on the history of the family in Western Europe. *Journal of Marriage and the Family* 35(3):395–405.

Blake, Judith. 1985. The fertility transition: Continuity or discontinuity with the past? In *Proceedings: International Population Conference, Italy, 1985.* Liège, Belgium: IUSSP.

Blau, Peter. 1977. *Inequality and Heterogeneity: A Primative Theory of Social Structure.* New York: The Free Press.

Bongaarts, John. 1975. A method for the estimation of fecundability. *Demography* 12:645–660.

———. 1976. A dynamic model of the reproduction process. *Population Studies* 30:59–73.

———. 1978. A framework for analyzing the proximate determinants of fertility. *Population and Development Review* 4:533–557.

———. 1979. The fertility impact of traditional and changing childspacing practices in tropical Africa. The Population Council, Center for Policy Studies, Working Papers, no. 42.

Bongaarts, John, and Robert G. Potter. 1983. *Fertility, Biology, and Behavior: An Analysis of the Proximate Determinants.* New York: Academic Press.

Boorstin, Daniel J. 1974. *The Americans: The Democratic Experience.* New York: Vintage Books.

Braun, Rudolph. 1978. Protoindustrialization and demographic changes in the canton of Zürich. In Charles Tilly, ed., *Historical Studies of Changing Fertility,* 289–334. Princeton, N.J.: Princeton University Press.

Buissink, J. D. 1971. Regional differences in marital fertility in the Netherlands in the second half of the nineteenth century. *Population Studies* 25:353–374.

Bureau of Economic and Business Research, University of Utah. 1964. A statistical abstract of Utah's economy: 1964. *Studies in Business and Economics* 4:3.

Bush, Lester E., Jr. 1976. Birth control among the Mormons: Introduction to an insistent question. *Dialogue* 10:12–44.

Byers, Edward. 1982. Fertility transition in a New England commercial center: Nantucket, Massachussetts, 1680–1840. *Journal of Interdisciplinary History* 13:17–40.

Caldwell, John C. 1982. *Theory of Fertility Decline.* New York: Academic Press.

Caldwell, John C., and Pat Caldwell. 1987. The cultural context of high fertility in sub-Saharan Africa. *Population and Development Review* 13:409–438.

Carlson, Elwood D. 1985. The impact of international migration upon the timing of marriage and childbearing. *Demography* 22:61–72.

Carlsson, Gösta. 1966. The decline of fertility: Innovation or adjustment process. *Population Studies* 20:149–174.

Chamie, Joseph. 1981. *Religion and Fertility.* Cambridge, Mass.: Cambridge University Press.

Chiaramella, Y. 1981. A general demographic data base system: MERCURE. Unpublished paper. Laboratoire IMAG, Université Scientifique et Médicale de Grenoble, BP 53. 38041, Grenoble, France.

Coale, Ansley J. 1969. The decline of fertility in Europe from the French Revolution to World War II. In S. J. Behrman; Leslie Corsa, Jr.; and Ronald Freedman, eds., *Fertility and Family Planning: A World View*. Ann Arbor, Mich.: University of Michigan Press.

———. 1971. Age patterns of marriage. *Population Studies* 25:193–214.

———. 1973. The demographic transition reconsidered. In *Proceedings: International Population Conference, Liège, 1973*. Liège, Belgium: IUSSP.

———. 1986. The decline of fertility in Europe since the eighteenth century as a chapter in human demographic history. In Ansley J. Coale and Susan Cotts Watkins, eds., *The Decline of Fertility in Europe: The Revised Proceedings of a Conference on the Princeton European Fertility Project*, 1–30. Princeton, N.J.: Princeton University Press.

Coale, Ansley J.; B. A. Anderson; and E. Härm. 1979. *Human Fertility in Russia Since the Nineteenth Century*. Princeton, N.J.: Princeton University Press.

Coale, Ansley J., and D. R. McNeil. 1972. The distribution by age of the frequency of first marriage in a female cohort. *Journal of the American Statistical Association* 67:743–749.

Coale, Ansley J., and Roy Treadway. 1986. A summary of the changing distribution of overall fertility, marital fertility, and the proportions married in the provinces of Europe. In Ansley J. Coale and Susan Cotts Watkins, eds., *The Decline of Fertility in Europe: The Revised Proceedings of a Conference on the Princeton European Fertility Project*, 31–181. Princeton, N.J.: Princeton University Press.

Coale, Ansley J., and T. James Trussell. 1974. Model fertility schedules: Variations in the age structure of childbearing in human populations. *Population Index* 40:185–258.

———. 1978. Technical note: Finding the two parameters that specify a model schedule of marital fertility. *Population Index* 44:203–213.

Coale, Ansley J., and Susan Cotts Watkins, eds. 1986. *The Decline of Fertility in Europe: The Revised Proceedings of a Conference on the Princeton European Fertility Project*. Princeton, N.J.: Princeton University Press.

Coale, Ansley J., and Melvin Zelnick. 1963. *New Estimates of Fertility and Population in the United States*. Princeton, N.J.: Princeton University Press.

Coleman, James S. 1986. *Individual Interests and Collective Action: Selected Essays*. New York: Cambridge University Press.

Condran, Gretchen A., and Jeff Seaman. 1979. Linkage of the 1880–81 Philadelphia death register to the 1880 manuscript census: Procedures and preliminary results. Paper presented at the Population Association of America Meetings, Philadelphia, Pa.

David, Paul A., and Thomas A. Mroz. 1986. A sequential econometric model of birth spacing among rural French villagers, 1749–1789. Working Paper no. 19, Stanford Project on the History of Fertility Control, January.

David, Paul A., and Warren C. Sanderson. 1987. The emergence of a two-child norm among American birth-controllers. *Population and Development Review* 13:1–41.

Davis, Kingsley. 1963. The theory of change and response in modern demographic history. *Population Index* 19:345–366.

Davis, Kingsley, and Judith Blake. 1955. Social structure and fertility: An analytic framework. *Economic Development and Cultural Change* 4:211–235.

Day, Lincoln. 1968. Natality and ethnocentrism: Some relationships suggested by an analysis of Catholic-Protestant differentials. *Population Studies* 22:27–50.

Dickens, Charles. 193?. *The Uncommercial Traveler*. London: Chapman Hall.

Dintelman, Sue M., and A. Timothy Maness. 1983. An implementation of a query language supporting path expressions. In *ACM Proceedings, of the Second ACM SIGTACT-SIGMOD Symposium on the Principles of Database Systems*. Baltimore, Md.: Association for Computing Machinery. 87–93.

Dintelman, Sue M.; A. Timothy Maness; Mark H. Skolnick; and Lee L. Bean. 1980. In Bennett Dyke and Warren T. Merrill, eds. *Genealogical Demography*. New York: Academic Press.

Easterlin, Richard A. 1961. The American baby boom in historical perspective. *American Economic Review* 51:869–911.

———. 1971. Does human fertility adjust to environment? *American Economic Review* 61:399–407.

———. 1976. Population change and farm settlement in Northern United States. *Journal of Economic History* 34:45–83.

———. 1978. The economics and sociology of fertility: A synthesis. In Charles Tilly, ed., *Historical Studies of Changing Fertility*, 57–134. Princeton, N.J.: Princeton University Press.

Easterlin, Richard A.; George Alter; and Gretchen A. Condran. 1978. Farms and farm families in old and new areas: The northern states in 1860. In Tamara Hareven and Maris Vinovskis, eds., *Family and Population in 19th Century America*, 22–84. Princeton, N.J.: Princeton University Press.

Easterlin, Richard A., and Eileen M. Crimmins. 1985. *The Fertility Revolution: A Supply-Demand Analysis*. Chicago: University of Chicago Press.

Eaton, Joseph W., and Albert J. Mayer. 1953. The social biology of very high fertility among Hutterites: The demography of a unique population. *Human Biology* 25:206–263.

Eblen, Jack E. 1965. An analysis of nineteenth-century frontier populations. *Demography* 2:399–413.

Elder, Glen H., Jr. 1978. Family history and the life course. In Tamara Hareven, ed., *Transitions: The Family and the Life Course in Historical Perspective*, 21–64. New York: Academic Press.

Entwisle, Barbara; William M. Mason; and Albert I. Hermalin. 1986. Multilevel dependence of contraceptive use on socioeconomic development and family planning program strength. *Demography* 23:199–216.

Ericksen, E. E. 1922. *The Psychological and Ethical Aspects of the Mormon Group Life*. Chicago: Unversity of Chicago Press.

El Faedy, Mahjoub A., and Lee L. Bean. 1987. Differential paternity in Libya. *Journal of Biosocial Science* 19:395–403.

Fienberg, S. E. 1977. *The Analysis of Cross-Classified Data*. Cambridge, Mass.: MIT Press.

Forster, Colin, and G. S. L. Tucker. 1972. *Economic Opportunity and White*

American Fertility Ratios: 1800–1860. New Haven, Conn.: Yale University Press.

Freedman, Ronald. 1961–1962. The sociology of human fertility. *Current Sociology* 10/11:42.

———. 1979. Theories of fertility decline: A reappraisal. *Social Forces* 58:1–17.

Freedman, Ronald; Pascal K. Whelpton; and Arthur A. Campbell. 1959. *Family Planning Sterility and Population Growth*. New York: McGraw-Hill Book Company, Inc.

French, F. E., and J. Bierman. 1962. Probabilities of fetal mortality. *Public Health Report* 77:635–847.

Fridlizius, Gunnar. 1979. Sweden. In W. R. Lee, ed., *European Demography and Economic Growth*, 340–404. New York: St. Martins Press.

Frost, Henry. 1949. *To Have and to Hold; The Family and Population Changes in Utah*. Salt Lake City: University of Utah, Extension Division.

Georgescu-Roegen, Nicholas. 1971. *The Entropy Law and the Economic Process*. Cambridge, Mass.: Havard University Press.

Goldscheider, Calvin. 1971. *Population Modernization and Social Structure*. Boston: Little, Brown.

Goodman, Leo A. 1978. *Analysing Qualitative/Categorical Data: Log Linear Models and Latent Structure Analysis*. Cambridge, Mass.: Abt Books.

———. 1981. Criteria for determining whether certain categories in a cross-classification table should be combined with special reference to occupational categories in an occupational mobility table. *American Journal of Sociology* 87:612–650.

Gordon, Linda. 1976. *Women's Body, Woman's Right: A Social History of Birth Control in America*. New York: Grossman.

Gottlieb, Robert, and Peter Wiley. 1984. *America's Saints: The Rise of Mormon Power*. New York: G. P. Putnam.

Haines, Michael R. 1978. Recent development in historical demography: A review of the European Fertility Project with some comparisons from Japan. *Historical Methods* 11:162–173.

———. 1979. *Fertility and Occupation: Population Patterns in Industrialization*. New York: Academic Press.

Hajnal, J. 1965. European marriage patterns in perspective. In D. V. Glass and D. F. C. Eversley, eds., *Population in History*. Surrey, England: Edward Arnold.

Hareven, Tamara K. 1978. Introduction: The historical study of the life course. In Tamara Hareven, ed., *Transitions: The Family and the Life Course in Historical Perspective*, 1–16. New York: Academic Press.

Hareven, Tamara K., and Maris A. Vinovskis. 1978. Patterns of childbearing in late nineteenth-century America: The determinants of marital fertility in five Massachusetts towns in 1880. In Tamara Hareven and Maris Vinovskis, eds., *Family and Population in Nineteenth-Century America*, 85–125. Princeton, N.J.: Princeton University Press.

Hastings, D. W.; C. H. Reynolds; and R. R. Canning. 1972. Mormonism and birth planning: The discrepancy between church authorities teachings and lay attitudes. *Population Studies* 16:19–28.

Hatch, Charles M. 1982. Land, inheritance and family in the formation of Mormon towns. Paper presented at the Twenty-second Annual Conference of the Western History Association, Phoenix, Ariz.

Heaton, Tim B. 1986. How does religion influence fertility?: The case of the Mormons. *Journal for the Scientific Study of Religion* 25:248–258.

Heaton, Tim B., and Sandra Calkins. 1983. Family size and contraceptive use among Mormons: 1965–1975. *Review of Religious Research* 25:102–113.

Heaton, Tim B., and Kristen L. Goodman. 1985. Religion and family formation: A comparison of Mormons with Catholics and Protestants. *Review of Religious Research* 26:343–359.

Henry, Louis. 1961. Some data on natural fertility. *Eugenics Quarterly* 8:81–91.

———. 1967. Manuel de demographie historique. Geneva: Droz.

———. 1976. *Population Analysis and Models.* London: Edward Arnold.

Henry, Louis, and Fleury, M. 1958. Pour connaître la population de la France depuis Louis XIV. Plan de travaux par sondage. *Population,* 663–686.

Himes, Norman E. 1963. *The Medical History of Contraception.* New York: Gamut Press.

Hirschman, Charles. 1985. Premarital socioeconomic roles and the timing of family formation: A comparative study of five Asia societies. *Demography* 22:35–58.

Hirschman, Charles, and Dorothy Fernandez. 1980. The decline of fertility in Peninsular Malaysia. *Genus* 36:93–125.

Hollingsworth, T. H. 1969. *Historical Demography.* Ithaca, N.Y.: Cornell University Press.

———. 1976. Genealogy and historical demography. *Annales de Demographie Historique,* 167–170.

Homans, George C. 1964. Bringing men back in. *American Sociological Review* 29:809–818.

Hull, Terence H., and Valerie J. Hull. 1977. The relation of economic class and fertility: An analysis of some Indonesian data. *Population Studies* 31:43–57.

Johnson, Robert A. 1985. Analysis of age, period, and cohort effects in marital fertility. In William M. Mason and Stephen E. Fienberg, eds., *Cohort Analysis in Social Research.* New York: Spring-Verlag.

Kantrow, Louise. 1980. Philadelphia gentry: Fertility and family limitation among an American aristocracy. *Population Studies* 34:21–30.

Kearl, J. R., and Clayne Pope. 1987. Choices, rents and luck: Economic mobility of nineteenth-century Utah households. Unpublished paper. Brigham Young University, Department of Economics.

Kertzer, David I., and Caroline Brettell. 1987. Advances in Italian and Iberian family history. *Journal of Family History* 12:87–120.

Knodel, John. 1974. *The Decline of Fertility in Germany,* 1871–1939. Princeton, N.J.: Princeton University Press.

———. 1975. Ortsippenbucher als Quelle für die historische Demographie. *Geschichte und Gesellschaft* 1:288–324.

———. 1977. Family limitation and the fertility transition: Evidence from the age patterns of fertility in Europe and Asia. *Population Studies* 31:219–249.

———. 1978. Natural fertility in preindustrial Germany. *Population Studies* 32:481–510.
———. 1979. From natural fertility to fertility limitation: The onset of fertility transition in a sample of German villages. *Demography* 16:493–521.
———. 1987. Starting, stopping, and spacing during the early stages of fertility transition: The experience of German village populations in the 18th and 19th centuries. *Demography* 24:143–162.
Knodel, John, and Etienne van de Walle. 1979. Lessons from the past: Policy implications of historical fertility. *Population and Developmental Review* 5:217–246.
Knodel, John, and Christopher Wilson. 1981. The secular increase in fecundity in German village populations: An analysis of reproductive histories of couples married 1750–1899. *Population Studies* 35:53–84.
Larson, Gustive O. 1947. *Prelude to the Kingdom.* Francestown, N.H.: Marshall Jones.
Lee, Ronald D. 1987. Population dynamics of humans and other animals. *Demography* 24:443–465.
Légaré, J.; J. Lavoie; and H. Charbonneau. 1972. The early Canadian population: Problems in automatic record linkage. *Canadian History Review* 53.
Lesthaeghe, Ron J. 1977. *The Decline of Belgian Fertility, 1800–1970.* Princeton, N.J.: Princeton University Press.
Lesthaeghe, Ron J. and Chris Wilson. 1986. Modes of production, secularization, and the pace of the fertility decline in Western Europe, 1870–1930. In Ansley J. Coale and Susan Cotts Watkins, eds., *The Decline of Fertility in Europe: The Revised Proceedings of a Conference on the Princeton European Fertility Project,* 261–292. Princeton, N.J.: Princeton University Press.
Levine, David. 1986. Review Symposium: *The Decline of Fertility in Europe.* Edited by Ansley J. Coale and Susan Cotts Watkins. *Population and Development Review* 12:335–340.
Lewis-Faning, E. 1949. Report on an enquiry into family limitation and its influence on human fertility during the past fifty years. In *Papers of the Royal Commission on Population,* vol. 1. London: H. M. Stationery Office.
Livi Bacci, M. 1971. *A Century of Portuguese Fertility.* Princeton, N.J.: Princeton University Press.
———. 1977. *A History of Italian Fertility during the Last Two Centuries.* Princeton, N.J.: Princeton University Press.
Logue, Barbara J. 1985. The case for birth control before 1852: Nantucket reexamined. *Journal of Interdisciplinary History* 15:371–391.
Lynch, Katherine A.; Geraldine P. Mineau; and Douglas L. Anderton. 1985. Estimates of infant mortality on the western frontier: The use of genealogical data. *Historical Methods* 18:155–164.
Malthus, Thomas Robert. 1965. *First Essay on Population: 1798.* New York: August M. Kelley.
May, Dean L. 1977. The making of saints: The Mormon town as a setting for the study of cultural change. *Utah Historical Quarterly* 45:78.
May, Dean L.; Lee L. Bean; and Mark H. Skolnick. 1986. The stability ratio:

An index of community cohesiveness in nineteenth-century Mormon towns. In Robert M. Taylor et al., eds., *Generations and Change: Genealogical Perspectives on Social History,* 141–158. Macon, Ga.: Mercer University Press.

McDonald, Peter. 1984. *Nuptiality and Completed Fertility: A Study of Starting, Stopping, and Spacing Behavior.* World Fertility Survey: Comparative Studies, no. 35.

Melbin, Murray. 1978. Night as frontier. *American Sociological Review.* 43:3–22.

Mendels, Franklin F. 1972. Proto-Industrialization: The first phase of the process of industrialization. *Journal of Economic History* 32:241–261.

Menken, Jane. 1985. Age and fertility: How late can you wait? *Demography* 22:469–483.

Menken, Jane; James Trussell; and Susan Watkins. 1981. The nutrition fertility link: An evaluation of the evidence. *Journal of Interdisciplinary History* 11:411–425.

Mineau, Geraldine P. 1980. Fertility on the frontier: An analysis of the nineteenth-century Utah population. Ph.D. dissertation, University of Utah.

———. 1988. Utah widowhood: A demographic profile. In Arlene Scadron, ed., *On Their Own: Widows and Widowhood in the American Southwest 1848–1939,* 140–163. Chicago: University of Illinois Press.

Mineau, Geraldine P., and Douglas L. Anderton. 1983. Sterility in a natural fertility population. Paper presented at the Population Association of America meetings, Pittsburgh, Pa.

Mineau, Geraldine P.; Douglas L. Anderton; and Lee L. Bean. 1989. Description and evaluation of linkage of the 1880 census to family genealogies with implications for Utah fertility research. *Historical Methods* 22.

Mineau, Geraldine P.; Douglas L. Anderton; Lee L. Bean; and J. Dennis Willigan. 1984. Évolution différentielle de la fécondité et groupes sociaux religieux: L'exemple de l'Utah au XIX siècle. *Annales de Demographie Historique* 219–236.

Mineau, Geraldine P.; Lee L. Bean; and Douglas L. Anderton. 1989. Migration and fertility: Behavioral change on the American frontier. *Journal of Family History* 14:43–61.

Mineau, Geraldine P.; Lee L. Bean; and Mark Skolnick. 1979. Mormon demographic history II: The family life cycle and natural fertility. *Population Studies* 33:429–446.

Mineau, Geraldine P., and James Trussell. 1982. A specification of marital fertility by parents' age, age at marriage and marital duration. *Demography* 19:335–350.

Mosk, Carl. 1979. The decline of marital fertility in Japan. *Population Studies* 33:19–39.

———. 1983. *Patriarchy and Fertility: Japan and Sweden, 1880–1960.* New York: Academic Press.

O'Dea, Thomas F. 1957. *The Mormons.* Chicago: University of Chicago Press.

Palloni, Alberto. 1984. Assessing the effects of intermediate variables on birth interval-specific measures of fertility. *Population Index* 50:623–657.

Papanikolas, Helen. 1976. *The Peoples of Utah*. Salt lake City: Utah Historical Society.

Paul, Rodman W., and Richard W. Etulain. 1977. *The Frontier and the American West*. Arlington Heights, Ill.: AHM Publishing.

Petersen, William. 1969. *Population*. Toronto: Collier-Macmillan Canada.

Pitcher, Brian; Phillip R. Kunz; and Evan T. Peterson. 1974. Residency differentials in Mormon fertility. *Population Studies* 28:143–151.

Reed, James. 1978. *From Private Vice to Public Virtue: The Birth Control Movement and American Society Since 1830*. New York: Basic Books.

Retherford, R. D. 1985. A theory of marital fertility transition. *Population Studies* 38:225–240.

Romaniuk, Anatole. 1974. Modernization and fertility: The case of the James Bay Indians. *The Canadian Review of Sociology and Anthropology* 11:344–359.

Ryder, Norman B. 1956. Problems of trend determination during a transition in fertility. *Milbank Memorial Fund Quarterly* 34:5–21.

———. 1965. The cohort as a concept in the study of social change. *American Sociological Review* 30:35–49.

———. 1980. Components of temporal variations in American fertility. In R. W. Hiorns, ed., *Demographic Patterns in Developed Societies,* 11–54. London: Taylor and Francis.

Ryder, Norman B., and Charles F. Westoff. 1971. *Reproduction in the United States, 1965*. Princeton, N.J.: Princeton University Press.

Shackle, G. L. S. 1972. *Epistemics and Economics: A Critique of Economic Doctrines*. London: Cambridge University Press.

Shapiro, Morton Owen. 1982. Land availability and fertility in the United States, 1760–1870. *Journal of Economic History* 42:577–600.

Sheps, Mindel. 1965. An analysis of reproductive patterns in an American isolate. *Population Studies* 19:65–80.

Skolnick, Mark. 1980. The Utah genealogical data base: A resource for genetic epidemiology. In J. Cairns et al., eds., *Banbury Report No. 4: Cancer Incidence in Defined Populations,* 285–297. New York: Cold Spring Harbor Laboratory.

Skolnick, Mark; Lee L. Bean; Sue M. Dintelman; and Geraldine P. Mineau. 1979. A computerized family history data base system. *Sociology and Social Research,* 601–619.

Skolnick Mark; Lee L. Bean; Dean May; Val Arbon; Klancy de Nevers; and P. Cartwright. 1978. Mormon demographic history I. Nuptiality and fertility of once-married couples. *Population Studies* 32:5–19.

Smith, Daniel Scott. 1987. "Early" fertility decline in America: A problem in family history. *Journal of Family History* 12:73–86.

Smith, David P. 1985. Breastfeeding, contraception, and birth intervals in developing countries. *Studies in Family Planning* 16:154–163.

Smith, J. E. 1981. How first marriage and remarriage markets mediate the effects of declining mortality on fertility. In J. Dupaquier et al., eds., *Mar-*

riage and Remarriage in Populations of the Past, 229–243. New York: Academic Press.

Smith, T. Lynn, and Paul E. Zopf, Jr. 1976. *Demography.* Port Washington, N.Y.: Alfred.

Spath, Helmuth. 1980. *Cluster Analysis Algorithms.* West Sussex, England: Ellis Horwood.

Spicer, Judith C., and Susan O. Gustavus, 1974. Fertility through half a century: Another test of the Americanization hypothesis. *Social Biology* 21:70–76.

Stern, Mark J. 1987. *Society and Family Strategy: Erie County, New York 1850–1920.* Albany: State University of New York Press.

Stone, Glenn Davis; Robert McC. Netting; and M. Priscilla Stone. 1987. Seasonality, labor scheduling and agricultural intensification in the West African savanna. Unpublished paper.

Telford, Ted A. 1986. The mechanism of China's population growth, 1520–1661: The demography of Chinese lineage. Ph.D. dissertation, University of Utah.

Temkin-Greener, Helena, and A. C. Swedlund. 1978. Fertility transition in the Connecticut valley: 1740–1850. *Population Studies* 32:27–41.

Thomas, Darwin L. 1983. Family in the Mormon experience. In William V. D'Antonio and Joan Aldous, eds., *Families and Religions,* 267–288. Beverley Hills: Sage.

Thompson, Warren S. 1931. *Ratio of Children to Women in the United States, 1920.* Census Monograph, No. 11. Washington, D.C.: U.S. Bureau of the Census.

Tilly, Charles. 1978. The historical study of vital processes. In Charles Tilly, ed., *Historical Studies of Changing Fertility,* 3–55. Princeton: Princeton University Press.

———. 1981. *As Sociology Meets History.* New York: Academic Press.

———. 1986. Review symposium: *The Decline of Fertility in Europe.* Edited by Ansley J. Coale and Susan Cotts Watkins. *Population and Development Review* 12:323–328.

Tolnay, Stewart E.; Stephen N. Graham; and Avery M. Guest. 1982. Own-child estimates of U.S. white fertility, 1886–99. *Historical Methods* 15:127–138.

Tolnay, Stewart E., and Avery M. Guest. 1984. American family building strategies in 1900: Stopping or spacing? *Demography* 21:9–18.

Trovato, Frank. 1987. A macrosociological analysis of Native Indian fertility in Canada: 1961, 1971, and 1981. *Social Forces* 66:463–485.

Turner, Frederick Jackson. 1921. *The Significance of the Frontier in American History.* Ann Arbor, Mich.: University Microfilms.

U.S. Bureau of the Census. 1984. *Current Population Reports,* Series P-23, No. 395, *Fertility of American Women: June 1983.* Washington, D.C.: Government Printing Office.

———. 1985. *Current Population Reports,* Series P-23, No. 142, *Future Fertility of Women by Present Age and Parity.* Washington, D.C.: Government Printing Office.

van de Walle, E. 1974. *The Female Population of France in the Nineteenth Century*. Princeton, N.J.: Princeton University Press.

Vinovskis, Maris A. 1976. Socio-economic determinants of interstate differentials in the United States in 1850 and 1860. *Journal of Interdisciplinary History* 6:781–786.

———. 1978. A multivariate regression analysis of fertility differentials among Massachusetts regions and towns in 1860. In Charles Tilly, ed., *Historical Studies of Changing Fertility*. Princeton, N.J.: Princeton University Press.

Wahlquist, Wayne L. 1974. Settlement progress in the Mormon core area: 1847–1890. Ph.D. dissertation, University of Nebraska.

———. 1977. A review of Mormon settlement literature. *Utah Historical Quarterly* 45(1).

———. 1981. The Mormon expansion. In Wayne L. Wahlquist, ed., *Atlas of Utah*. Provo, Utah: Brigham Young University Press.

Watkins, Susan C. 1986. Conclusions. In Ansley J. Coale and Susan Cotts Watkins, eds., *The Decline of Fertility in Europe: The Revised Proceedings of a Conference on the Princeton European Fertility Project*, 420–449. Princeton, N.J.: Princeton University Press.

Westoff, Charles F., and Norman B. Ryder. 1977. *The Contraceptive Revolution*. Princeton, N.J.: Princeton University Press.

Widtsoe, John A. 1915. *Rational Theology*. Published for the use of the Melchizedek Priesthood. Salt Lake City, Utah: The General Priesthood Committee.

Wilcox, Jerry, and Hilda H. Golden. 1982. Prolific immigrants and dwindling natives? Fertility patterns in Western Massachusetts, 1850 and 1880. *Journal of Family History* 7:265–288.

Williams, R. R.; M. Skolnick; D. Carmelli; A. T. Maness; S. C. Hunt; S. J. Hasstedt; G. E. Reiber; and R. K. Jones. 1978. Utah pedigree studies: Design and preliminary data for premature male CHD deaths. In C. F. Sing and M. Skolnick, eds., *Genetic Analysis of Common Diseases: Applications to Predictive Factors in Coronary Disease*, 711–732. New York: Alan R. Liss.

Willigan, J. Dennis; Douglas L. Anderton; Geraldine P. Mineau; and Lee L. Bean. 1982. A macrosimulation approach to the investigation of natural fertility. *Demography* 19:161–176.

Willigan, J. Dennis, and Katherine A. Lynch. 1982. *Sources and Methods of Historical Demography*. New York: Academic Press.

Wilson, Chris. 1984. Natural fertility in pre-industrial England, 1600–1799. *Population Studies* 38:225–240.

Wilson, Chris; Jim Oeppen; and Mike Pardoe. 1988. What is natural? The modelling of a concept. *Population Index* 54:4–20.

Wirth, Louis. 1964. *On Cities and Social Life—Selected Papers*. Edited by A. L. Reiss. Chicago: University of Chicago Press.

Wolfers, D. 1968. The determinants of birth intervals and their means. *Population Studies* 22:253–262.

Wrigley, E. A. 1966. Family limitation in pre-industrial England. *Economic History Review* 19:82–109.

———. 1983. English population history from family reconstitution: Summary results 1600–1799. *Population Studies* 37:157–184.

Wrigley, E. A., and R. Schofield. 1981. *The Population History of England 1541–1871: A Reconstruction.* Cambridge, Mass.: Harvard University Press.

Yasuba, Yasukichi. 1962. *Birth Rates of the White Population in the United States, 1800–1860: An Economic Study.* Baltimore, Md.: Johns Hopkins University Press.

Yaukey, David. 1969. On theorizing about fertility. *The American Sociologist* 4:100–104.

Zarate, Alvin, and Alcia Unger de Zarate. 1975. On the reconciliation of research findings of migrant-nonmigrant fertility differentials in urban areas. *International Migration Review* 9:115–156.

Index